*"Information through Innovation"*

# Acumen Series

## Microsoft Access 2.0

# Michelle Poolet

# Michael Reilly

*Mount Vernon Data Systems, Inc.*

**boyd & fraser publishing company**

 An International Thomson Publishing Company

Danvers • Albany • Bonn • Boston • Cincinnati • Detroit • London • Madrid • Melbourne
Mexico City • New York • Paris • San Francisco • Singapore • Tokyo • Toronto • Washington

**Publishing Process Director:** Carol Crowell
**Series Editor:** Linda Ericksen
**Development Editor:** Harriet Serenkin
**Production Editor:** Jean Bermingham
**Composition:** Gex, Inc.
**Interior Design:** Gex, Inc.
**Cover Design:** Richard Pepper/Flying Pepper Design
**Manufacturing Coordinator:** Carol Chase

The ITP logo is a trademark under license.

Printed in the United States of America

This book is printed on recycled, acid-free paper that meets
Environmental Protection Agency standards.

For more information, contact boyd & fraser publishing company:

boyd & fraser publishing company
One Corporate Place • Ferncroft Village
Danvers, Massachusetts 01923, USA

International Thomson Publishing Europe
Berkshire House 168-173
High Holborn
London, WCIV 7AA, England

Thomas Nelson Australia
102 Dodds Street
South Melbourne 3205
Victoria, Australia

Nelson Canada
1120 Birchmount Road
Scarborough, Ontario
Canada M1K 5G4

International Thomson Editores
Campose Eliseos 385, Piso 7
Col. Polanco
11560 Mexico D.F. Mexico

International Thomson Publishing GmbH
Konigswinterer Strasse 418
53227 Bonn, Germany

International Thomson Publishing Asia
221 Henderson Road
#05-10 Henderson Building
Singapore 0315

International Thomson Publishing Japan
Hirakawacho Kyowa Building, 3F
2-2-1 Hirakawacho
Chiyoda-ku, Tokyo 102, Japan

1 2 3 4 5 6 7 8 9 10 D 8 7 6 5 4

ISBN 0-87709-983-9

# Brief Contents

# Contents

# Preface

Welcome to the boyd & fraser family of *ACUMEN* authors, educators, and students who are participating in this vanguard of computer education. The *ACUMEN* series is both a well-integrated solution to the demands of the classroom and the foundation for the essential computer skills that today's students require for economic survival in the modern business world.

Computer literacy is essential in education and a growing number of professions. In the course of their careers, most individuals will have to learn more than a single application and, eventually, new versions of those applications. They will need to know how to integrate the applications to produce complex documents. They will need to work with other individuals to produce unified team projects.

The primary goals of the *ACUMEN* series are to instill confidence, build the skills and insight necessary to master the software application, develop a basic understanding of the concepts behind each task, and comprehend how different applications are often used interactively to complete a variety of tasks.

To meet these goals, *ACUMEN* introduces the concept of *active learning* that links all of the books in strategic and important ways. While other computer books isolate students in the world of a single application, *ACUMEN* students enter the real world of interactive computer technology.

Each text can be taught as a stand-alone course or combined in a unified syllabus. For example, the letters and plans written in the word processing application can be performed alone or combined with the financial projections and charts from the spreadsheet application. This information can then be applied to the product database from the database application to produce a complete business plan. In addition, optional group projects teach students how to work together in teams to produce the unified projects.

The *ACUMEN* structure, objectives, content, exercises, projects, and design are the product of extensive research, interviews, and field studies on what computer educators need to effectively teach both individual applications courses and fully integrated, comprehensive courses that cover a variety of applications.

# The ACUMEN Solution: from Concept to Comprehension

**Quick Preview.** Each *ACUMEN* begins with a short, pre-written program that demonstrates the application to the students and introduces a confidence-building real-world example.

**Progressive Chapters.** The chapters of each book are grouped into three distinct parts, with each chapter in a part progressively building on the preceding chapter.

**Fundamentals.** Part I introduces the application and the basic skills required for competency. All of the chapters in this part cover the essential tasks necessary for using the program.

**Critical Thinking.** Part II combines problem solving and critical thinking while adding skills required to produce useful work.

**Advanced Features.** Part III combines advanced skills designed to improve productivity and proficiency.

**Conceptual Introductions.** Each chapter begins with a list of objectives, a list of key terms and definitions, and a short, conceptual overview that clearly tell the student what will be covered in that chapter.

**Objectives Covered.** The chapter objectives are each covered individually and are introduced with a brief why-this-is-important or explanatory paragraph. Each objective includes at least one hands-on exercise.

**Key Terms.** New terms are printed in italic when first introduced. The term also is printed in bold in the margin of the text so that the student can make the connection between the definition in the *Key Terms* box and the use of the term in context.

**Self Evaluation.** Each chapter ends with self-evaluation review questions, four Quick Projects, and two In-Depth projects. Projects are written so that two are specific to the chapter, two are continuing projects specific to the part, and two are *stretch* projects that require critical thinking.

**Part Projects.** Each of the three parts ends with two comprehensive applications projects that combine the knowledge and skills learned in that part. One is an individual project and one is a team project.

**Linked Case Studies.** Each applications title includes Case Studies that, while specific to the particular application covered in that book, are also part of an overall series project. The Case Studies can be used to link different applications and create actual business projects, with source materials drawn from the various applications.

**Boxed Sidebars and Special Features.** To maintain student interest and show the effectiveness of the application in practical situations, each chapter contains at least one boxed sidebar and one special features box. Boxed sidebars provide human interest and real-world examples, while special features boxes emphasize an advanced or particularly interesting skill.

 **Appendix on Windows.** A special appendix introducing Windows to novice users is included at the back of each *ACUMEN* text. This Introduction to Windows gives the user an overview of basic Windows features and includes a hands-on tutorial.

## Instructor's Materials

A comprehensive *Instructor's Manual* containing topic overviews, key terms, and solutions to all exercises and problems is available for each book. An *Instructor's Resource Disk* containing exercise and problem files, as well as all solutions files, is also available. The *Instructor's Resource Disk* contains data files that can be distributed to the user via disk or over a computer network. It also contains the integrated Case Studies and accompanying solutions, and a complete text-based copy of the *Instructor's Manual*.

## Software Upgrades

*ACUMEN* adopters are eligible to participate in boyd & fraser's software upgrade program. Contact your sales representative for specific details.

## Acknowledgments

The following reviewers helped shape this text by providing valuable comments:

| | |
|---|---|
| Joan Lumpkin | Wright University |
| Marie McCooey | Bryant Business School |
| Gail MonteCarlo | Gloucester Community College |
| George Novotny | Ferris State University |

Special thanks go to Linda Ericksen, Series Editor, for her work on the entire list of *ACUMEN* series titles.

# ACUMEN Series Titles

boyd & fraser is proud of the diversity, variety, and quantity of the computer education resources we offer designed to meet your instructional needs. New titles will be added for major software applications as the programs are released in new versions. Our current offerings include:

## DOS:

DOS 6.22   ISBN 0-87709-971-5

WordPerfect 6.0 for DOS   ISBN 0-87709-956-1

## Windows:

Windows 3.1   ISBN 0-87709-965-0

Windows 95   ISBN 0-7895-0349-2

Ami Pro 3.1 for Windows   ISBN 0-87709-962-6

Word 6.0 for Windows   ISBN 0-87709-959-6

WordPerfect 6.1 for Windows   ISBN 0-87709-953-7

Excel 5.0 for Windows   ISBN 0-87709-980-4

Lotus 1-2-3, Release 5 for Windows   ISBN 0-87709-974-X

Access 2.0 for Windows   ISBN 0-87709-983-9

Paradox 5.0 for Windows   ISBN 0-87709-968-5

QuattroPro 6.0 for Windows   ISBN 0-87709-977-4

## Combined Applicatons:

Word 6.0 for Windows, Excel 5.0 for Windows,
Access 2.0 for Windows   ISBN 0-7895-0199-6

# Quick Preview

## Microsoft Access 2.0

Microsoft Access 2.0 is a database management system that can be used by people at all skill levels for storing data and displaying information. MS-Access is easy for beginners and has powerful features that help you build tables to store data, construct queries to manipulate data, and generate forms and reports to display data. This Quick Preview shows you some of these features.

## Activity 1: Creating a Database File

The first step in using MS-Access is to create a database file. The database file acts as a container that holds your data, tables, forms, and reports.

1. Start Microsoft Windows.

   The Program Manager window opens.
2. Double-click the MS-Access Group icon.

   The MS-Access Group window opens.
3. Double-click the MS-Access icon.

   The MS-Access main screen opens.
4. Click File/New Database from the top menu.

   The New Database dialog box opens.
5. Accept the name db1.mdb and click OK.

   You have just created a database file.

## Activity 2: Creating a Table

**tables**
**wizard**

The next step is to create a table. Your data is stored in organized groups called *tables*. You will use the MS-Access Wizards to create a table in which to store your data. A *Wizard* is a program within MS-Access that leads you through the steps necessary to perform a task—in this case, creating a table.

1. The Database window is open at the Table listing. There are no tables in the list.
2. Click New.

   The New Table dialog box appears.
3. Click Table Wizards.

   The Table Wizard dialog box appears.
4. From the Sample Tables list on the left, select Mailing List.
5. From the Sample Fields list in the middle, select MailingListID.
6. Click the box with the > symbol to move a copy of MailingListID from the Sample Fields list to the Fields in My New Table list.
7. Move the following entries in the Sample Fields list to the Fields in My New Table list by repeating Steps 5 and 6:

   FirstName
   LastName
   Address
   City
   State
   PostalCode.
8. Click Next at the bottom of the dialog box.
9. When the next dialog box appears, leave the suggested Mailing List as the name of your table and let MS-Access set the primary key for you.
10. Click Next at the bottom of the dialog box.
11. Select the Enter Data Directly Into the Table response to the question, What do you want to do?
12. Click Finish at the bottom of the dialog box.

    The MS-Access Table Wizard creates the Mailing Labels table for you and opens it. You are ready to begin adding data.

# Activity 3:   Entering Data into the Database

Now that you have created a database and a table in the database, you are ready to enter data into the table.

1. Press (TAB) to move to the First Name column and type *your first name*.
2. Press (TAB) to move to the Last Name column and type *your last name*.
3. Press (TAB) to move to the Address column and type *your street address*.
4. Press (TAB) to move to the City column and type *the name of the city you live in*.
5. Press (TAB) to move to the State column and type *the name of the state you live in*.
6. Press (TAB) to move to the Postal Code column and type *your zip code*.
7. Press (← ENTER) to complete the first record.

8. Repeat Steps 1 through 7 to create three additional records containing the names and addresses of friends or classmates.

   You now have four records in your Mailing List table.

9. Click File/Save Record to save the data you entered.

10. Click File/Save Table to save the table you created.

11. Click File/Close to close the datasheet and return to the Database window.

## Activity 4:  Generating a Mailing Labels Report

Now that you have data in your table, you can print this information as mailing labels. You will use the MS-Access Wizards to create a mailing labels report. You can then preview this report and send it to the printer.

1. The Database window for database.db1 is open at the table listing. Click the Report tab on the left.

   The Report window opens. There are no reports in the list.

2. Click New.

   The New Report dialog box appears.

3. Click the down arrow located to the right of the Select a Table/Query box.

   A drop-down menu appears with the entry Mailing List highlighted.

4. Click Mailing List.

   Mailing List pops into the Select a Table/Query box.

5. Click the Report Wizards button.

   The Report Wizards dialog box appears.

6. Highlight the Mailing Labels Wizard. Click OK.

   The Mailing Labels Wizard dialog box appears.

7. In the Available Fields list, highlight the FirstName entry.

8. Click the > button located to the right of the FirstName entry in the Available Fields list.

   A copy of First Name moves to the Label Appearance list.

9. Click the Space button located below the Available Fields list.

10. Highlight LastName in the Available Fields list. Click the > button.

    First Name and Last Name are now on the first line of the Label Appearance list; they are separated by a space.

11. Click the Newline button.

    A new line appears on the Label Appearance list.

12. Highlight Address in the Available Fields list. Click the > button.

    Address appears on the second line of the Label Appearance list.

13. Click Newline to start a new line.

14. Scroll down the Available Fields list to show City, State, and PostalCode.

15. Highlight City in the Available Fields list. Click the > button to move it to the Label Appearance list.

16. Click Comma, then Space to add a comma and a space after City in the Label Appearance list.

17. Highlight State in the Available Fields list. Click the > button to move it to the Label Appearance list.

18. Click Space twice to add two spaces after State in the Label Appearance list.

19. Highlight PostalCode in the Available Fields list. Click the > button to move it to the Label Appearance list.

20. Click Next at the bottom of the Mailing Label Wizard dialog box.

21. Highlight LastName as the field by which you want to order the list. Click the > button to move it to the Sort Order list.

22. Click Next at the bottom of the Mailing Label Wizard dialog box.

23. Highlight Avery #5161, 1" × 4", 2 across, when asked for the size of the label. Accept English as the unit of measure and Sheet Feed as the label type.

24. Click Next at the bottom of the Mailing Label Wizard dialog box.

25. Accept the default values for text appearance. Click Next.

26. Accept See Mailing Labels as They Will Look Printed. Click Finish.

    The Mailing Label Wizard creates the Mailing Label report for you and displays the Print Preview screen.

# Activity 5:  Printing a Mailing Labels Report

The Print Preview screen allows you to preview your report before sending it to the printer. By clicking on the report itself, you can zoom in to see specific sections of the report or zoom out to see the general layout of the report. Once you are satisfied with the appearance of the report, you can print it.

1. At the Print Preview screen, test the zoom feature: Click the report several times to zoom in and out.

2. From the top menu choose File/Print.

   The Print dialog box appears.

3. Accept the print range of All. Click OK.

   Your mailing labels are now printing.

4. Exit Print Preview by clicking the Close Window icon at the far left of the top toolbar.

   You are returned to the Report Design Mode screen.

5. Select File/Save to save the report.

   The Save As dialog box appears, prompting you for a report name.

6. Type MailingLabelsReport as the report name. Click OK.

7. Select File/Close to close the report and return to the Database window.

## Activity 6:  Ending Your MS-Access Session

It is important to end your MS-Access session properly. Improper exit procedures—such as turning off your computer in the middle of an MS-Access session—could cause you to lose data. Here's the correct way to end an MS-Access session.

1. From the Database window, choose File/Close Database.

   The active database is shut down.

2. Choose File/Exit.

   The MS-Access session is terminated. You are returned to the MS-Access group, in the Program Manager screen.

# Part 1

# Fundamentals

# Chapter 1

## *Database Fundamentals*

*Objectives*

- **Introduction to Databases**
- **Starting the Software**
- **Mouse and Keyboard Commands**
- **Elements of the Screen**
- **Elements of the Menu System**
- **Event-Driven versus Menu-Driven Applications**
- **The On-Line Help System**
- **Exiting the Software**

*Key Terms*

| TERM | DEFINITION |
|---|---|
| **Data** | raw facts—for example, a data item might be a name, street address, or phone number |
| **Information** | organized data that can be used to assist in the decision-making process |
| **Database** | an organized, related collection of data |
| **Database Management System** | a computerized record-keeping system that stores data, manages a database, and presents data to a user on request |
| **Flat-file Data Manager** | a type of database that stores data in a single file |
| **Relational Database** | a type of database that stores data in separate, but related, groups called tables |
| **Database File** | a computer file that contains an MS-Access database |
| **Table** | a collection of data related to a single topic, such as customer information |
| **User Interface** | the screens used to interact with a computer or computer program |

| TERM | DEFINITION |
|------|-----------|
| **Network** | a system that connects computers so that people can communicate with each other and share data files, printers, and hardware |
| **Report** | a printed listing of data from the database, organized to provide information used in evaluating and making decisions |
| **Form** | a screen display of a single record from a table in the database that is used for inputting, outputting, and displaying data |
| **Report Writer** | a database tool used to design, build, and produce printed reports without the user having to write code in a computer programming language |
| **Icon** | a small picture on the computer screen that represents a program, such as MS-Access, or a task, such as opening a file |
| **Dialog Box** | a pop-up window that assists you in some task, such as choosing a file |
| **Minimize a Window** | reduce an MS-Access window to an icon |
| **Maximize a Window** | enlarge an MS-Access window to fill the entire screen. |
| **On-line Help System** | the computerized version of the *MS-Access User's Guide*, which contains information about MS-Access |
| **Cue Card** | an on-line tutorial that guides you through a complicated task, such as editing a table; a part of the MS-Access on-line help system |
| **Context-sensitive Help** | a feature of the MS-Access on-line help system that allows you to access information relevant to what you are doing by pressing F1 |
| **Wizard** | a predefined set of instructions built into MS-Access that automates the steps required to perform a task; a part of the MS-Access on-line help system |

Computing technology has revolutionized the way we live and do business. With the desktop computer standard in most offices and many homes, there is a demand to organize the vast amount of information at our fingertips: Enter the database and the database management system.

**database programmers**

Database management systems were once found only in large corporations. They were an intricate set of programs that were exceedingly complicated to use and maintain. Only specially trained people (called *database programmers*) knew how to extract information from the database. Today's database management systems are very different: just as complex on the inside, but user-friendly on the outside.

## Objective 1:  Introduction to Databases

SIGNS, Ltd. is a small business that makes and sells signs. The owner is considering developing a database to track sales and customer calls and has called in a database systems consultant to discuss this project. Listen in on the conversation between the owner of SIGNS, Ltd. and the consultant.

*Owner:* People keep telling me I need a database, but they all have different ideas about what a database really is. Can you tell me the *real* definition of a database?

**database**

*Consultant*: A *database* is an organized collection of related data from which you extract information. This Rolodex on your desk can be considered a database. It's organized—you have each card in alphabetical order—and from it you can extract phone numbers, names, and where a customer's office is located.

*Owner:* How does a database differ from a database management system?

**database management system network**

*Consultant*: A database is a collection of related facts. A *database management system* is a set of computer programs that stores and manages those facts. If the database is stored on a *network*, the database management system makes the database accessible to anyone connected to the network. The data stored in the database becomes a shared resource throughout the company.

**user interface**

The database management system allows you to build a nice, user-friendly *user interface* to work with. The user interface makes it easy for you to add data, change data already stored in the database, or get rid of old data that has outlived its usefulness. It helps you manipulate the data and extract useful information so that you can make better-informed decisions. This

**report writer**

information can be formatted by the *report writer*, which is also part of the database management system. The report writer produces paper reports for distribution—for example, invoices for your customers or end-of-year purchase reports that help your customers track what they've bought from you over the past twelve months. And the database management system acts as a security guard—only people who are supposed to get into the database can do so.

*Owner:* Just a minute. I thought information and data were the same thing—you're telling me they're not?

**data information**

*Consultant*: Actually they're not the same. *Data* is raw facts. You rearrange or recombine data to produce useful *information* that can help you make decisions. For instance, your company sells several types of signs to customers, and you have a list of customers. That is your data. When you're having a sale on a specific type of sign, you sort through your customer list, extracting the names of only those customers who have purchased that type of sign in the past. That is information.

*Owner:* So how can a database help my company?

*Consultant*: What you now do manually you can do with a computerized database management system in a fraction of the time. For example, it probably takes an hour or so to sort through all your customers to find those who have purchased a specific type of sign. It then takes several hours to prepare the mailing for the sale notices. With a database system you could complete these tasks in a few minutes.

With your sales data stored in a database, you could generate reports of sales activity—which products are selling and which are not—and adjust your inventory and sales efforts to meet the demand. Also, you could track overdue accounts.

If you had all your product inventory information stored in the database, you could enter customer orders into the database and see immediately which items are in stock and which need to be ordered. You could track and manage your inventory by assigning a reorder point value to each inventory item and generate a daily report listing which items need to be reordered. The possibilities are endless.

*Owner:* Right now I keep customer lists in my word processor and product lists and sales in my spreadsheet. Isn't that a sort of database?

*Consultant:* Yes it is. Each list is a file—a collection of data related to a single topic. It is very much like the earliest and simplest of the database management systems for the personal computer. These database manage ment systems, which are still used today, are called *flat-file data managers.* They allow only for a single type of data in a database file, such as your customer listing or sales figures.

**flat-file data managers**

Word processors, spreadsheets, and flat-file data managers are a fine way to keep track of short lists and simple sets of data. But as your company grows and you need to get more and more information out of these lists, they will fall short. You will need to combine and extract data from the different sets of data, and unless you have your data stored in an inte grated, *relational database*, this will be very difficult to do.

**relational database**

*Owner:* What do you mean by relational?

*Consultant:* A relational database stores data in separate groups, called *tables.* Each table stores information about a single topic, such as customer data or outstanding orders. The relational database connects these database tables so that you might, for example, print a list of all customers who have outstanding orders. To make these connections, the database must know how the two tables are related. When you define these relationships between tables, you are building a relational database.

**tables**

*Owner:* Well, I think we need a relational database, and MS-Access sounds like an interesting product. How do I find out more about it?

*Consultant:* Please follow me to the next section.

# Objective 2:  Starting the Software

**icons**

Your computer should be turned on and running MS-Windows. The Program Manager window will be visible. It contains the Program Group *icons*, which are small pictures. Each of these icons represents a group of programs. Find the Program Group icon labeled Microsoft Access, MS-Access, or simply Access. When you select a Program Group icon you open a window for that group; the window contains icons for the programs. The MS-Access Group window may include the MS-Access icon, a Readme Help icon, and a Setup icon.

**Cue Cards**

When you start MS-Access, the Cue Cards window may appear. *Cue Cards*, which are part of the MS-Access on-line help system, are tutorials that walk you through various complicated tasks, such as editing a table. If the Cue Cards window is open, simply close it. You will see it again the next time you start MS-Access. When time permits, you should investigate the contents of the Cue Cards window.

## Exercise 1: Starting MS-Access

This exercise teaches you to start MS-Access from the MS-Windows Program Manager.

1. Double-click the Microsoft Access Program Group icon in the Windows Program Manager screen to open the MS-Access Program Group (Fig. 1-1).

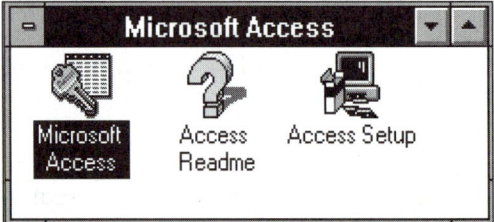

**Figure 1-1   MS-Access Program Group icons**

2. Double-click the Microsoft Access icon to start MS-Access.

3. If the Cue Cards window appears, close the window by double-clicking the small box in the upper, left corner of the Cue Cards window.

You are now in the MS-Access main window.

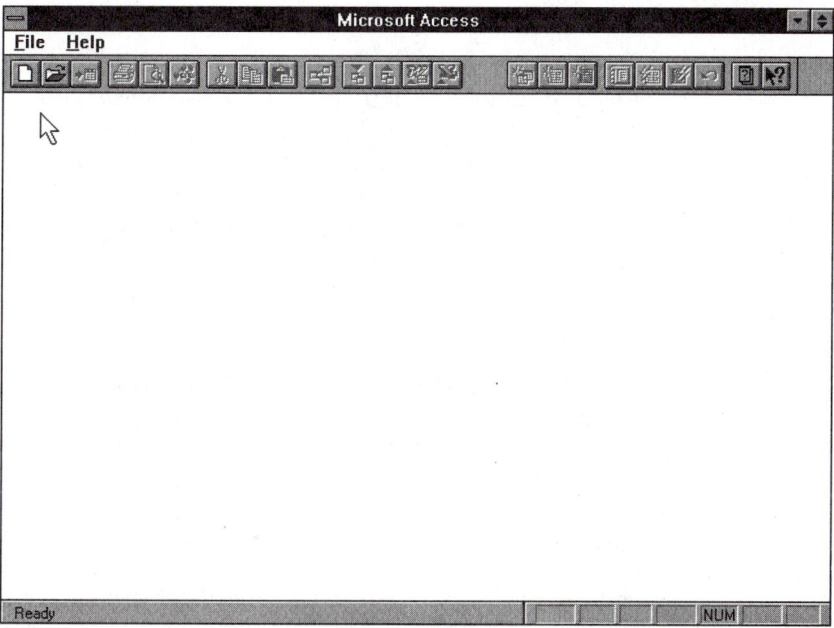

**Figure 1-2**  **MS-Access Main window**

### The Father of Modern Computing . . .

. . . was a nineteenth-century Englishman named Charles Babbage (1791–1871). He never built an operational computer himself, but his ideas laid the foundation for modern computing devices and methods.

Charles Babbage began work on the Difference Engine in 1822. This machine was designed to automate the calculation of the roots of polynomials. The British Navy used these calculations to produce astronomical tables for navigation. While developing the Difference Engine, Babbage began work on a much more powerful Analytical Engine. The Analytical Engine was designed as a general-purpose computing machine that employed the basic concepts of a modern-day digital computer. For nearly 40 years, Babbage labored at his plans, producing thousands of detailed drawings of this steam-driven computing machine that would accept punched-card input of both program instructions and data, perform any arithmetic operation under the direction of the mechanically stored set of instructions, and produce either punched-card or printed output. Babbage died before he could make his dream a reality.

Babbage's Analytical Engine was finally finished in 1991–92 from his original designs. It was sponsored and displayed by the Science Museum in London, England. The Analytical Engine works exactly as Babbage predicted it would.

# Objective 3: Mouse and Keyboard Commands

You can use either the mouse or the keyboard to navigate MS-Access screens and menus. When you start MS-Access, you see a nearly empty window. The title bar reads, "MS-Access." Directly below the title bar is the menu bar, which has only two options, File and Help. Notice that the letters F and H are underlined on the screen. The convention for all MS-Windows programs is that you can choose these menu items with the key combination ⟨ALT⟩ + (underlined letter). To use the File menu, you click File or press ⟨ALT⟩+⟨F⟩. The underlined letter is not necessarily the first letter of the word.

When you choose a menu item, a list of actions drops down below the item you choose. Once the drop-down menu is opened, there are three ways to choose an action: (1) select an item by pressing the appropriate letter (this time without ⟨ALT⟩), (2) use the arrow keys to highlight the item and press ⟨↵ ENTER⟩, or (3) use the mouse to select the item. You can also use a combination of keystrokes and mouse clicks.

## Exercise 2: Using the keyboard and mouse to open a database file

MS-Access comes with sample database files. You can open and close these files to familiarize yourself with the mouse and keyboard actions. MS-Access normally places the sample files in a directory called \access\sampapps.

   1. From the File menu, click the Open Database icon.

**dialog box**    The Open Database dialog box opens to help you select a database file (Fig. 1-3). A *dialog box* is a pop-up window that assists you in some task, such as choosing a file.

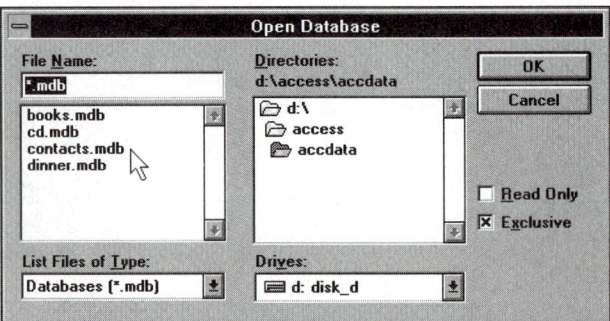

**Figure 1-3   Open Database dialog box**

   2. Change to the directory where the sample database files are stored.

   3. Double-click nwind.mdb to open the NorthWind Traders database.

The database window entitled Database: NWIND opens (Fig. 1-4). Leave it on the screen while you continue with the next objective.

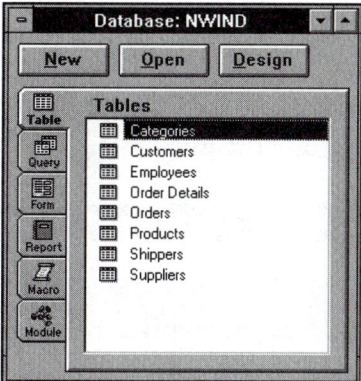

**Figure 1-4  NorthWind Traders database window**

# Objective 4:  Elements of the Screen

At the top of the screen is the title bar, which displays the title "Microsoft Access." To the left of the title bar is the box used to close MS-Access. To the right are two arrows that *minimize* (reduce the MS-Access window to an icon on the screen) and *maximize* (enlarge the MS-Access window to fill the entire screen) the MS-Access window. These arrows are standard MS-Windows controls.

**minimize**
**maximize**

Below the title bar is the main menu bar. Below the main menu bar is the toolbar, which contains a row of icons. Some icons are dimmed, which means they are not available at this time. When you position the cursor over an icon, a small balloon-box appears with a description of the icon. At certain times a longer description of the icon is shown in the lower left corner of the screen. These descriptions appear for the dimmed icons as well.

**database file**

The icon on the far left is used to create a new database file. It looks, appropriately, like a blank sheet of paper. The *database file* is the MS-Access file that contains all the tables you create, all the data you enter, and all the other database objects. The database filename always ends with the extension .mdb.

**on-line help**
**system**

The icon just to the right of the new database file icon looks like an open file folder. This is the icon for opening an existing database file. The two icons at the far right with question marks are for Cue Cards and on-line help. The *on-line help system* contains descriptions and definitions of everything used in MS-Access.

### Exercise 3: The MS-Access Main window: icons

In this exercise, you learn to use the first of the MS-Access help functions by positioning the cursor over various icons.

1. Position the cursor over one of the icons in the top toolbar and wait.

   A balloon box with information (Fig. 1-5) and a description in the lower left corner appear for that icon.

2. Repeat Step 1 for several other icons.

**Figure 1-5**  **Toolbar with balloon-box help windows for icons**

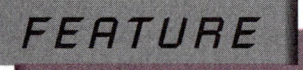

### How can I get a copy of that database?

You will probably develop databases for groups to which you belong, such as Little League, church groups, and social organizations. At work, you may produce contact directories, sales leads organizers, or branch office personnel rosters. At home, your video tapes, CDs, photographs, and even the contents of your freezer can be databased. As you develop useful databases in MS-Access, your friends, coworkers, and neighbors may ask for copies so they can use them. How do you provide copies? Most likely your friends will not want to buy MS-Access, and you know that you cannot legally install your copy on their computers, for copyright reasons.

There is an easy solution. You can buy a product called the MS-Access Developer's Toolkit. It costs several hundred dollars but is a one-time investment. With this product you can legally compile and distribute your databases with no further royalties or payments to Microsoft. As long as your friends have computers that will run MS-Windows, they can install your program and databases like any other Windows software package. They can run the programs, use the forms, add their own data, and generate reports and mailing labels; a nice, legal solution that makes everyone happy!

## Objective 5:  Elements of the Menu System

The opening screen for MS-Access shows only two menu options, File and Help. Clicking either of these options causes a menu box to drop down. The File menu opens and closes database files and lists the maintenance operations that you can perform on your databases. The Help menu is the gateway to the on-line help system and the Cue Cards.

### Exercise 4: The MS-Access Main window: menu choices

This exercise teaches you to use the MS-Access menu system.

1. Click File on the main menu bar to drop down a list of options (Fig. 1-6).

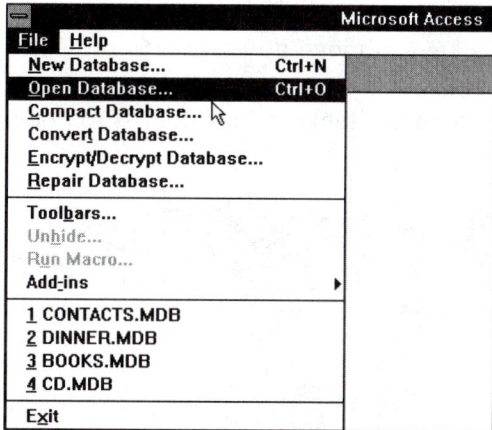

**Figure 1-6**   *File menu drop-down menu*

The options you will work with in later exercises are New Database, Open Database, Close Database, and Exit. Do not select any of these options yet.

2. Press ⌷ESC⌷ or click anywhere on the screen outside of the drop-down menu box to exit from this menu.

## Objective 6:  Event-Driven versus Menu-Driven Applications

You have probably heard the term event-driven application. What does it mean? Consider the Database: NWIND window on the screen. At the top of the window is a row of buttons: New, Open, and Design. Down the left side are tabs: Table, Query, Form, Report, Macro, and Module. Because MS-Access is event-driven, *you* decide what to do next. You can open a table to look at data, edit the design of a table, or use any one of the other MS-Access features. When you click a button or tab, the program interprets the click as an event—that is, a command to do something. It then runs the program code associated with that event.

In a menu-driven application, you have a list of choices, but the list is limited. You are forced to step through the program just as the programmer designed it.

## Exercise 5: Looking at an example of event-driven programming

In this exercise, you will investigate the NorthWind Traders database to see a good example of an event-driven application. You will learn important navigation skills inside an MS-Access application.

1. In the Database window, click the Form tab to show a list of forms.

2. Use the arrow keys to move down the list until the Main Switchboard entry is visible.

3. Double-click Main Switchboard on the list to open NorthWind Traders (Fig. 1-7).

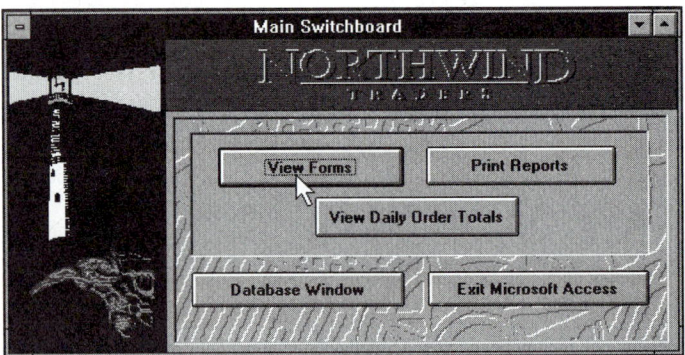

**Figure 1-7   NorthWind Traders Main Switchboard**

4. Click the View Forms button.

   A second switchboard, the Forms Switchboard, opens (Fig. 1-8). It shows six buttons, which allow you to do different things, such as look at customer information or modify product information.

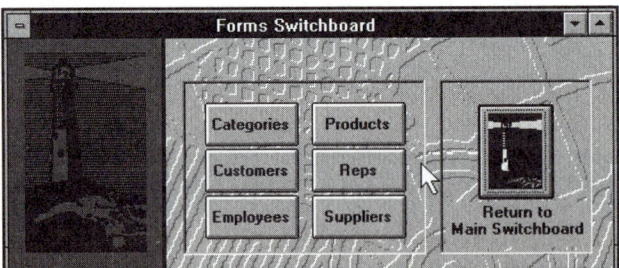

**Figure 1-8   NorthWind Traders Forms Switchboard**

5. Double-click the dash in the small box at the upper left corner of the Forms Switchboard.

   You are returned to the Main Switchboard.

6. Double-click the dash in the small box at the upper left corner of the Main Switchboard.

   The Main Switchboard closes, and you are returned to the Database window, without having to exit MS-Access.

# Objective 7:  The On-Line Help System

There are several ways to ask MS-Access for help. The first is to click the Help option on the top menu bar. The drop-down menu that appears contains a table of contents for the help system, a search option for tracking down help topics by keywords, and the Cue Cards discussed earlier.

On the top toolbar, at the far right, is an icon with an arrow and a question mark. When you click this icon, it stays active and changes color. The cursor changes to a copy of the arrow and question mark. You then position the cursor over any menu item or icon and click; the MS-Access help information for that specific menu item or icon appears.

A quick way to invoke Cue Cards is to use the Cue Cards icon. Just to the left of the Help icon is the Cue Cards icon, which looks like a stack of cards with a question mark on top.

**context-sensitive help**

MS-Access also has *context-sensitive help* available. When you press F1, MS-Access knows where you are in the software and provides information relevant to whatever you are doing.

**form**

**report**

When working with MS-Access, you create forms to help with data entry. A *form* displays one record at a time from a table of a database. You also build reports in MS-Access. A report is used to output data to either the screen or a printer. A *report* is a listing of data from the database, organized to provide information that can be used in making decisions.

**Wizards**

As you design tables, reports, and forms, you will encounter the *Wizards*, predefined sets of instructions built into MS-Access that guide you through particular tasks. The Wizards ask questions and then take over. For example, they can produce a table, form, or report for you. They differ from Cue Cards: Using Cue Cards is like having someone stand behind you and tell you what to do next; using a Wizard is like having someone take over the keyboard and do the work for you.

## Exercise 6: Examining the on-line help system

During this exercise, you will investigate some of the features of the MS-Access help system.

1. Choose Help/Contents from the top menu.

   The MS-Access Help Contents menu appears on the right of the screen (Fig. 1-9).

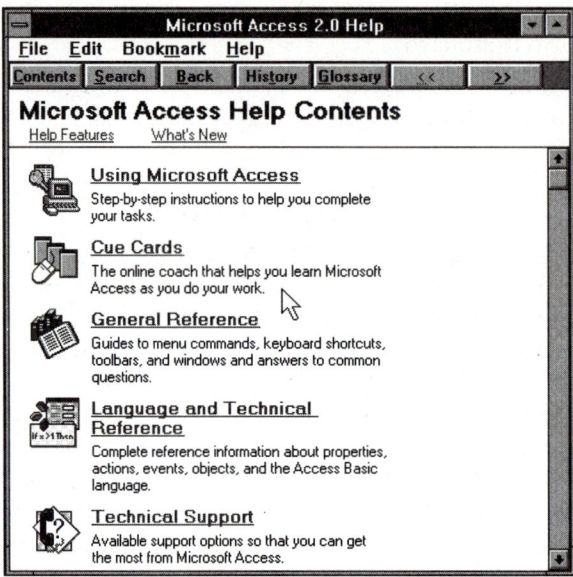

**Figure 1-9** **The On-Line Help menu**

2. Click Cue Cards from the list.

   The MS-Access Cue Cards window appears. Examine the available choices.

3. Click the dash in the upper left corner of the Cue Cards window. Choose Close.

4. Click the dash in the upper left corner of the Help window. Choose Close.

5. Click the Help icon on the top toolbar.

   The cursor changes to an arrow and a question mark (Fig. 1-10).

**Figure 1-10** **The Help cursor**

6. Position the changed cursor over the Print icon and click.

   MS-Access Help opens at the Print Command (File menu) page.

7. Double-click the dash in the upper left corner of the Help window.

   MS-Access Help closes.

# Objective 8:  Exiting the Software

Now you must close the database and exit from the software. You should never turn off your computer while any program is running because you risk losing data. Since you make business decisions based on information from your database, this risk is not acceptable. Always (1) close the database, (2) close MS-Access, (3) exit from MS-Windows, and (4) turn off your computer.

## Exercise 7: Exiting from the database

This exercise teaches you how to exit properly from the database. If you are finished with MS-Access, then you can close it.

1. Click File/Close Database.

   The NorthWind Traders database closes.

2. Click File/Exit.

   MS-Access is terminated.

## Chapter Summary

This chapter introduced the concept of a database and a database management system (DBMS). You learned how companies use DBMSs and what they can do for companies. You took a guided tour through MS-Access and the NorthWind Traders database. You looked at the screens and moved around using both the mouse and the keyboard. We discussed the differences between menu-driven and event-driven applications. You looked at the on-line help system, which is always available with MS-Access, and learned about the Cue Cards and the Wizards. You also learned how to leave MS-Access properly so that the data stored in your database will not be corrupted.

## Review Questions

### True/False Questions

_____  1. Data and information are the same thing.

_____  2. A database is a collection of unrelated facts.

_____  3. An event-driven program forces you to move through the application step-by-step.

_____ 4. A relational database allows you to organize your data into related groups called tables.

_____ 5. With on-line help you can search using specific keywords.

## Multiple-Choice Questions

_____ 6. A computerized record-keeping system that stores, manages, and retrieves data on demand is called a
   A. Wizard.
   B. database.
   C. database management system.
   D. user interface.

_____ 7. Organized data that is used in the decision-making process is called
   A. information.
   B. a database.
   C. a report.
   D. a flat-file data manager.

_____ 8. A database user interface
   A. helps you manage data.
   B. allows you to view data.
   C. helps you enter data and change data already stored in the database.
   D. all of the above.

_____ 9. When you need step-by-step instructions to accomplish a task you look for the
   A. Wizards.
   B. Cue Cards.
   C. on-line help table of contents.
   D. instructor.

_____ 10. When you are finished with MS-Access and ready to shut it down, you should
   A. turn off your computer.
   B. exit MS-Windows without closing MS-Access.
   C. close the database you are working with, then close MS-Access.
   D. close MS-Access, then close the database you are working with.

## Fill-in-the-Blank Questions

11. A person interacts with his/her computer through a _____.

12. MS-Access is a database management system that needs to run in the environment known as _____.

13. Programs that allow you to choose what you want to do next are called _____.

14. You can select menu commands by using the key combination _____ + the appropriate underlined letter.

15. Helpful information that is relevant to where you currently are in MS-Access is called _____.

## Acumen-Building Activities

## Quick Projects

## 1. Opening the NorthWind Traders Database Main Switchboard.

1. Start MS-Access. From the File menu click the Open Database icon.

2. Change to the directory where the sample database files are stored and double-click nwind.mdb to open the NorthWind Traders database.

3. Click the Form tab in the Database window.

4. Click the Main Switchboard entry in the list to highlight it (you may have to scroll down the list to find it). Click Open.

## 2. Using Print Preview.

1. In the NorthWind Traders database, at the Main Switchboard screen, click the Print Reports button.

2. In the Print Reports dialog box, click the Sales by Category option of Report to Print.

3. Highlight Dairy Products. Click Print Preview.

4. When the report appears on the screen, use the zoom-in and zoom-out features to examine the report.

## 3. Using context-sensitive help.

1. From the Print Preview screen, press F1 to invoke context-sensitive help.

2. Read the on-screen information about Print Preview.

3. Position the cursor over the green lettering that reads `Print Preview button` and click once. Read about the Print Preview icon. Click to close the pop-up help box.

4. Position the cursor over the green lettering that reads `Close button` and click once. Read about the Close icon.

5. Exit help and return to the Print Preview screen. Click File/Exit from the top menu.

6. Return to the Main Switchboard. Click File/Close from the top menu.

7. Close the Main Switchboard.

## 4. Using on-line help and Cue Cards.

1. From the Database window, click the Help menu and choose Cue Cards.

2. Click See a Quick Overview. Click the Databases button.

3. Read the page on What Is a Database? Click Next in the lower right corner.

4. Read A Microsoft Access Database. Click Next.

5. Close the Cue Cards. Close the NorthWind Traders database. Close MS-Access.

## In-Depth Projects

## 1. Designing the CD database.

You have a large collection of music CDs. Managing them is becoming difficult, and you are looking at computerizing.

In coming chapters, you will design and build a database in which you can record information about your collection of CDs. You'll create a table, designating the title, artist, recording label, music classification, length, release date, and cost of each CD. You'll then create a second table to store the track information for each CD. Then you will establish a relationship between the two tables, so you can extract information from the CD database.

From specifications we provide, you will design and develop a user interface for the CD database. You will create forms to assist you in data entry and reports to list what is in the database.

For now, write out a list of the data you would store in a database for your CD collection and the reports you would want to see from such a database.

## 2. Designing the Dinner Party database.

You belong to a social organization that meets periodically for dinner parties and would like to track the events better. In coming chapters, you will design and build a database in which you can record information about these dinner parties. The first table includes information about the people in your group—their names, addresses, phone numbers, dietary restrictions, likes, and dislikes. The second table includes information about each dinner party—when, where, and what was served. A third table keeps track of which people attended each dinner party. Then you will establish a relationship between these three tables, so you can extract information from the Dinner Party database.

You will design and develop a user interface for the Dinner Party database. You will create forms to assist you in data entry and reports to list what is in the database. For now, write out a list of the type of data you want to store in a dinner party database and what kind of information you want to extract.

## CASE STUDIES

### Coffee-On-The-Go:   Introduction

In this case study, you will create and use a database of employees for a business called Coffee-On-The-Go. This chain of espresso stands is located in many cities in the Pacific Northwest. The business sells various types of coffee drinks and teas, along with muffins and cookies. The coffee booths are all located in busy areas and are accessible by automobile and by foot.

You will be provided with more information in the chapters that follow.

## CASE STUDIES

### Videos West:   Introduction

In this case study, you will create and use a database for a video business located in Fairbanks, Alaska. This business has operated a video rental store in downtown Fairbanks for two years. The owners of Videos West are planning to expand the business by including a retail line of special interest videos available to the entire state by mail order.

You will be provided with the information to complete the database for the new venture in the chapters that follow.

# Chapter 2

## Designing A Database

*Objectives*
- Creating a Database File
- Designing the Tables in a Database
- Understanding Data and Field Types
- Determining Relationships
- Setting a Primary Key
- Creating a Database Table
- Editing a Database Table
- Saving the Database Table
- Printing a Definition of the Database Table

*Key Terms*

| TERM | DEFINITION |
| --- | --- |
| Field | a data item that is part of a database table and that is defined when you create the table; related fields are grouped together to form a record |
| Field Name | the name assigned to a field at the time it is defined |
| Data Type | the different types of data that MS-Access recognizes and supports; a data type is assigned to a field when it is defined |
| Record | a collection of related fields, such as customer information or inventory information; records of the same type make up a database table |
| Relationship | an association between two tables in a database that allows you to combine data items from each table and display them in the same form or report |

| TERM | DEFINITION |
|------|------------|
| **One-to-One Relationship** | a situation where each record in one table is related, or linked, to one and only one record in another table |
| **One-to-Many Relationship** | a situation where each record in one table is related, or linked, to more than one record in another table |
| **Many-to-Many Relationship** | a situation where many records in one table are related or linked to many records in the second table |
| **Primary Key** | a field of a table whose contents can be used to identify each row in the table; no two primary keys can have the same value within the same table |
| **Database Report** | a report that contains information on a table of the database, listing the fields, data types, field lengths, primary key assignments, and so on |
| **Table Wizard** | a predefined set of instructions built into MS-Access that builds a table for you |

Before you begin any database development, you must ask yourself: What am I going to use the database for? What kind of data am I going to collect? How am I going to collect it? What kind of reports am I going to produce? To make your database work well for you, you must understand its purpose and what it is intended for.

Database design is the first step of database development and is usually done with pencil and paper. You wouldn't think of building a plane without a set of engineering blueprints. Neither should you plunge ahead with database development until you have a clear design to work from.

Time spent on design is not time wasted. Rather, it cuts down on database development time. Perhaps more important, a good design will allow you to be productive and expand your database in response to future needs.

First you must decide what data is to be stored and how to divide the data items into appropriate groupings. Next you create the database and its tables according to the way you group the data items. Then you assign specific characteristics for each data item, such as a field name and data type. You will change some of these characteristics once the table has been created. Next you print out the Table Structure report, and finally you save the table structure.

# Objective 1:  Creating a Database File

MS-Access stores all the information about a database in one file on your disk. All MS-Access database files have the extension .mdb. You must create the database file before you can proceed.

## Exercise 1: Creating a new database file

This exercise teaches you how to create a new, empty database file.

1. Start MS-Access. Click File.
2. Click New Database to bring up the New Database dialog box (Fig. 2-1).

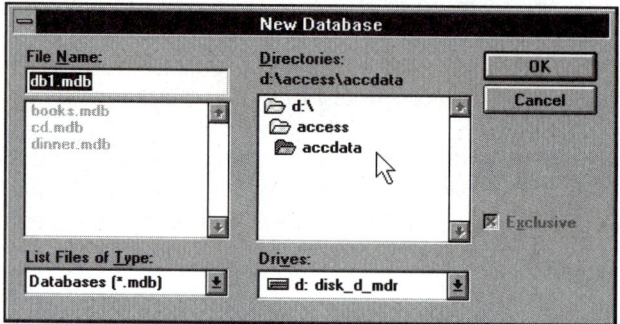

**Figure 2-1   New Database dialog box**

3. In the File Name window type contacts.mdb.
4. Move to the Drives window in this dialog box.

Verify that the drive shown is where you want to save the database file.

5. Move to the Directories window in this dialog box.

Verify that the directory shown is where you want to save the database file.

6. Click OK.

MS-Access creates your database. It moves you to the Database window, so that you may begin adding new tables (Fig. 2-2).

**Figure 2-2   MS-Access Database window**

# Objective 2:  Designing the Tables in a Database

Now that you have built your database file, you can think seriously about what to put in it. Write down what you want this database to do. Is it meant to keep track of your collection of compact discs? Is it meant to track statistics gathered during a research project? Is it a database that underlies an order-entry system? Each of these three databases would be designed differently.

Once you know the purpose of the database, list the type of output you want. Paper reports, electronic reports, computer files, and merge files are types of database output. Also decide what information will be in the reports. A report can be as simple as a listing of your CD titles or as complex as a customer invoice. If you understand what you want to get out of a database, then you know what you need to put into it. Working backwards like this is often the most efficient method of determining what data items you need to store in a database.

Let's design a sample database: a sales contact database. In such a database, you would store a person's name, address, phone number, the company he or she works for, and so on. To begin, list these data items on a piece of paper—do not start keying them into the database until you have **field** thought the design through. Each data item will become a field. A *field* is a data item that is part of a database table. Related fields—for example, **record** name, address, and phone number—are grouped together to form a *record*. Each contact person will become a record in the contacts table.

**field name** Assign each data item a proper *field name*. MS-Access allows you to use long table names and field names for ease of recognition. It even permits you to use spaces in these names, such as First Name. However, the technique most favored among MS-Access database designers is to leave out all spaces and join words, indicating the beginning of each word with an uppercase letter, as in FirstName.

Make a list of how you will want to sort your sales contacts. This helps you organize the data. If you list first name, last name, company name, street address, city, state, and zip code as separate data items, then you can sort your database by first name, to find Mary's phone number, or by city and zip code, to organize your sales calls when you're in Denver.

Consider if you are storing too much information in any one field. Are you storing a person's full name in one field? It may be easier to store it in two fields, such as FirstName and LastName. Having the last name stored separately from the first name allows sorting by either first or last name.

Consider if you are storing too little information in any one field. Did you split the street address into separate fields for number, street, and apartment or suite? Do you need this much detail? If you are a door-to-door salesperson, you may need to know which of your customers live on Baker Street. But if you are keeping a database of batting statistics for the local Little League team, this design would be too detailed.

### Exercise 2: Designing the tables of a database

This exercise shows you how to lay out the design of the sales contact database on paper.

1. Make a list of the data items you will store in your sales contact database.
2. Give each data item a proper field name.
3. Mark the fields on which you will sort the data.
4. Consider if you are storing too much information in any one field.
5. Consider if you are storing too little information in any one field.

## Objective 3:  Understanding Data and Field Types

**data type**    You should choose an appropriate *data type* for each field. MS-Access has a number of data types from which you can choose, as described in Table 2-1.

**Table 2-1    MS-Access data types**

| DATA TYPE | DESCRIPTION | EXAMPLE |
|---|---|---|
| Text | The data type used to store letters, numbers, and special characters (*&^%$#@!). Can be up to 255 characters long. | 123 West High St. |
| Memo | A text data type with a maximum length of 64,000 characters. Use this data type for notes, comments, or long fields (greater than 255 characters). There are some restrictions imposed on this data type, so use it carefully. | Any kind of text message or number can be stored. |
| Number | A data type used to store numbers. There are many numeric data types. | 1 |
| Byte | A number data type, stores values from 0 to 255 (no fractions). | 1 |
| Integer | A number data type, stores values from –32,768 to 32,767 (no fractions). | 32,000 |
| Long Integer | A number data type, stores values from –2,,147,648 to 2,147,647 (no fractions). | 1,100,000 |
| Single | A number data type, stores values with six digits of precision (scientific notation). This data type can store fractions. | 4.25 |
| Double | A number data type, stores values with ten digits of precision (scientific notation). This data type can store fractions. | .0000000001 |
| Date/ Time | The data type used to store date and/or time values. | 1/01/94, 5:34 P.M. |
| Currency | The data type used to store money values, up to 15 digits on the left side of the decimal point and 4 digits on the right side. Displayed in forms and reports in the currency format, as shown. | $1.00 |

**continued**

**Table 2-1**    **Continued**

| DATA TYPE | DESCRIPTION | EXAMPLE |
|---|---|---|
| Counter | A number automatically incremented by MS-Access whenever a new record is added to a table. Counter fields are most often used as primary keys. They are maintained within MS-Access and cannot be updated by the user. | 0000001 |
| Yes/No | A data type used when one of two possible answers is needed, such as yes/no, true/false, 0/1. There are some restrictions imposed on this data type, so use it carefully. | 0 |
| OLE Object | A data type used to store graphics, video, sound, or other computer programs, such as spreadsheets, in the database. There are some restrictions imposed on this data type, so use it carefully. | |

When choosing a data type for a field, consider the following:

1. Will this field store a date and/or time, a money value, or some graphic?

If a date or time, select the Date/Time data type.

If a money value, use the Currency data type.

If a graphic or sound/video clip, use the OLE Object data type.

Otherwise, proceed.

2. What is the maximum size of the data to be stored in the field?

If one of two letters or numbers, use the Yes/No data type.

If over 255 characters, use the Memo data type.

Otherwise, proceed.

3. Will you need to do arithmetic on the data that you have stored in this field?

Use one of the number data types, determined by (1) the largest and smallest value you will ever need to store and (2) whether you will need to store fractions or only whole numbers.

Otherwise, proceed.

4. Will you be storing letters, numbers, and special characters in a field?

Use the Text data type.

# Objective 4:  Determining Relationships

**relationship**

Look at the tables and determine if there are any relationships between your tables. A *relationship* is a special association between two tables in a database. This association allows you to combine data items from two tables and display them in the same form or report.

A relational database is composed of data grouped into tables. These tables are related to one another in one of three ways: one-to-one, one-to-many, and many-to-many.

**one-to-one relationship**

A *one-to-one relationship* is when a record in one table is related or linked to one and only one record in a second table. A student's on-campus address information might be stored in one table, while the student's parent/guardian information might be stored in a second table. The student has one campus address record in one table related to one parent information record in a second table.

The link that joins these two tables in the one-to-one relationship is a data field that is present in both tables. In the example, the StudentID field is a field in the Student table as well as the StuParentInfo table. When the value of StudentID in a record in the Student table matches the value of StudentID in a record in the StuParentInfo table, you have a link established between these two tables.

**primary key**

The StudentID field is an excellent candidate for the primary key. A *primary key* has a value that is unique. Since no two students will have the same student ID number, the ID number is unique and suitable as the primary key. Most often the primary key field is used to link two related tables.

**one-to-many relationship**

A *one-to-many relationship* is when a record in one table is related or linked to many records in a second table. In our example, each department at Central University offers many courses, but each course, with its own unique course number, is offered by only one department. In this case, one table contains data describing each department (the Department table), and a second table describes each class (the Class table). The relationship between the Department table and the Class table is a one-to-many relationship; each record in the Department table is related to many records in the Class table.

**many-to-many relationship**

A *many-to-many relationship* is where many records in one table are related or linked to many records in a second table. On campus, many students take many classes, and each class has many students. Student information is stored in the Student table. Class information is stored in the Class table. A student registers for many classes each term, and a class includes many students. This constitutes a many-to-many relationship.

Keeping in mind the different types of relationships you can have in a relational database, you must determine the kinds of relationships between tables.

# Objective 5:  Setting a Primary Key

Once you have determined the relationships between tables in your database, select a field in each table to serve as a primary key. Remember, the data values in a primary key field must uniquely identify each row in the table.

If you don't have a field in a table that is a good primary key, you might have to create one. StudentID, CustomerID, and InvoiceNumber are all typical primary key fields. While it is not absolutely necessary to set a primary key for each table, MS-Access functions faster and more efficiently if you do. It is always a good idea to assign a primary key to each table in your database.

# Objective 6:  Creating a Database Table

**Table Wizard**

MS-Access has many Wizards to help you create database objects, one of which is the Table Wizard. The *Table Wizard* is a set of instructions that prompts you for certain information and then builds a table for you. You can build a table without the help of the Table Wizard, but the best practice in most cases is to let the Table Wizard build a basic table for you and then modify the table to fit your needs.

### Exercise 3: Creating the database tables

This exercise shows you how to use the Table Wizard to construct the first table in your contact database.

1. At the Database window, make sure the Table tab is selected and click New.

The New Table dialog box pops up.

2. Choose the Table Wizards button to activate the Table Wizard (Fig. 2-3).

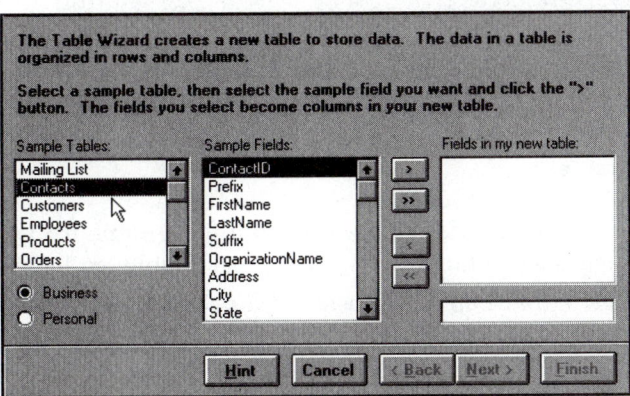

**Figure 2-3**  **Table Wizard window**

3. Highlight Contacts in the Sample Tables box.

The list of fields in the Sample Fields box changes to show the suggested fields for a Contacts table.

4. Highlight the ContactID field in the Sample Fields list. Click the single right arrow button to the right of the Sample Fields.

A copy of the ContactID field is moved to the list entitled Fields in my new table, and the Sample Fields highlight bar moves down to the next entry in the list.

5. Select the following fields from the Sample Fields list: FirstName, LastName, OrganizationName, Address, City, State, PostalCode, Country, WorkPhone, HomePhone, Note, and Photograph.

*TIP*   A quick way to select an item from the Sample Fields list is to double-click on it. The first click highlights the item; the second click selects it.

6. Click the Next> button.

The Next dialog box of the Table Wizard appears, asking you about table names and primary keys (Fig. 2-4).

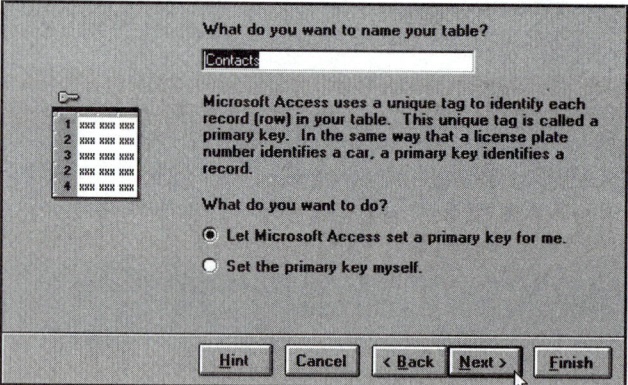

**Figure 2-4   Table Wizard window asking, "What do you want to name your table?"**

7. This Wizard dialog box asks you for a name for your table. MS-Access suggests Contacts. This seems reasonable, so leave it as is.

8. Check that Let MS-Access set a primary key for me is selected, then click Next.

The final Table Wizard window appears (Fig. 2-5).

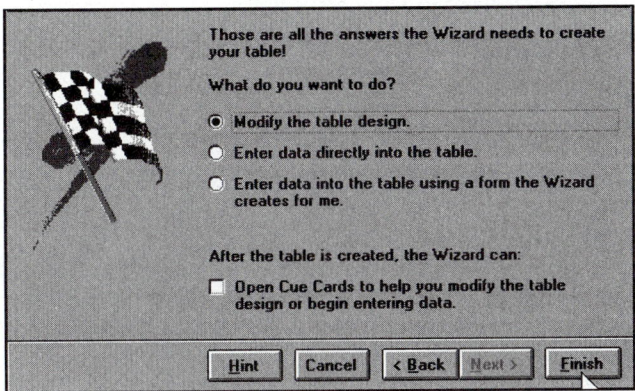

**Figure 2-5**   **Table Wizard Window with a checkered flag**

9. Click the Modify the table design button, and then the Finish button.

The Table Wizard builds your table and then exits, presenting you with the table in design view, so you can modify it.

# Objective 7:  Editing a Database Table

The Table Wizard is a helpful starting point for creating a table, but you will probably want to make some changes to the table it builds for you. In Exercise 4, you will modify some of the fields in the Contacts table.

## Adding field descriptions

You should add some descriptive text to identify better the fields in the table. It is good practice to annotate each field when you create a table.

### Exercise 4: Editing an existing field: adding field descriptions

The Table Wizard does not supply descriptions of each field when it builds a table, so you should add descriptions to document the fields you created. At the moment, your screen displays the Table Design window (Fig. 2-6).

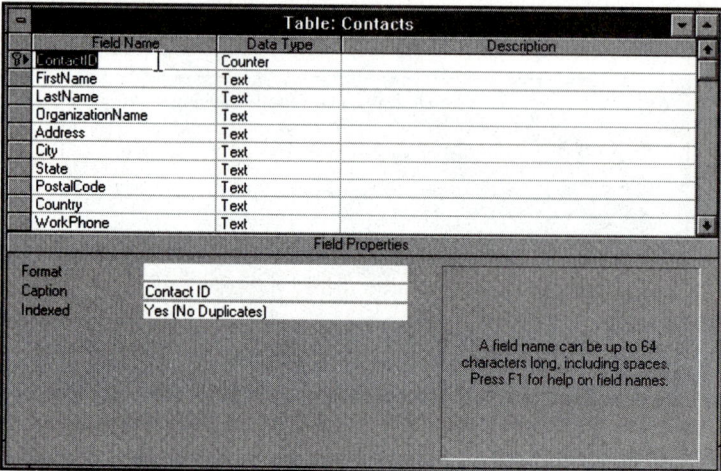

**Figure 2-6** **Table Design window**

1. Use TAB, →, or the mouse to move the cursor to the top row of the Description field. Type Automatic counter, primary key.

2. Move the cursor to the Description column for the FirstName field and type Given name.

3. Add descriptions for the remaining fields.

# Objective 8: Saving the Database Table

It is always a good idea to save your tables as you work on them and again when you end an editing session.

## Exercise 5: Saving a database table

1. Click File/Save to save your work.

2. Close the Design window by clicking File/Close.

---

**The First Computer Programmer . . .**

. . . was a woman, Lady Augusta Ada Byron (1815 – 1853), the Countess of Lovelace and daughter of the poet Lord Byron. She worked closely with Charles Babbage, the father of the modern computer, developing program instructions for his Analytical Engine. In 1978, the Department of Defense (DOD) staged a competition to select a programming language as the standard for all software development within the DOD. They selected the language Ada, which was named after Augusta Ada. Today the DOD still uses Ada as the programming language for its embedded computer systems on airplanes, ships, and rockets.

# Objective 9:  Printing a Definition of the Database Table

**database report**

When you build tables in your database you should print out information about each table. This *database report* gives you documentation for each table—for example, when the table was created, when it was last updated, and how many records are in the table. The report also contains information on each field or column in the table, the relationships this table has with other tables, and how those relationships are defined.

## Exercise 6: Printing out a table definition

1. In the Database window, click the Table tab. Make sure the Contacts table is highlighted.
2. Select File/Print Definition.

The Print Table Definition dialog box appears (Fig. 2-7).

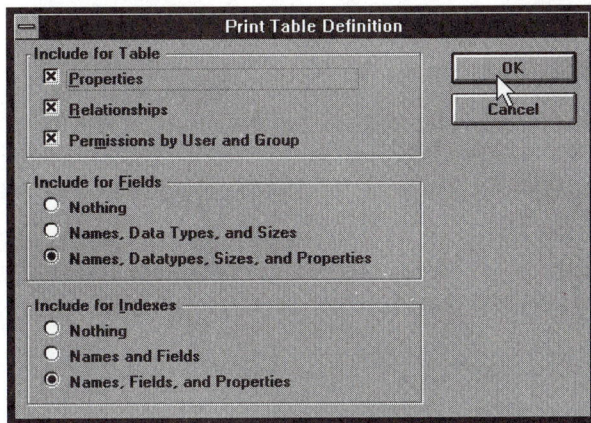

**Figure 2-7**   **Print Table Definition dialog box**

3. Select the following options for the Table Definition report:
   - Include for Table: Properties; Relationships; Permissions by User and Group
   - Include for Fields: Names, Data Types, Sizes, and Properties
   - Include for Indexes: Names, Fields, and Properties
4. Choose OK.

The Table Definition report Object Definition appears in Print Preview. (A table is an MS-Access object.) Scroll through the report, clicking the cursor to zoom in and out on any portion of the report.

**WARNING** If you want to print out this report, be sure that your computer is connected to a printer and that the printer is turned on.

## FEATURE

### What's in a name?

Here are some thoughts on how to handle a seemingly easy subject that is full of pitfalls — how to divide up the name field.

The simplest method is to split your names into two fields: one for last names, the other for first name plus middle initials. You will find that this accommodates both Wolfgang A. Mozart and J. Sebastian Bach.

However, name fields can be handled many different ways. Consider the following list:

- John Doe
- John M. Doe
- J. Martin Doe
- Dr. John M. Doe, III
- J. Martin Doe, III Ph. D.

And what about hyphenated, combined, and prefixed names like Forbes-Hamilton, Van Der Waal, and MacTavish? Or double last names such as Jacqueline Kennedy Onassis? You may consider using FamilyName and GivenName instead of FirstName and LastName.

Many societies reverse the order of their names: The well-known Japanese actor Toshiro Mifune is called Mifune Toshiro. It is important to be culturally, politically, and technically correct.

5. Click the Print icon.

The Print dialog box pops up (Fig. 2-8). You can print the entire report (six pages) or just a few pages. Check with your instructor to determine your best set of options for printing all or part of this report.

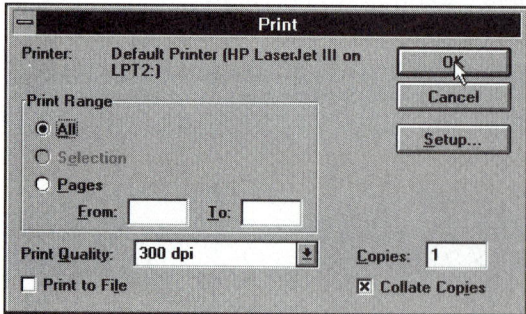

**Figure 2-8** **Print dialog box**

6. To exit Print Preview, click the Open Door icon in the left corner.

7. Click File/Close Database to close the database.

8. Click File/Exit to shut down MS-Access.

## Chapter Summary

The first part of this chapter discussed database design and some of the techniques used to develop a good design. You started with paper and pencil and determined (1) what the purpose of the database is and (2) what kind of information you want to get out of the database. That helped you to decide what kind of data to store and how to organize the data in the tables of the database. We discussed the types of relationships between the tables of the database and the criteria used to determine primary key assignments.

In the second part of this chapter, you built a table for your contacts database, then made some changes to the fields in the table. You learned how to print out a database report and save the table.

## Review Questions

### True/False Questions

_____ 1. Before writing code, you need not take time to design your database program.

_____ 2. If you understand what you want from a database, then you will understand how to design your database.

_____ 3. It is a good idea to keep your database files in a directory separate from the MS-Access software.

_____ 4. Every record in a table should have a unique identifier, called a primary key.

_____ 5. A one-to-one relationship involves only one table.

## Multiple-Choice Questions

_____ 6. All MS-Access database files have the extension

    A. .mbd

    B. .mdt

    C. .mdb

    D. .dta

_____ 7. A Table Wizard will

    A. select data types for you.

    B. show you the different colors and design options available for your table.

    C. enter data into the table for you.

    D. guide you through the table-building process and construct a table for you.

_____ 8. The primary key of a table

    A. uniquely identifies each record in the table.

    B. can be maintained only by MS-Access.

    C. can be maintained only by the user.

    D. speeds up operations on the database.

_____ 9. You would make a field a number field if

    A. you will be doing calculations on the contents of the field.

    B. the contents of the field will be number values.

    C. the contents of the field will not be number values.

    D. the field will hold decimal values.

_____ 10. If you need to store long messages or notes that will exceed 255 characters, you must use the data type called

    A. text.

    B. memo.

    C. double.

    D. long.

## Fill-in-the-Blank Questions

11. MS-Access stores all the information about a database in _____ file on your hard drive.

12. When designing your database and choosing table and field names, it (is, is not) a good idea to use spaces in the names.

13. In a _____ relationship, each record in one table is related to many records in a second table.

14. The field in a table that contains a group of unique values that can uniquely identify each row of the table is called a _____.

15. To store money values in a field, you would use the _____ data type.

## Acumen-Building Activities

### Quick Projects

### 1. Creating a new Books database.

1. Start MS-Access. Click File/New Database.
2. In the File Name window type books.mdb.
3. Move to the Drives window in this dialog box. Make sure that the drive shown is where you want to save the database file.
4. Move to the Directories window in this dialog box. Make sure that the directory shown is where you want to save the database file. Click OK.

### 2. Creating a new table.

This exercise is a continuation of Quick Project #1.

1. At the Database window, with the Table tab selected, click New.
2. Choose the Table Wizards button.
3. Under Sample Tables, choose Personal. Scroll through the list and choose Book Collection.
4. From the Sample Fields list, choose the following fields and move them to the Fields in My Table list: BookCollectionID, Title, ISBNNumber, PublisherName, DatePurchased, Pages, and Note.
5. Click the Next button. Name your table MyBooks.
6. Choose Set the Primary Key Myself. Click Next.
7. Accept that BookCollectionID will be unique for each record and choose Numbers and/or letters I enter when I add new records. Click Next.
8. Click Modify the table design. Click Finish.

### 3. Adding field descriptions to the MyBooks table.

This exercise is a continuation of Quick Project #2.

1. Type these descriptions for the corresponding field names:
2. Save your changes by clicking File/Save.
3. Close the Design window. Click File/Close.

| FIELD NAME | DESCRIPTION |
| --- | --- |
| **BookCollectionID** | Primary key of this table; unique identifier for each book. |
| **Title** | Title of the book |
| **ISBNNumber** | Assigned ISBN number. |
| **PublisherName** | Name of the publishing house. |
| **DatePurchased** | When this book was purchased. |
| **Pages** | Number of pages in the book. |
| **Note** | Subject, notes, and comments. |

## 4. Printing out a report for the MyBooks table.

This exercise is a continuation of Quick Project #3.

1. Highlight MyBooks in the Database window. Select File/Print Definition.
2. Use the default options for this table. Choose OK.
3. Look at the Print Preview presentation of this report and use the zoom feature.
4. If you are connected to a printer, click the Print icon.
5. Choose File/Close. Choose File/Close Database.

## In-Depth Projects

## 1. Creating the CD database.

1. Create a new database file and call it cd.mdb.
2. Create a new table using the Table Wizard. From the Personal Sample Tables list, use MusicCollection. Select MusicCollectionID, Title, GroupName, RecordingLabel, YearReleased, and PurchasePrice, in that order, and add them as fields in your new table.
3. Name your new table CDCollection, and let MS-Access set the primary key for you.
4. Indicate that you want to modify the table design, then tell the Table Wizard that you are finished.
5. In the Description column of the CDCollection table, add some text describing each field. Notice that MusicCollectionID is the primary key for this table.
6. Save the changes and close the Design Mode screen.
7. Print the Table Definition using the default options or, if you are not connected to a printer, carefully examine the Print Preview output.
8. Exit from Print Preview and close the database.

## 2. Creating the Dinner Party database.

1. Create a new database file and call it dinner.mdb.

2. Create a new table using the Table Wizard. From the Personal Sample Tables list use Guests. Select GuestID, FirstName, LastName, Address, City, State, PostalCode, HomePhone, and HealthProblems, in that order, and add them as fields in your new table.

3. Name your new table DinnerGuests and let MS-Access set the primary key for you.

4. Indicate that you want to modify the table design, then tell the Table Wizard that you are finished.

5. In the Description column of the DinnerGuests table, add a line of description for each field. GuestID is the primary key for this table. For the description of HealthProblems, type Dietary restrictions.

6. Save the changes and close the Design Mode screen.

7. Print the Table Definition using the default options or, if you are not connected to a printer, carefully examine the Print Preview output.

8. Exit from Print Preview and close the database.

# CASE STUDIES

 **Coffee-On-The-Go:**   ## Creating a Database

In this chapter, you learned how to create a database and a database table. You will use those skills to create an employee table for Coffee-On-The-Go.

1. Create a database file Coffee.mdb.

2. Create the following employee table:

| Field | Type | Size |
|---|---|---|
| EmployeeID | Text | 10 |
| Last | Text | 20 |
| First | Text | 9 |
| Location | Text | 2 |
| Sex | Text | 1 |
| Salary | Currency | |
| Start | Date/Time | |
| Current | Yes/No | |

3. Make EmployeeID the primary key for this table.

4. Save the table as Employee.

5. Print the table definition.

# CASE STUDIES

 **Videos West:**   **Creating a Database**

In this chapter, you learned how to create a database and a database table. You will use those skills to create an inventory table for Videos West.

1. Create a database file Video.mdb.
2. Create the following inventory table:

| Field | Type | Size |
|---|---|---|
| VideoID | Counter | – |
| Type | Text | 2 |
| Title | Text | 30 |
| Cost | Currency | |
| Retail | Currency | |
| Quantity | Numeric/Integer | 3 |
| Rating | Text | 2 |
| Release | Date | |

3. Make VideoID the primary key for this table.
4. Save the table as Inventory.
5. Print the table definition.

# Chapter 3

# Adding Records to the Database

**Objectives**
- Opening a Database File
- Using the Datasheet View to Add Records
- Using the Form Wizard to Create a Basic Data Entry Form
- Using the Form View to Add Records
- Generating a Quick Report with the Report Wizard

**Key Terms**

| TERM | DEFINITION |
|------|------------|
| **Datasheet** | a display of many records from a table of the database with the data arranged in rows and columns |
| **Form Wizard** | a predefined set of instructions built into MS-Access that assists in building a form by asking questions and then constructing a form |
| **Browse Mode** | a mode of operation that allows you only to view the records in your database |
| **Edit Mode** | a mode of operation that allows you to browse, make changes, and add records to your database |
| **Data-Entry Mode** | a mode of operation that allows you only to add records to your database |
| **Report Wizard** | a predefined set of instructions built into MS-Access that assists in building a report by asking questions and then constructing a report |

You need to add data to your database so that you can extract information. Data can be added directly to the database tables using the datasheet view of the database or a data-entry form. In this chapter, you will add data to the database using both techniques. You will use the MS-Access Form Wizard to build a quick data-entry form to help you enter the data. Then you will use the MS-Access Report Wizard to generate a quick report so you can have a list of the data that you entered into the database.

MS-Access forms are usually screen displays that show a single record at a time from a database table. They are used to enter data into the database and display data from the database, record by record. Reports are printed on paper or distributed electronically and display organized information from the database.

**datasheet**    The *datasheet* of an MS-Access database presents many records from a single table in a spreadsheet format. You can enter data directly into the datasheet. The Form Wizard helps you quickly build a form that is more suitable for data entry. Once you have some data in the database, you can use the Report Wizard to generate a quick report.

# Objective 1:  Opening a Database File

In order to continue working with the Sales Contact database you created in Chapter 2, you must first open that database file. There are three different ways to open an MS-Access database file. The first way is to use the icons on the upper toolbar. When you first start MS-Access, you will see a screen that is blank except for the menu and toolbar at the top and the status bar at the bottom, which reads "Ready." On the toolbar, the second icon from the left looks like an open folder. Clicking on this icon will open the Open Database dialog box.

The second way to open a database file is to use the top drop-down menu. By selecting the File option on the menu, then selecting the Open Database option from the drop-down menu that appears, you open the Open Database dialog box.

If you have recently used the database file you are seeking, then the third method may be the quickest: Select the File menu; near the bottom of the drop-down menu, just above Exit, is a list of recently used database files. You can select any file from this list.

### Exercise 1: Opening a database file

1. Start MS-Access. Click the Open Folder icon of the top toolbar (Fig. 3-1).

**Figure 3-1**    **Opening a database with the Open Folder icon**

The Open Database dialog box pops up (Fig. 3-2), allowing you to select your drive, directory, and database file.

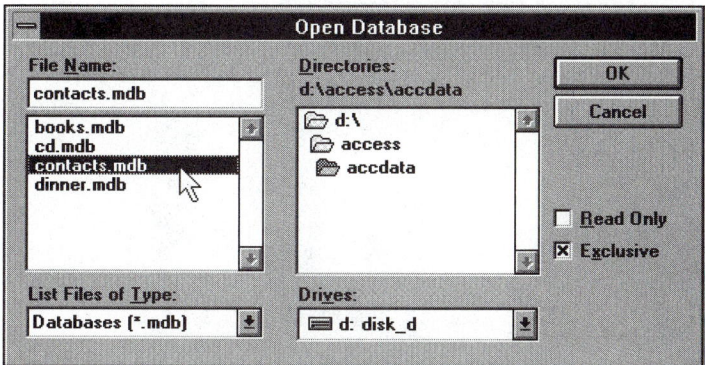

**Figure 3-2   Open Database dialog box**

2. Click Cancel.

   Now you will open the database file using the third method we discussed.

3. Click File on the menu bar (Fig. 3-3).

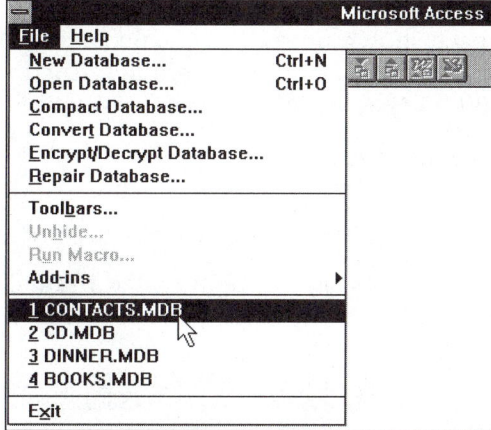

**Figure 3-3   MS-Access File menu**

4. Click the entry for contacts.mdb at the bottom of the drop-down menu.

   The Database window opens (Fig. 3-4).

**Figure 3-4   The Database window**

# Objective 2:  Using the Datasheet View to Add Records

You can add records directly to the datasheet. The datasheet looks much like a spreadsheet, with data arranged in rows and columns. Each row represents a single record; each column represents a single field of data.

When you add data to a field in the datasheet and the text you type is longer than the space shown on screen, the text scrolls to the left as you type it in. Notice that the table columns are identified by field captions, which (unlike field names) contain spaces for clarity.

### Exercise 2: Adding records to the database using the Datasheet view

In this exercise, you will type several records directly into the datasheet.

1.  Make sure the Contacts table is highlighted in the Database window. Click the Open button to open the datasheet (Fig. 3-5).

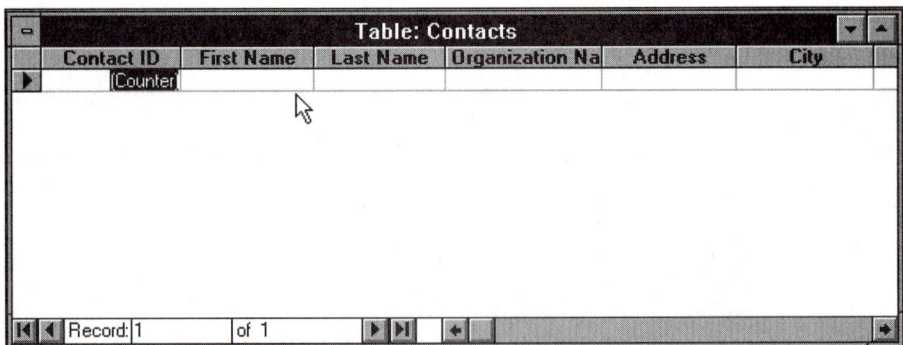

**Figure 3-5   Contacts database in Datasheet view**

2. Position the cursor in the first row of the First Name column and type
John S.

The counter field, ContactID, is immediately assigned a value by
MS-Access.

3. Using ⌜TAB⌝, move to the first row of the Last Name column and type
Adams.

4. Enter the following data for each field:

**The First U.S. Government Database . . .**

. . . was developed by the Census Bureau to help with the 1890 census. The 1880 census took seven years to tabulate by hand. A government engineer and statistician named Herman Hollerith came up with an idea to facilitate counting. The 1890 census data was stored on cards with holes punched in them. Hollerith then built devices to punch the holes and other devices to sort the cards. Cards were "read" by electromechanical devices equipped with wire brushes that touched the cards. When the brush encountered a hole, it completed a circuit in an electromechanical counter. Using Hollerith's equipment and ideas, the Census Bureau completed the 1890 census count one month after the data was entered onto punch cards. The complete set of tabulations, including information that had never before been gathered because of the enormity of the task, was finished in under two years.

| FIELD CAPTION | DATA |
|---|---|
| Organization Name: | Antiques Unlimited |
| Address: | 47 Main Street |
| City: | Boston |
| State: | MA |
| Postal Code: | 01738 |
| Country: | USA |
| Work Phone: | 1241234567 (Don't worry about parentheses around the area code or the hyphen in a seven-digit phone number; the format mask inserts those for you. Type only the digits, without any spaces.) |
| Home Phone: | 1249742525 |
| Note: | A real nice guy, likes to golf on Wednesdays. |
| Photo: | (no entry) |

5. Press ⌜TAB⌝ to finish the record entry.

6. Save your work by selecting File/Save Record.

## Exercise 3: Resizing a column of the datasheet

You can change the size of the columns in a datasheet so that you can see more and work better as you add and edit data. (If you have used Microsoft Excel, then you already know how to resize an MS-Access datasheet column.)

1. Position the cursor on the right boundary of the Address column.

The cursor will change to a short vertical line intersected by a horizontal double arrow.

2. Drag the column boundary to the right to widen the column until it is large enough to display the full address (Fig. 3-6).

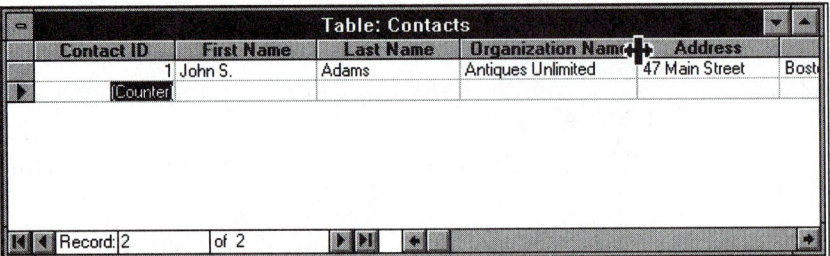

**Figure 3-6** **Resizing columns on the datasheet**

3. Move to the State column. Position the cursor over the right boundary line of the State column label until the cursor changes shape.

4. Drag the right boundary line of the State column to the left, making the State column narrower.

5. Move to the Note column. Resize the Note column, making it wider so you can read a reasonable portion of the text contained within.

6. Save your changes by selecting File/Save Table. Close the datasheet using File/Close. Choose Yes when asked if you want to save the layout changes.

# Objective 3: Using the Form Wizard to Create a Basic Data Entry Form

**Form Wizards**

There is a second way to enter data into the database: Use a data-entry form. You can easily and quickly build a data entry form using the MS-Access Form Wizards. The *Form Wizards* are programs built into MS-Access that assist in building a form by asking questions and constructing a form.

One of the MS-Access Form Wizards builds a very simple default form (MS-Access calls it an AutoForm) from a single table, with all the fields arranged in a single column. In later chapters, you will rearrange the position of the fields on the form and add some advanced features that will make your form more useable.

## Exercise 4: Creating a basic data-entry form

The Form Wizard asks you several questions and then generates a default data-entry form for the Contacts table.

1. Make sure you're at the Database window and click the Form tab.

   The Forms window opens. At this point, you will have no forms in the list.

2. Click the New button to begin designing a new form (Fig. 3-7).

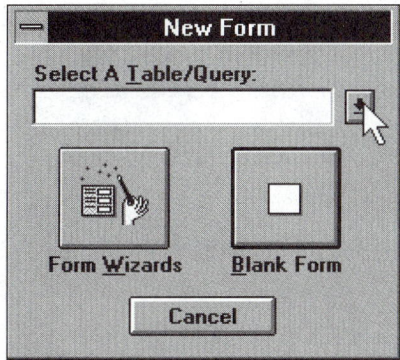

**Figure 3-7  New Form menu**

3. Click the down arrow to the right of the Select a Table/Query box.
   The drop-down menu appears with Contacts highlighted.
4. Click the highlighted Contacts entry in the list.
   Contacts pops into the Select a Table/Query box.
5. Click the Form Wizards button to initiate the Form Wizards (Fig. 3-8).

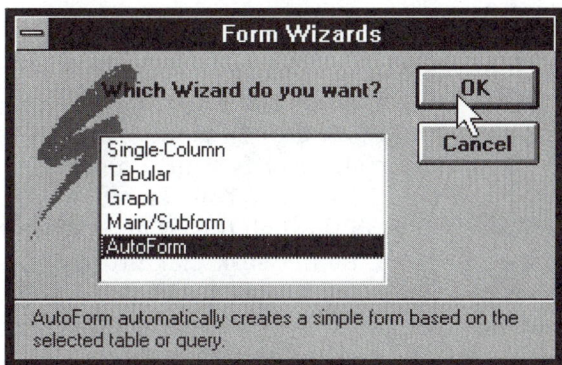

**Figure 3-8  Form Wizards dialog box**

6. Select AutoForm from the list of Wizards. Click OK.
   MS-Access builds the default data-entry form.
7. Save your work by clicking File/Save Form As from the top menu.
   The Save As dialog box appears.
8. Type QuickForm. Click OK (Fig. 3-9).

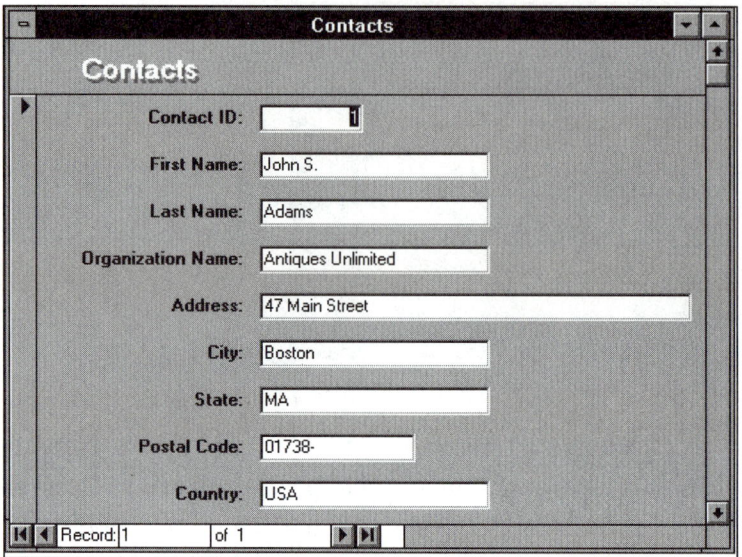

**Figure 3-9  A new form**

# Objective 4:  Using the Form View to Add Records

**Browse mode**

While working on a form, you have available three modes of operation: Browse mode, Data-Entry mode, and Edit mode. When you first open a form in MS-Access you are in *Browse mode:* You can search through the database and look at all your records. You can browse through the records using CTRL+PAGE DOWN and CTRL+PAGE UP. You can also use the controls at the bottom of the form to scroll through the records. If your database is shared on a network, anyone on the network may browse the same data at the same time. You cannot make changes to the data in the database while in Browse mode.

**Data-Entry mode**

If you want to add new records to the database and do not need to view any of the data already stored in the table, then you want to use *Data-Entry mode*. While you enter a new record into the database, only you have access to that record. Other people on the network have to wait until you have saved the new record before they can view it.

**Edit mode**

When you want to be able to do a combination of tasks—browse the data, change or delete a record, and add a record—you want to be in *Edit mode*. While you are in Edit mode, you and others on your network will be able to browse all records in the database. Only when you begin to change the data in a record will others on the network be denied access to that record. As soon as you save the record, the record becomes available to others on the network.

## Exercise 5: Adding records in Form view, Edit mode

In this exercise, you will add several records to the table using the data-entry form you created.

1. Click the right arrow with the vertical bar at the bottom of the form so that the last record in this table is displayed.
2. Click the single right arrow at the bottom of the form to switch to Data-Entry mode.
3. Press ( TAB ) to move to the First Name field and add the following data to the database:

| FIELD CAPTION | DATA |
|---|---|
| First Name: | George |
| Last Name: | Langford |
| Organization Name: | Langford Trucking |
| Address: | 1 Farm Road |
| City: | Mount Vernon |
| State: | VA |
| Postal Code: | 00111 |
| Country: | USA |
| Work Phone: | 7032341234 |
| Home Phone: | 7032344321 |
| Note: | Very cautious, very quality conscious. |
| Photo: | (no entry) |

4. Press ( ↵ ENTER ) to move to the next record.
5. Press ( TAB ) to move to the First Name field and add the following data:

| FIELD CAPTION | DATA |
|---|---|
| First Name: | G. David |
| Last Name: | Swenson |
| Organization Name: | Swenson Adventure Tours |
| Address: | 24 Bear Creek Road |
| City: | Smyrna |
| State: | TN |
| Postal Code: | 27238 |
| Country: | USA |
| Work Phone: | 6156667777 |
| Home Phone: | 6156677773 |
| Note: | Loves adventure and travel. |
| Photo: | (no entry) |

6. Save your records by selecting File/Save Record from the top menu.

## Exercise 6: Adding records in Form view, Data-Entry mode

In this exercise, you will add some records to the table using the same form. This time you will be in Data-Entry mode.

1.  Select Records/Data Entry from the top menu.

    Notice that the record count at the bottom of the form has changed from `Record: 3 of 3` to `Record: 1 of 1`.

2.  Press `TAB` to move to the First Name field and enter the following data:

| FIELD CAPTION | DATA |
|---|---|
| First Name: | Margaret |
| Last Name: | Moore |
| Organization Name: | Liberty Insurance, Inc. |
| Address: | 145 Independence Ave. |
| City: | Philadelphia |
| State: | PA |
| Postal Code: | 01873 |
| Country: | USA |
| Work Phone: | 2152221111 |
| Home Phone: | 2152201234 |
| Note: | In line for promotion to VP. |
| Photo: | (no entry) |

3.  Press `↵ ENTER` to move to the next record.

4.  Press `TAB` to move to the First Name field and add the following data:

| FIELD CAPTION | DATA |
|---|---|
| First Name: | John P. |
| Last Name: | Jones |
| Organization Name: | Jones Shipbuilding |
| Address: | 19 Harbor Lane |
| City: | Mystic |
| State: | CT |
| Postal Code: | 03728 |
| Country: | USA |
| Work Phone: | 2038003333 |
| Home Phone: | 2034544242 |
| Note: | A dynamic personality. |
| Photo: | (no entry) |

5.  Save your records by selecting File/Save Record.

6.  Add the following data while in Data-Entry mode:

Roger S. O'Leary
    Western Surveying Company
    2525 Forest Lane
    Walla Walla, WA 94372 USA
    Work: 509 989 1000
    Home: 509 988 8877
    "Likes to go camping."
    (No photo)

Robin H. Clark
    Western Surveying Company
    270 Butte Meadows
    Boise, ID 82919 USA
    Work: 208 544 1111
    Home: 208 543 1234
    "Is into river rafting."
    (No photo)

Ignacio Chavez
    Western Surveying Company
    348 Embarcadero
    San Francisco, CA 91118 USA
    Work: 415 222 8880
    Home: 415 221 7777
    "Has been a surveyor for many years."
    (No photo)

Hiroshi Kanzaki
    Western Surveying Company
    897 Green Mtn. Boulevard
    Portland, OR 93456 USA
    Work: 503 565 7878
    Home: 503 522 2334
    "Doing well with his map-making business."
    (No photo)

Wendy Monteleone
    Monteleone Legal Services
    1478 27th Avenue SW
    Washington, DC 01728 USA
    Work: 202 344 1212
    Home: 202 341 1122
    "Legal services at reasonable fees."
    (No photo)

7.   Select File/Save Record. Select File/Close.

# Objective 5: Creating a Quick Report with the Report Wizard

Now that you have some data in your database, you can generate a report. Remember: The real justification for a database is information retrieval, not data storage. A report, printed to paper or circulated electronically by a network mail system, is an excellent way to disseminate information throughout your company. In the following exercise, you will use the MS-Access Report Wizard to build a default report from data in the Contacts table.

**Report Wizard**

The *Report Wizard* allows you to generate a quick report that can be used to check data that you have recently input. Generating a quick report is similar to generating a quick form. You tell MS-Access that you want to create a new report. It asks which table you want to use. Then the Report Wizard takes over. The generated report lays out the fields in a single column, one below the other. As you gain experience, you will let the Wizards build forms and reports and then modify their appearance to suit your requirements.

After you generate the quick report, you will have a chance to preview it before printing it out. You may direct the output from the report to Microsoft Word or Excel using the buttons just to the right of the center screen. In most cases, however, you will print the report from MS-Access.

## FEATURE

**Entering large amounts of data into your database**

If you have a large quantity of data in another format—for example, a mailing list in a word-processing format or a list of data items in a spreadsheet program— you do not have to retype the data into your MS-Access database. MS-Access has an Import option to bring the external data into your MS-Access database tables. The Import function is part of the File menu and is quite simple to use.

## Exercise 7: Generating a quick report

In this exercise, you will generate a quick report using the MS-Access Report Wizard. Your starting point is the Database window.

1. Click the Report tab in the Database window.

   The Reports window appears; there are no reports listed yet.

2. Click the New button to begin designing a new report.

3. Click the down arrow to the right of the Select a Table/Query box.

4. Click the highlighted Contacts entry in the list.

   Contacts pops into the Select a Table/Query box.

5. Click the Report Wizards button to initiate the Report Wizards (Fig. 3-10).

**Figure 3-10** **The Report Wizards window**

6. Select AutoReport from the list of Wizards and click OK.

   MS-Access builds the default report. When the report is finished, you will be at the Print Preview screen (Fig. 3-11). Take a minute to explore some of the options on this screen. Position the cursor over each option in turn (but do not click the mouse), and balloon-box help information will appear to tell you what each button does. If you have a printer connected, you may now print your report.

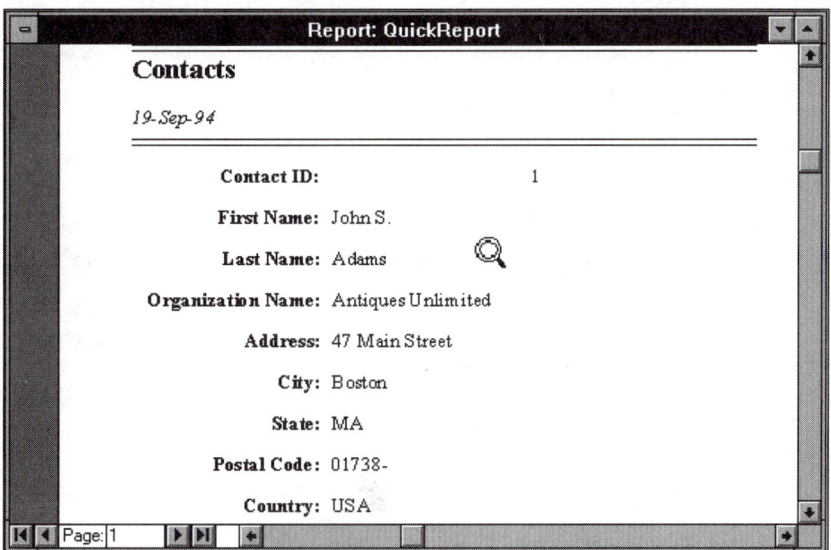

**Figure 3-11** **The report in Print Preview mode**

7. To print the report, click the Printer icon to bring up the Print dialog box.

8. Accept All for the print range and press OK. Your report is printing.

9. Exit Print Preview by clicking the Close Window icon on the far left of the toolbar. You are returned to the Report Design Mode screen.

10. Click File/Save As. Name the report QuickReport. Click OK to save your work.

11. Click File/Close to exit the report.

12. Close the database.

13. Close MS-Access.

## Chapter Summary

There are two ways to enter data into an MS-Access database. You can use the Datasheet view (rows and columns) or you can use a data-entry form, which you can easily create using the Form Wizard. When you wish to present information, you may do so using a printed report generated by the Report Wizard. Whether you are designing a form or a report, you can use a Wizard to generate a first draft, which you may then modify to your own specifications.

## Review Questions

### True/False Questions

_____ 1. A datasheet is a view of a single database table.

_____ 2. Reports display organized information from the database.

_____ 3. You cannot enter data directly into the Datasheet view of an MS-Access table.

_____ 4. The real reason for a database is data storage.

_____ 5. The default report created by the MS-Access Report Wizard lays out data in two, side-by-side columns.

### Multiple-Choice Questions

_____ 6. Forms are most often used for

A. generating reports for circulation to the rest of the office.

B. entering and displaying data on the screen.

C. making backups of the database.

D. assistance in creating tables.

_____ 7. A dialog box

    A. keeps up a running conversation with your MS-Access database.

    B. is a pop-up screen.

    C. assists the user in performing some special function.

    D. B and C

_____ 8. MS-Access lists recently used databases under which menu entry?

    A. File

    B. Edit

    C. Window

    D. Help

_____ 9. Which MS-Access Wizard would you use to build a data-entry form?

    A. the Table Wizard

    B. the Query Wizard

    C. the Report Wizard

    D. the Forms Wizard

_____ 10. An excellent way to disseminate information throughout your company is to

    A. chat with your fellow employees at the water cooler.

    B. send your boss a memo.

    C. generate a database report and circulate it electronically using the network mail facility.

    D. not say anything; it's not part of your job description.

## Fill-in-the-Blank Questions

11. The Datasheet view of an MS-Access table resembles a _____.

12. To resize a column in Datasheet view, you _____ the right column boundary until the column is the size you want.

13. For data entry, the Form view is _____ user-friendly than the Datasheet view.

14. Reports are used to _____ information.

15. The facility used to preview a report before printing it is called the _____ screen.

## *Acumen-Building Activities*

### Quick Projects

### 1. Resize a column of the datasheet using the Books database.

1. Click File/Open Database to open the Books database. Open the table MyBooks.
2. Position the cursor on the right boundary of the BookCollectionID column label.
3. Drag the column boundary to the left to make the column narrower so that only the Book of BookCollectionID is showing.
4. Position the cursor over the right boundary line of the Pages column. Drag the right boundary line of the Pages column to the left making it narrower.
5. Select File/Save Table. Close the datasheet.

### 2. Build a quick form for MyBooks.

This exercise is a continuation of Quick Project #1.

1. From the Database window, click the Form tab. Click the New button to begin designing a new form.
2. Click the down arrow. Choose MyBooks for the Select a Table/Query.
3. Click the Form Wizards button. Select AutoForm. Click OK.
4. Click File/Save Form As. Name the form frmBook. Click OK.

### 3. Add records to MyBooks.

This exercise is a continuation of Quick Project #2.

1. In the BookCollectionID field, type 1.
2. Press TAB to move to the Title field and add the following data to the database:

| FIELD | DATA |
|---|---|
| Title | Summer of the Danes |
| ISBNNumber | 0-7472-3564-3 |
| PublisherName | Headline |
| DatePurchased | 3/12/94 |
| Pages | 311 |
| Note | A medieval whodunnit. The Eighteenth Chronicle of Brother Cadfael. |

3. Press ↵ ENTER to move to the next record.
4. In the BookCollectionID field, type 2.

| FIELD | DATA |
|---|---|
| Title | Relativity |
| ISBNNumber | 0-517-029618 |
| PublisherName | Crown |
| DatePurchased | 6/01/90 |
| Pages | 164 |
| Note | The special and general theories of relativity. |

5. Add a third record using the following data:

| FIELD | DATA |
|---|---|
| Title | Friday |
| ISBNNumber | 1-03-061516-X |
| PublisherName | Holt Rinehart Winston |
| DatePurchased | 7/23/91 |
| Pages | 368 |
| Note | Recreational reading. |

6. Add a fourth record using the following data:

| FIELD | DATA |
|---|---|
| Title | One Up On Wall Street |
| ISBNNumber | 0-1401-27925 |
| PublisherName | Penguin |
| DatePurchased | 11/30/93 |
| Pages | 318 |
| Note | How to make money in the stock market. |

7. Save your records. Close the form.

## 4. Build a quick report for MyBook.

This exercise is a continuation of Quick Project #3.

1. Click the Report tab in the Database window. Click New for a new report.

2. Select MyBooks for the Select a Table/Query. Click the Report Wizards button.

3. Select AutoReport from the list of Wizards and click OK.

4. Look at the Print Preview presentation of this report using the zoom feature.

5. If you are connected to a printer, click the Print icon and print out the report.

6. Exit Print Preview and click the Close Window icon. Select File/Save As.

7. Name the report rptBooks. Click OK. Choose File/Close to close the report.

8. Close the Book database by clicking File/Close Database.

## In-Depth Projects

### 1. Quick forms and reports for the CD database.

1. Open the CD database. Create a new form for the CDCollection table using the Form Wizard. It will be an AutoForm.

2. When the form opens, enter some data. You may use the data suggested below or your own. Remember: The MusicCollectionID field is a counter, which will be incremented automatically, so Tab to the Title field to begin data entry.

| TITLE | GROUP NAME | RECORDING LABEL | YEAR RELEASED | PURCHASE PRICE |
|-------|-----------|-----------------|---------------|----------------|
| Star Wars | London Symphony Orchestra | RSO | 1977 | 20.00 |
| Evangeline | Evangeline | MCA | 1992 | 12.00 |
| Canyon Trilogy | R. Carlos Nakai | Canyon Records | 1989 | 14.00 |
| Cusco 2002 | Cusco | Higher Octave Music | 1993 | 12.00 |
| Question of Balance | Moody Blues | Threshold | 1970 | 11.00 |

3. After you have finished entering the data, save your records.

4. Save the form and name it frmCD. Close the form.

5. Create a new report for the CDCollection table using the Report Wizard. It will be an AutoReport.

6. Print the report or, if you are not connected to a printer, examine carefully the Print Preview output.

7. Save the report, calling it rptCD, and close it. Close the CD database.

### 2. Quick forms and reports for the Dinner Party database.

1. Open the Dinner database. Create a new form for the DinnerGuests table using the Form Wizard. It will be an AutoForm.

2. When the form opens, enter some data. You may use the data suggested below or your own. Remember: The GuestID field is a counter, which will be incremented automatically, so Tab to the FirstName field to begin data entry.

| FIRST NAME | LAST NAME | ADDRESS | CITY | STATE | POSTAL CODE | HOME PHONE | HEALTH PROBLEMS |
|---|---|---|---|---|---|---|---|
| Linda | Smith | 231 Poplar Street | Golden | CO | 80401 | 303-677-3241 | |
| John | Baccus | 89 Maple Grove | Littleton | CO | 80123 | 303-757-9976 | allergic to peanuts |
| Mary | Cummings | 717 Shady Lane | Applewood | CO | 80413 | 303-636-3357 | |
| Fred | Wood | 14 Fox Hunt Road | Lakewood | CO | 80119 | 303-925-4546 | |
| Sue | Woolrich | 67 Genessee Point | Englewood | CO | 80017 | 303-423-5531 | |

3. After you have finished entering the data, save your records.
4. Save the form and name it frmGuests. Close the form.
5. Create a new report for the DinnerGuests table using the Report Wizard. It will be an AutoReport. Print the report or, if you are not connected to a printer, examine carefully the Print Preview output.
6. Save the report, calling it rptGuests. Close the Dinner database.

# CASE STUDIES

**Coffee-On-The-Go:** **Adding Records**

In this chapter, you learned to add records to a database. You will use those skills to add records to the Coffee database for Coffee-On-The-Go.

1. Open the Coffee database.
2. Open the Employee table.
3. Add the following records:

| | | | | | | | |
|---|---|---|---|---|---|---|---|
| 1 | Smith | Sue | 01 | F | 15,000 | 1/3/89 | y |
| 2 | Lowe | George | 02 | M | 12,000 | 3/30/91 | y |
| 3 | White | Albert | 01 | M | 15,000 | 4/1/90 | n |
| 4 | Jones | Jerry | 01 | M | 14,000 | 3/15/93 | y |
| 5 | Smyth | Sally | 03 | F | 18,000 | 1/4/90 | y |
| 6 | Meyers | Judy | 01 | F | 14,000 | 4/1/94 | y |
| 7 | Miller | Mark | 03 | M | 12,000 | 3/8/88 | n |
| 8 | Smithsonian | Gerry | 02 | M | 16,000 | 2/3/94 | y |
| 9 | Ryan | Randy | 01 | M | 14,000 | 3/3/90 | n |
| 10 | Hart | Henry | 01 | M | 18,000 | 4/2/90 | y |
| 11 | Gold | Jane | 04 | F | 15,000 | 12/20/89 | y |
| 12 | Williams | Larry | 04 | M | 17,000 | 9/15/90 | y |
| 13 | Black | Ann | 03 | F | 13,000 | 6/4/93 | y |
| 14 | Pope | Nancy | 01 | F | 17,000 | 8/1/92 | y |
| 15 | Frances | Mary | 04 | F | 14,000 | 4/2/90 | n |

4. Save the Employee table.
5. Print a quick report of the data.

# CASE STUDIES

 **Videos West:** **Adding Records**

In this chapter, you learned to add records to a database. You will use those skills to add records to the Video database for Videos West.

1. Open the Video database.
2. Open the Inventory table.
3. Add the following records:

| | | | | | | |
|---|---|---|---|---|---|---|
| 01 | Golf Like a Pro | 7.99 | 19.99 | 10 | PG | 5/1/93 |
| 01 | Tips on Hunting | 3.99 | 14.99 | 5 | R | 6/1/90 |
| 02 | Tai Chi for Health | 9.99 | 19.99 | 3 | PG | 6/1/94 |
| 03 | Quit Smoking on Your Own | 5.99 | 9.99 | 5 | PG | 7/15/93 |
| 04 | Buy Your Own Home | 6.99 | 14.99 | 4 | PG | 5/1/92 |
| 01 | Baseball Tips | 9.99 | 19.99 | 2 | PG | 6/1/92 |
| 05 | Beaded Jewelry | 5.99 | 14.99 | 1 | PG | 5/15/93 |
| 02 | Jogging Tips | 6.99 | 14.99 | 2 | PG | 8/1/93 |
| 04 | Take Control of Your Debt | 5.99 | 9.99 | 3 | PG | 5/1/92 |
| 03 | Addiction Awareness | 14.99 | 21.99 | 6 | R | 7/1/94 |
| 03 | Eating for Your Health | 5.99 | 14.99 | 7 | PG | 8/1/94 |
| 05 | Christmas Decorations | 3.99 | 7.99 | 1 | PG | 12/2/92 |
| 01 | Skiing Your Best | 9.99 | 19.99 | 3 | PG | 3/1/91 |
| 01 | Tennis Pros Talk | 5.99 | 9.99 | 1 | PG | 1/1/94 |
| 05 | Hobbies for Profit | 5.99 | 9.99 | 2 | PG | 2/1/94 |
| 02 | Yoga for Your Health | 9.99 | 14.99 | 3 | PG | 6/1/91 |
| 04 | Start Your Own Business | 5.99 | 14.99 | 7 | PG | 5/1/93 |

4. Save the Inventory table.
5. Print a quick report of the data.

# Chapter 4

## Editing a Database

**Objectives**

- Adding a Field Using the Table Design View
- Deleting a Field Using the Table Design View
- Changing a Record Using the Datasheet or Table View
- Changing a Record Using the Form View
- Deleting Records Using the Datasheet or Table View
- Deleting Records Using the Form View
- Locating Records
- Locating and Replacing Data

**Key Terms**

| TERM | DEFINITION |
|------|------------|
| **Delete a Record** | remove a record from a database |
| **Update a Record** | change a data value within a record that is currently in a database |
| **Input Mask** | a user-defined template attached to a field of a table or form that aids in data entry; MS-Access contains several pre-defined input masks for commonly-used fields such as PhoneNumber and SocialSecurityNumber |

Some database tables, such as a list of state abbreviations, are relatively static. Other database tables, such as a list of contacts or employees, change often. As your business changes, so will the data you store in your database. You must keep your databases current by adding, editing, and deleting records and modifying table structures as necessary.

# Objective 1:  Adding a Field Using the Table Design View

The easiest way to add a new field is to copy an existing field using the cut and paste method; this method copies all the characteristics of the old field and transfers them to the new field. Alternatively, you can create a new field from scratch.

**input mask**
An *input mask* is a special property that you can assign to a field in a table. It is a template that formats the data entered into the field by specifying where data is to be entered, what kind of data is allowed, and how many characters are allowed. Although you define the input mask for a field in a table, when you build a form from the table the input mask remains.

## Adding a New Field to the Table Using Cut and Paste

Databases evolve as you use them. You design the database carefully, use the database for a while, and then realize that you need a field not included in the original design. MS-Access makes it easy to add fields to your database tables.

### Exercise 1: Adding a new field to the table using cut and paste

When you created the Contacts table you included the fields WorkPhone and HomePhone. For a business contact database, you should include a fax number as well.

1. Start MS-Access, and open the Contacts database. Open the Contacts table in Design mode.
2. Scroll down to the HomePhone row of the Field Name column.
3. Position the cursor in the left margin of the row to the left of the H in HomePhone; the cursor arrow changes shape and points into the row.
4. Click the mouse to highlight the row (Fig. 4-1).

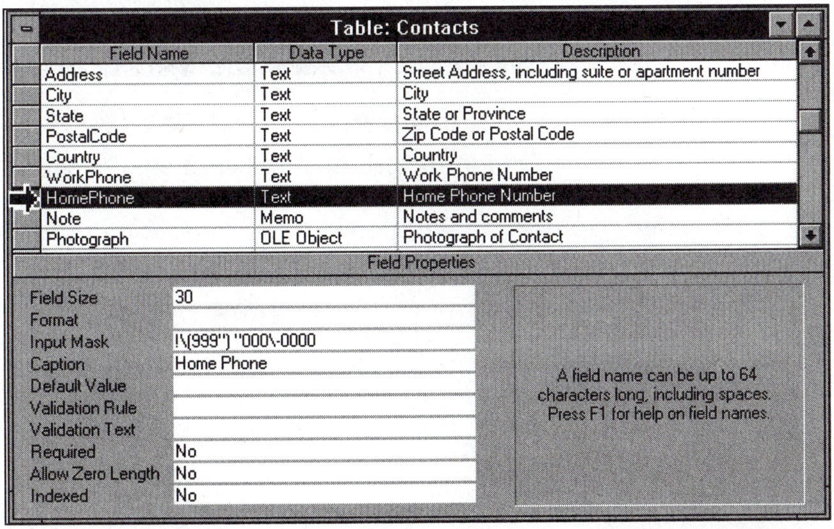

**Figure 4-1** **Table Design window with HomePhone highlighted**

5. Click Edit/Copy to place a copy of HomePhone on the Windows clipboard.

6. Click Edit/Insert Row to insert an empty row above HomePhone.

7. Click Edit/Paste to place a copy of HomePhone in the blank row.

8. Type Fax in the Field Name column and Fax Number in the Description column.

   *Note:* MS-Access will not accept two identical field names in the same table, so you must change the name of the new field when you add a field by copying.

9. Press F6 to move into the Field Properties box. Type Fax Number in the Caption row.

10. Press F6 to return to the field definitions (Fig. 4-2). Click File/Save to save your work.

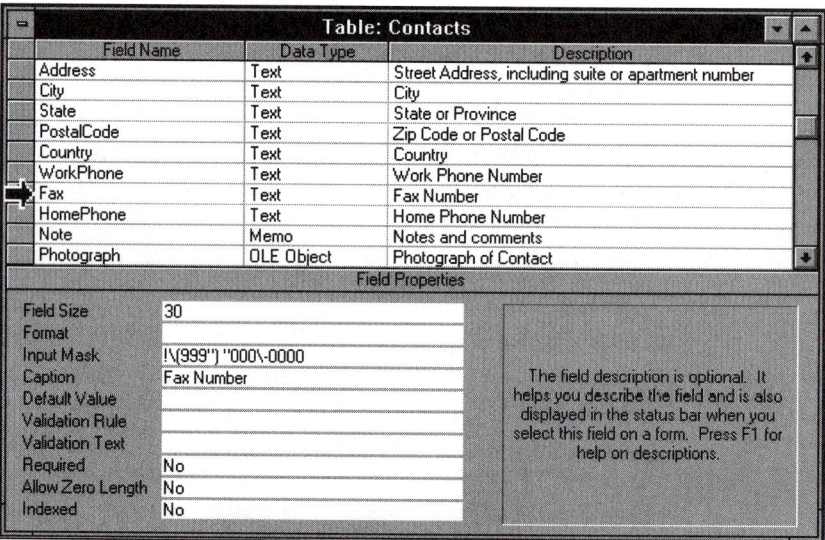

**Figure 4-2** **Table Design window with the Fax field added**

## Creating a New Field from Scratch

You need a field to record the number of employees in a company. You will use this field to find candidates for the on-site computer classes you offer. Because you will perform calculations on this data, it must be a numeric field.

### Exercise 2: Adding a new field to the table from scratch

There is no similar field to copy, so you will create a new field from scratch.

1. Open the table Contacts in Design mode. Scroll to the empty row below the field named Photograph. Type NumEmployees in the Field Name column.

2. Press `TAB` or `← ENTER` to move to the Data Type column.

3. Click the down arrow at the right side of the box and choose Number from the list. Press `F6` to move to the Field Properties box (Fig. 4-3).

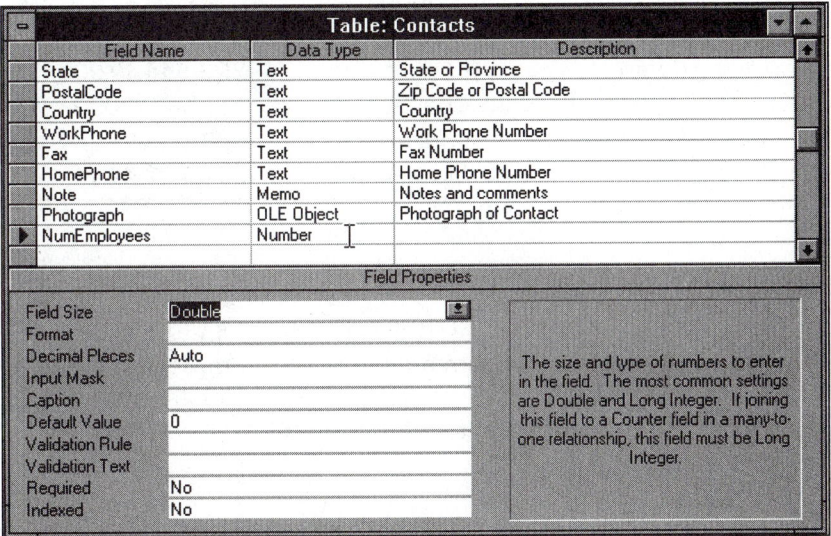

**Figure 4-3   Table Definition window with NumEmployees added**

4. Use the down arrow at the right of the box to see a list of the available numeric data types (Fig. 4-4) and choose Integer.

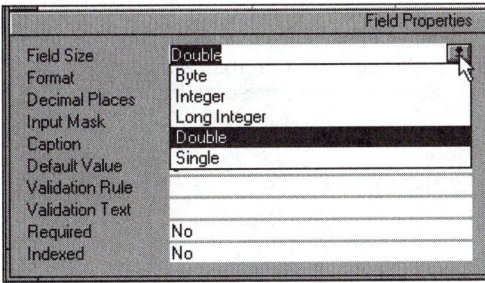

**Figure 4-4   Field Properties window with numeric data types listed**

5. In the Field Properties box, move to the Caption line and type Number of Employees. Press `F6` to return to the Definition window.

6. Move to the Description column, type Number of employees who work for this company. Click File/Save to save your work.

7. Switch to Datasheet view. Input the following values for Fax and NumEmployees:

| FIRST NAME | LAST NAME | FAX | NUMBER OF EMPLOYEES |
|---|---|---|---|
| John | Adams | (124)123-9874 | 8 |
| George | Langford | (703)234-1111 | 85 |
| G. David | Swenson | | 50 |
| Margaret | Moore | (215)222-1010 | 1259 |
| John P. | Jones | | 2 |
| Roger S. | O'Leary | (509)989-3333 | 14 |
| Robin H. | Clark | (208)544-1100 | 10 |
| Ignacio | Chavez | (415)222-8000 | 49 |
| Hiroshi | Kanzaki | (503)565-7888 | 26 |
| Wendy | Monteleone | (202)727-4444 | 2 |

# Objective 2:  Deleting a Field Using the Table Design View

Occasionally you will design a table and include fields that are not useful. Deleting fields from a table is very simple and quick, but be sure that you will not need the data stored in the deleted fields—the data is deleted from the database along with the field.

## Exercise 3: Deleting a field from the database table

In this exercise, you will delete the Photograph field.

1. Switch back to Design view, and move the cursor to the Photograph field. Click the margin to the left of the P in Photograph to highlight the entire field.
2. Press ⟨DELETE⟩ on your keyboard to remove the field.

**◣NOTE**   If you accidentally delete the wrong row, you can recover, but only if you act immediately. Select Edit/Undo to restore the deleted row. A dialog box appears, telling you "If you delete this field, you will lose the data it contains. Continue anyway?"

3. Click OK.
4. Click File/Save to save your work. Click File/Close to leave Table Design mode.

# Objective 3:  Changing a Record Using the Datasheet or Table View

**update a record**   You can use the Datasheet view to *update a record*—that is, change one or more data values within a record that is currently in a database. This method is most efficient when you have only a few changes to make. The Datasheet view displays multiple records in a row-and-column format, letting you view many records at one time. How you move to a field in the datasheet affects how MS-Access handles the data you input. If you use Tab and the arrow keys to move to a field, all the data in the field is highlighted, and anything you type will replace what is currently in that field. If you use the mouse to position the cursor in the field, whatever you type will be inserted at the cursor position, and the rest of the text will be moved to the right.

## Exercise 4: Changing records in Datasheet view

John S. Adams is on an extended vacation, so your contact at his antique shop will be his cousin Sam Adams. Also, Margaret Moore informed you that the Liberty Insurance Co. has changed its name to Liberty Shield Insurance, Inc.

1. Open the Contacts table in Datasheet view. `TAB` to the FirstName field for John S. Adams. Type Sam and press `TAB` or `↵ ENTER`.

2. Position the cursor between Liberty and Insurance in the Organization Name field of the Margaret Moore record. Click once. Type Shield and add a space before or after this word, as necessary (Fig. 4-5).

| | Contact ID | First Name | Last Name | Organization Name | Address | City |
|---|---|---|---|---|---|---|
| ▶ | 1 | Sam | Adams | Antiques Unlimited | 47 Main Street | Boston |
| | 2 | George | Langford | Langford Trucking | 1 Farm Road | Mount vernon |
| | 3 | G. David | Swenson | Swenson Adventure Tc | 24 Bear Creek Road | Smyrna |
| | 4 | Margaret | Moore | Liberty Shield Insurance | 145 Independence A | Philadelphia |
| | 5 | John P. | Jones | Jones Shipbuilding | 19 Harbor Lane | Mystic |
| | 6 | Roger S. | O'Leary | Western Surveying Cor | 2525 Forest lane | Walla Walla |
| | 7 | Robin H. | Clark | Western Surveying Cor | 270 Butte meadows | Boise |
| | 8 | Ignacio | Chavez | Western Surveying Cor | 348 Embarcadero | San Francisco |
| | 9 | Hiroshi | Kanzaki | Western Surveying Cor | 897 Green Mountain I | Portland |
| | 10 | Wendy | Monteleone | Monteleone Legal Serv | 1478 27th Avenue S\ | Washington |

Table: Contacts

Record: 1    of 10

**Figure 4-5**   **Contacts table in Datasheet view with changes**

3. Position the mouse at the end of the OrganizationName field after the Co. Use `← BACKSPACE` to remove the Co. and the space preceding it. Type, Inc.

4. Save your changes by selecting File/Save Record. Close the datasheet.

# Objective 4:  Changing a Record Using the Form View

G. David Swenson has moved his Adventure Tours from Smyrna to Nashville; this means you need to update his record. In the following exercise, you will use the Form view to make the modifications.

## Exercise 5: Changing a record in Form view

In this exercise, you will make changes to the record for G. David Swenson.

1. In the Database window, click the Form tab. Open the QuickForm.

2. Click on the right, single arrow at the bottom of the form repeatedly until you find the record for G. David Swenson. `TAB` to the Address field.

3. Type 101 Chase Lane. Press ( ↵ ENTER ) to move to the City field.

4. Type Nashville. Press ( ↵ ENTER ) twice to move to the PostalCode field.

5. Press ( DELETE ) to remove the PostalCode value. You don't know the new postal code, but you need to remove the old value because it is no longer valid.

6. Repeat Step 5 to remove the data values for the WorkPhone, Fax, and HomePhone fields.

7. ( TAB ) to the Note field, press ( F2 ), and type Just moved from Smyrna to Nashville. This comment will be added to the notes already in the field.

8. Select File/Save Record. Close the QuickForm.

## Objective 5:  Deleting Records Using the Datasheet or Table View

**delete records**

You decide to remove certain people—retirees and those with whom you have lost contact—from your database so that it will run more quickly and take up less disk space. This means you will *delete records*.

You can delete records using either the Datasheet or Form view—these two views are essentially the same. When you delete records using the Datasheet view, you can delete one or more records at the same time. In Form view, you can only delete one record at a time: You must first open the form, select the record you want to delete, and then delete it.

When you delete a record from the database, you can change your mind and cancel the delete command. MS-Access asks if you want to save your changes. If you choose OK, the record is deleted.

### Exercise 6: Deleting a single record using the Datasheet or Table view

Open the Contacts table in Datasheet view. Move to the record for John P. Jones, who has recently retired and is living on his yacht, and delete it.

1. Open the Contacts table in Datasheet view and select the record for John P. Jones.

2. Click the arrow in the left margin of the datasheet to highlight the entire record (Fig. 4-6).

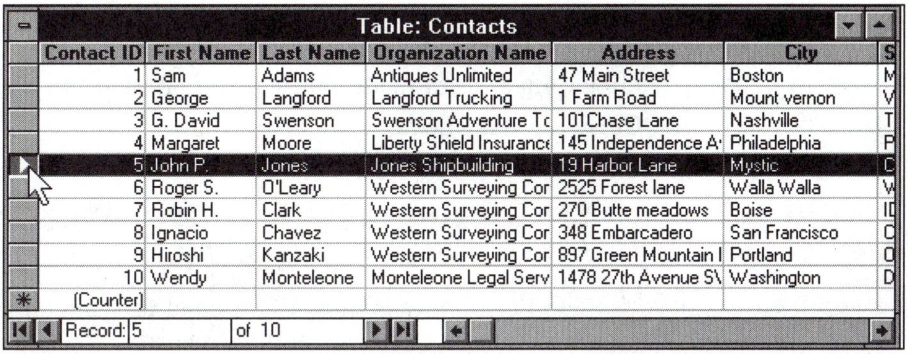

Table: Contacts

| Contact ID | First Name | Last Name | Organization Name | Address | City | S |
|---|---|---|---|---|---|---|
| 1 | Sam | Adams | Antiques Unlimited | 47 Main Street | Boston | M |
| 2 | George | Langford | Langford Trucking | 1 Farm Road | Mount vernon | V |
| 3 | G. David | Swenson | Swenson Adventure Tc | 101Chase Lane | Nashville | T |
| 4 | Margaret | Moore | Liberty Shield Insurance | 145 Independence A | Philadelphia | P |
| 5 | John P. | Jones | Jones Shipbuilding | 19 Harbor Lane | Mystic | C |
| 6 | Roger S. | O'Leary | Western Surveying Cor | 2525 Forest lane | Walla Walla | W |
| 7 | Robin H. | Clark | Western Surveying Cor | 270 Butte meadows | Boise | ID |
| 8 | Ignacio | Chavez | Western Surveying Cor | 348 Embarcadero | San Francisco | C |
| 9 | Hiroshi | Kanzaki | Western Surveying Cor | 897 Green Mountain I | Portland | O |
| 10 | Wendy | Monteleone | Monteleone Legal Serv | 1478 27th Avenue S\ | Washington | D |
| (Counter) | | | | | | |

Record: 5 of 10

**Figure 4-6 Contacts table in Datasheet view with John P. Jones record highlighted**

3. Press DELETE to remove the record.
4. Click OK in the dialog box to confirm that you want to delete this record.

   Mr. Jones is gone from your database and MS-Access has updated all the necessary tables.

## Exercise 7: Deleting multiple records using the Datasheet or Table view

Your contacts O'Leary, Clark, Chavez, and Kanzaki have moved. You want to delete their records. Their records are listed consecutively in the database, so you can remove them in one operation.

1. Highlight the entire O'Leary record by clicking the left margin of the datasheet.
2. Hold the left mouse button down and drag the cursor down the table until Clark, Chavez, and Kanzaki are also highlighted (Fig. 4-7).

   (To highlight several consecutive records, you can click the first record in the block, hold down Shift, and click the last record in the block.)

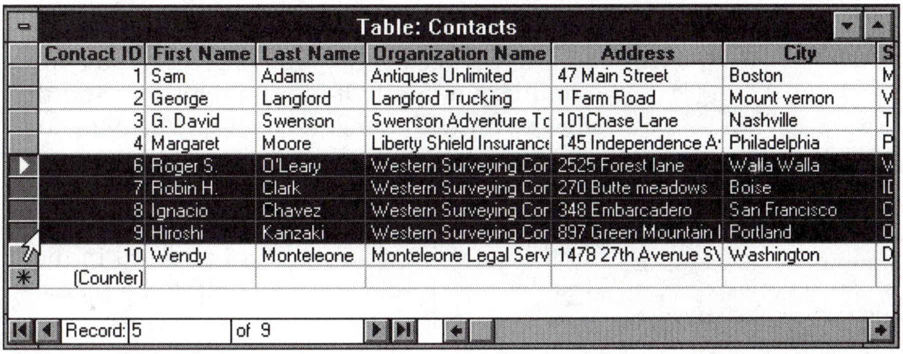

Table: Contacts

| Contact ID | First Name | Last Name | Organization Name | Address | City | S |
|---|---|---|---|---|---|---|
| 1 | Sam | Adams | Antiques Unlimited | 47 Main Street | Boston | M |
| 2 | George | Langford | Langford Trucking | 1 Farm Road | Mount vernon | V |
| 3 | G. David | Swenson | Swenson Adventure Tc | 101Chase Lane | Nashville | T |
| 4 | Margaret | Moore | Liberty Shield Insurance | 145 Independence A | Philadelphia | P |
| 6 | Roger S. | O'Leary | Western Surveying Cor | 2525 Forest lane | Walla Walla | W |
| 7 | Robin H. | Clark | Western Surveying Cor | 270 Butte meadows | Boise | ID |
| 8 | Ignacio | Chavez | Western Surveying Cor | 348 Embarcadero | San Francisco | C |
| 9 | Hiroshi | Kanzaki | Western Surveying Cor | 897 Green Mountain I | Portland | O |
| 10 | Wendy | Monteleone | Monteleone Legal Serv | 1478 27th Avenue S\ | Washington | D |
| (Counter) | | | | | | |

Record: 5 of 9

**Figure 4-7 Contacts table in Datasheet view with four records selected**

3. Select Edit/Delete or press DELETE.

4. When the dialog box appears asking you to confirm your deletion, click Cancel to indicate that you do *not* want to delete these records.

5. Close the datasheet.

# Objective 6:  Deleting Records Using the Form View

The Form view is most often used for data entry, but it can also be used for changing or deleting records. You will be able to change or delete only the record that is on the screen.

## Exercise 8: Deleting a record using the Form view

You want to remove Wendy Monteleone from your list of contacts. You must first select the record before you can delete it.

1. Open the QuickForm. Use the buttons at the bottom of the form to find the record for Wendy Monteleone.

2. Select the record by clicking Edit/Select Record.

3. Press DELETE to remove the record. Click Cancel when MS-Access asks if you want to save your changes. Close the form.

# Objective 7:  Locating Records

Once you have many records in a database, you will find it a chore to page through them looking for a particular record. Fortunately, you you can use the Find dialog box, in either Datasheet or Form view, to locate specific records quickly.

The Find dialog box is opened by clicking the binoculars icon on the top toolbar, pressing Ctrl+F, or selecting Edit/Find from the top menu. Using one of these three mthods, call up the Find dialog box.

Notice the options in the Find dialog box. Let's assume you want to find the record George Langford. You could change the Where condition to Start Of Field, type Lang, and thus find all records that begin with Lang. Of course, MS-Access would find Langdon and Langston as well, if they were records in your database.

## Exercise 9: Finding a record in Datasheet view

In this exercise, you will find a record in the database by opening the datasheet, selecting the field to be searched, and specifying the search criteria.

1. Open the Contacts table in Datasheet view. Position the cursor at the top of the Last Name column until it changes to a black down-turned arrow.

2. Click the Last Name label.

   The entire column is selected for the search operation.

3. Click the binoculars icon to open the Find dialog box.

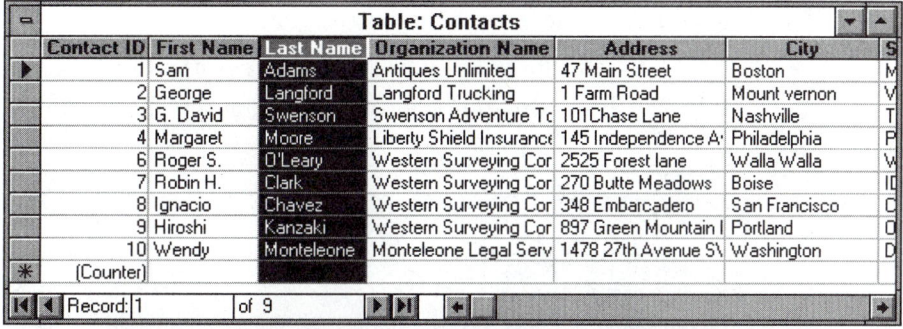

**Figure 4-8** *Contacts table in Datasheet view with the Find dialog box open*

4. Type Langford in the Find What field (Fig. 4-8) and press (← ENTER).

   MS-Access finds the record for George Langford.

5. Click the Close button to close the Find dialog box.

   The record for George Langford is highlighted in the datasheet.

6. Close the datasheet.

# Objective 8: Locating and Replacing Data

You sometimes need to find one or more records in your database and update the information they contain. The Replace procedure is very similar to the Find procedure. However, when replacing information, you specify not only the data you want to find, but the data you want to input in its place.

You can replace data values one record at a time, or you can replace a value in all the records at the same time. You should use this method only when you are sure that you want to substitute a new value for every occurrence of the old value in *all* records.

When you perform a Find-and-Replace operation on more than one record at a time, you make multiple changes to the data in your database. You must confirm these changes in a separate step. Also, the Edit/Undo option does not work after multiple changes are made.

## Exercise 10: Locating and Replacing Data

Western Surveying Company has changed its name to Precision Surveys, Inc. You have several contacts at Western Surveying. Find and replace the outdated data with the current data.

1. Open the QuickForm and move to the Organization Name field.
2. Click Edit/Replace on the top menu. The Replace dialog box opens.

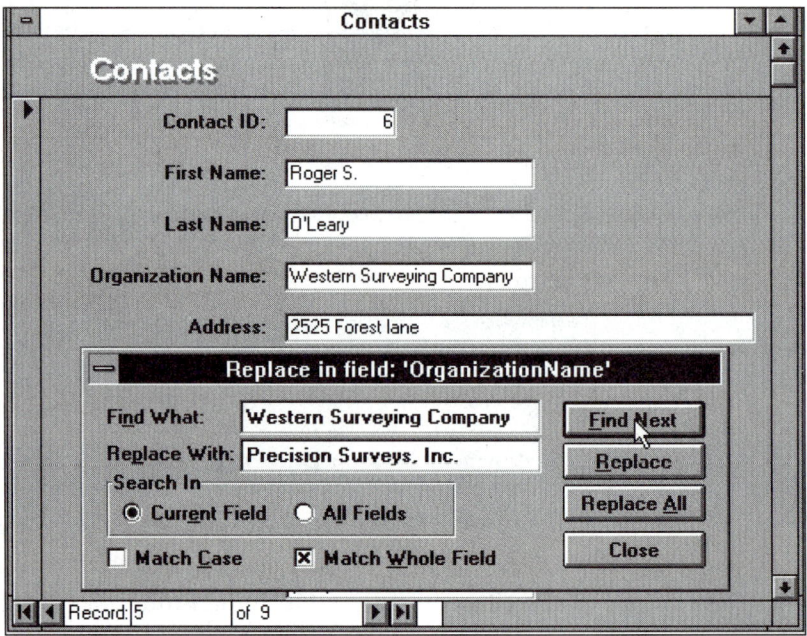

**Figure 4-9    Replace dialog box**

3. Type Western Surveying Company in the Find What box. Press [TAB].
4. Type Precision Surveys, Inc. in the Replace With box. Press [↵ ENTER].

   The first record with Organization Name Western Surveying Company has been found (Fig. 4-9). Now replace the old organization name with the new one.

5. Click Replace to modify the O'Leary record.
6. To change the rest of the outdated values, click Replace All.

   All the outdated records are changed. The pop-up dialog box indicates that MS-Access has reached the end of its search.

7. Select Yes when asked if MS-Access should continue searching from the beginning of the records. Click OK when the next pop-up dialog box appears.

   MS-Access has reached the end of the records and has made all the replacements you requested.

8. Click OK when you are warned that this operation cannot be undone.

9. Click Close to exit the Replace dialog box. Close the Contacts QuickForm.

## FEATURE

### Tips on table design

When you create fields in a table, do not give the same name to two fields. MS-Access will not accept two identical field names in the same table.

When you add a field to a table, you can insert it anywhere in the table; you do not have to add it to the end of the table. Simply highlight the row *below* where you want the new field to appear and press Insert.

The Field Name, Caption, and Description fields often contain the same information, but they do not have to. The Field Name is the name given to a data item when it is created as part of the table. It can be as long as 64 characters, but you should try to keep it between 12 and 20 characters. Don't use embedded spaces in the field name; rather, use the mixed-case naming convention we introduced earlier. The Caption is a label that appears on forms and reports. If you do not specify a Caption, MS-Access automatically creates one from the Field Name. If you create your own Captions, make them descriptive but short. The Description is the place to spell out the purpose or use of a field. Indicate in the Description column when a field is a primary key or when it relates to other tables. Identification fields and Code fields might need an explanation to make them understandable to others. You should always document your work, and the Description column is the place to do just that.

## Chapter Summary

In this chapter, you learned how to udpate your database by editing records and removing out-of-date records, find specific records in the database using the Find operation, and search for and replace data values with the Find-and-Replace function. You learned how to perform these database maintenance operations using both the Datasheet and Form views.

# Review Questions

## True/False Questions

_____  1. A database is only as accurate and current as the data it contains.

_____  2. Once you press Del to delete a record in Datasheet view, you have no way to reverse that action.

_____  3. In Datasheet view, you cannot delete more than one record at a time.

_____  4. In Form view, you cannot delete more than one record at a time.

_____  5. When using the Find dialog box to locate a record, MS-Access shows only records that match exactly the text you type.

## Multiple-Choice Questions

_____  6. You make changes to the data in your database because

A. you want accurate information.

B. you want current, timely information.

C. you want the data in your database to be correct.

D. All of the above.

_____  7. When in Data-Entry or Update mode on the datasheet, scrolling allows you to

A. move the cursor from field to field.

B. continue entering text even after you have apparently filled the field.

C. switch from Form to Datasheet view.

D. enter the same data in several consecutive records.

_____  8. You can open a form from the Database window by

A. highlighting the form name and clicking Open.

B. typing OPEN form_name> at the command line.

C. double-clicking the form name.

D. either A or C

_____  9. When deleting records from the database, you must

A. use the mouse to position the cursor in the field you want to delete, then press Del.

B. press Ctrl+Alt+Del.

C. first select the record, then delete it.

D. Choose File/Remove from the top menu.

_____ 10. When performing a Find-and-Replace operation, you must

    A. position the cursor in the field you want to change and select File/Replace from the top menu.

    B. first select the field and then type in the old and new data values.

    C. select Edit/Replace from the top menu without first indicating the field.

    D. press Ctrl+Alt+Repl.

## Fill-in-the-Blank Questions

11. To move from field to field in a form, you can use the _____ key.

12. To move from field to field in a form and highlight the contents of the field selected, you would use the _____ key.

13. One way to open the Search dialog box is to click the _____ icon on the top toolbar.

14. The _____ operation locates all records that meet the criteria you have specified.

15. The _____ operation locates all records that meet the criteria you have specified and replaces the data with the new value you specify.

## Acumen-Building Activities

## Quick Projects

### 1. Creating a new field in the table MyBooks.

1. Open the Books database. Open the table MyBooks in Table Design mode.

2. Highlight the row ISBNNumber by clicking the margin to the left of Field Name. Press INSERT.

3. Type Author in the Field Name column. Choose Text as the data type.

4. Press F6 to move to the Field Properties box. In the Indexed row select Yes (Duplicates OK). Press F6 to return to the Definition window.

5. In the Description column, type Author of the book.

6. Click File/Save. Exit Table Design mode.

### 2. Regenerating the AutoForm for MyBooks to include the new field.

This exercise is a continuation of Quick Project #1.

1. Click the Form tab in the Database window.

2. Make sure .frmBook is highlighted. Press DELETE. Click OK.

3. Create a New form using the table MyBooks and the Form Wizards.

4. Select AutoForm. Save your work (File/Save Form As). Name the new form frmBooks. Click OK.

## 3. Changing records in MyBooks.

This exercise is a continuation of Quick Project #2.

1. For Book ID #1, [TAB] to the Author field and type Ellis Peters.

2. For Book ID #2, [TAB] to the Author field and type Albert Einstein.

3. For Book ID #3, [TAB] to the Author field and type Robert Heinlein.

4. For Book ID #4, [TAB] to the Author field and type Peter Lynch.

5. Save your work by clicking File/Save Record.

## 4. Finding a record in the Form view from MyBooks.

This exercise is a continuation of Quick Project #3.

1. Press [SHIFT] + [TAB] to return to the Title field. Click the binoculars icon on the toolbar.

2. Type Danes in the Find What field. Make sure the Where field is set to Any Part of Field. Click Find First. Drag the Find dialog box down to the bottom of the screen so you can see the record underneath.

3. Click the Find Next button in the dialog box to find any additional entries for Danes. Check through the records from the beginning.

4. Close the Find dialog box. Close the form. Save your changes.

5. Close the Books database.

## In-Depth Projects

## 1. The CD database.

1. Open the CD database. Open the table CDCollection in Table Design mode.

2. Add two new fields. Insert the field Length between YearReleased and PurchasePrice. Make it a number/integer data type. Modify the caption by typing Length in Minutes. In the Description field, type How long is this CD? Add the field Classification to the end of the Field Name list. Make it a text data type. In the Description field, type What type of music is this?

3. Save the changes you made and close the Table Design Mode window.

4. Go to the Forms listing in the Database window and delete the form frmCD.

5. Create a new form using the Auto Form option of the Form Wizards. Save the form, calling it frmCDs. Leave the new form open.

6. Modify the data currently in CDCollection. You may use the data suggested below, which is a continuation of the data from the previous chapter, or your own.

| TITLE | LENGTH | CLASSIFICATION |
|---|---|---|
| Star Wars | 75 | Movie theme |
| Evangeline | 39 | Cajun/Country |
| Canyon Trilogy | 59 | Native American flute |
| Cusco 2002 | 41 | New Age symphonic |
| Question of Balance | 38 | Symphonic Rock |

7. After you have entered the data, save your records.

8. Close the form. Close the CD database.

## 2. The Dinner Party database.

1. Open the database dinner.mdb. Open the table DinnerGuests in Table Design mode.

2. Add two new fields to the end of the Field Name list. The first field is Likes: Make it a text data type and type Specific food preferences as the Description. The second field is Dislikes: Make it a text data type and type Specific culinary dislikes for the Description.

3. Save the changes you have just made and close the Table Design Mode window.

4. Go to the Forms listing in the Database window and delete the form frmGuests.

5. Create a new form using the Auto Form option of the Form Wizards. Save the form, calling it frmGuests. Leave the new form open.

6. Modify the data currently in DinnerGuests. You may use the data suggested below, which is a continuation of the data from the previous chapter, or your own. Maximize the form to facilitate data entry.

| FIRST NAME | LAST NAME | LIKES | DISLIKES |
|---|---|---|---|
| Linda | Smith | chocolate | |
| John | Baccus | fajitas | cauliflower |
| Mary | Cummings | lemon squares | |
| Fred | Wood | strawberry trifle | whole tomatoes |
| Sue | Woolrich | salads | fish |

7. After you have entered the data, save your records. Close the form.

8. Go to the Report listing in the Database window and delete the report rptGuests.

9. Create a new report using the Report Wizard.

10. Examine your report on the Print Preview screen. Then, if you are connected to a printer, print out the report.

11. Save the report, calling it rptGuests.

12. Close the report. Close the Dinner Party database.

# CASE STUDIES

**Coffee-On-The-Go:**   **Editing a Database**

In this chapter, you learned to edit a database. You will use those skills to edit the Employee table for Coffee-On-The-Go.

1. Open the Coffee database.
2. Open the Employee table.
3. Change Henry Hart's name to Harry Hart.
4. Change Nancy Pope's location from 01 to 02.
5. Change the spelling of Jerry Jones's first name to Gerry.
6. Delete Mary Frances from the database.
7. Save the changes to the Employee table.
8. Print a quick report of the data.
9. Close the database.

# CASE STUDIES

**Videos West:**   **Editing a Database**

In this chapter, you learned to edit a database. You will use those skills to edit the Inventory table for Videos West.

1. Open the Video database.
2. Open the Inventory table.
3. Delete the video Christmas Decorations.
4. Change the retail price of Yoga for Your Health to $19.99.
5. Change the video Baseball Tips to Baseball Pitching Tips.
6. Change the quantity of Start Your Own Business from 7 to 3.
7. Save the changes to the Video database.
8. Print a quick report of the data.
9. Close the database.

# Acumen Fundamentals Milestone

**Individual Project:**

## the Scouts Cookie Sale Database

Scout Troop #99 is getting ready to launch its annual cookie sale. Troop Master Wilson wants to track sales this year to find out who is selling in which neighborhoods and where they need more penetration.

Mrs. Wilson will need a table to store information about the scouts (ScoutNbr, ScoutName), customers (CustomerNbr, CustomerName, Address, HomePhone), and sales (ScoutNbr, CustomerNbr, CookieType, NbrBoxes).

There are eight scouts in Troop #99: Andrea, Ariel, Cathy, Debby, Laura, Mandy, Michelle, and Rachel. There are six cookie types: Chocolate Chip, Coconut Macaroon, Lemon Crisp, Mint Wafer, Peanut Butter, and Vanilla Sandwich. Instead of building a separate table for the cookies, Mrs. Wilson has chosen to use a reference list in the form when entering cookie sales.

1. Design the database on paper. Identify the tables of the database and the fields within each. Give each field a proper field name. Designate the primary key for each table. Mark the fields on which you will sort the data as candidates for indexing. Make sure that you will be able to create relationships between tables as needed.

2. Create the tables in MS-Access. Choose appropriate data types for each field. Add meaningful comments to each field. Assign a primary key to each table as designated by your design.

3. Create Quick Forms. Populate the Scout table. Record this week's cookie sales.

4. Generate Quick Reports to print out the data in your database.

**Team Project:**

## the Community Recreation Center Database

Your project group has been assigned to develop a database to track activities at the local Community Recreation Center. The Rec Center services both the community and the nearby University. Students from the

University can use the Rec Center if they have paid their annual student activity fee. The student activity fee can be considered a purchased membership. Faculty members from the University and residents of the community must purchase a membership before they can use the facilities. Faculty membership fees are slightly less than those for people from the community.

The Rec Center has four racquetball courts and six tennis courts. These courts may be reserved up to one week in advance. A member can make many reservations, but each court can only be reserved for one hour at a time.

Members of the Rec Center are allowed to check out sports equipment to use at the facility. When members check out the equipment, an equipment-issue form is completed listing the member's number, the member's name, the equipment being used, and the date and time that the equipment was checked out. The member gets one copy; a second copy is kept by the Rec Center staff. When the equipment is returned, the equipment-issue form is updated with the date and time of the return. Staff employed by the Rec Center monitor the checkout and use of the sporting equipment and make reservations for use of the racquetball and tennis courts.

All the members of your project group will have to work together to design this database on paper. In addition to determining the tables and their relationships, list the kinds of reports that will be required by the management of the Rec Center. Include equipment-issue receipts, listings of court activity, membership listings, mailing listings, mailing labels, and letters to the membership about upcoming events.

Designate one member of your project group as the Database Administrator. This person is responsible for creating tables and relationships, designating primary keys and indexes, and implementing validation rules as requested by the members of the team.

Designate a second member of your project group as the Forms Designer. This person is responsible for the design and implementation of the data-entry forms and any underlying queries for the Rec Center database.

A third member of your project group will serve as the Report Designer. This person is responsible for the design and implementation of the reports and any underlying queries for the Rec Center database.

All members of the project team will share data-entry responsibilities equally. When changes to any object of the database are required, each member first confers with the others before making a modification. The project team members report to each other on a regular basis about their activities and coordinate development of the Rec Center database with each other.

### The Full Project Team

Design the database on paper. Identify the tables of the database and the fields within each. Give each field a proper field name. Designate the primary key for each table. Mark the fields on which you will sort the data as candidates for indexing. Make sure that you will be able to create relationships between the tables as needed. Record this week's new members, reservations, and equipment issues.

### The Database Administrator

Create the tables in MS-Access. Choose appropriate data types for each field. Add meaningful comments to each field. Assign a primary key to each table as designated by your design. Generate database reports.

### The Forms Designer

Create Quick Forms. Populate the Courts and Equipment Inventory table.

### The Report Designer

Generate some Quick Reports to print out the data.

# Part 2

# Critical Thinking

# Chapter 5

## Changing and Customizing Tables

**Objectives**

- Creating a Relationship Between Two Tables
- Sorting Records
- Changing Field Size and Format
- Adding Validation Rules to Tables
- Creating Indexes
- Making a Backup of the Database

**Key Terms**

| TERM | DEFINITION |
|------|------------|
| **Database Application** | a combination of data, input and output modules, and business rules that turn raw data into useable information |
| **Database Integrity** | a measure of the accuracy and correctness of the data stored in a database |
| **Null** | a condition that indicates missing or unknown data |
| **Referential Integrity** | a rule that states that you cannot have records on the many side of a one-to-many relationship that are not linked to a record on the one side of that same relationship |
| **Orphan Records** | records that were once part of a one-to-many relationship on the many side that have been abandoned because the related record on the one side was changed or deleted |
| **Cascade Update** | a change made in the value of a primary key field on the one side is passed along to the related record(s) on the many side in a one-to-many relationship |
| **Cascade Delete** | an automatic deletion of records on the many side that occurs when the related record on the one side is deleted |

| TERM | DEFINITION |
|---|---|
| **Join** | a database operation that connects related records in two or more tables so that data can be accurately extracted and displayed from the related tables in a single form or report |
| **Index** | a list of unique values built from a column of a table that helps you find a record quickly |
| **Validation Rule** | a business rule that limits data being entered into the database |
| **Database Backup** | a copy of the database file, which is made as a safety measure |

**database application**  A *database application* is a combination of the data, the input and output modules, and the business rules that turn raw data into useable information. Before you start building applications, you must create relationships between tables. You can then combine data from different tables and output them to forms and reports.

Often you will need to sort records in a specific order, such as Last Name, State, or Zip Code. With MS-Access you can sort in ascending or descending order.

After using the database for a while, you may need to change a field size or format. Or you may want to prevent incorrect data from being entered. Adding validation rules to your database application will help prevent these problems.

MS-Access uses a technique called Rushmore to find data quickly, even in large databases. To take advantage of this technique, you must use queries or reports that are based on fields that are indexed. Therefore, carefully choosing which fields to index helps when retrieving your data.

Two routine maintenance steps that are often neglected are compacting, or compressing, the database and making a regular backup copy of the database.

# Objective 1:  Creating a Relationship Between Two Tables

To create a relationship between two tables, you must build a table that can be related, or linked, to an existing table.

## Building a Related Table

Your Contacts table includes fields for home, work, and fax phone numbers. Three phone number fields may not be enough, since people have pagers, cellular phones, car phones, and 800 numbers. You can add more fields to the Contacts table for each extra phone number, but you would have to add a separate field for each type. Using a second, related table, you can employ a more efficient method of handling multiple phone numbers.

## Exercise 1: Building a phone number table

Instead of using the Table Wizard, you will build the Phone Number table from scratch.

1. Start at your Contacts database with the Tables tab selected.
2. Click New.
3. Click the New Table button (Fig. 5-1).

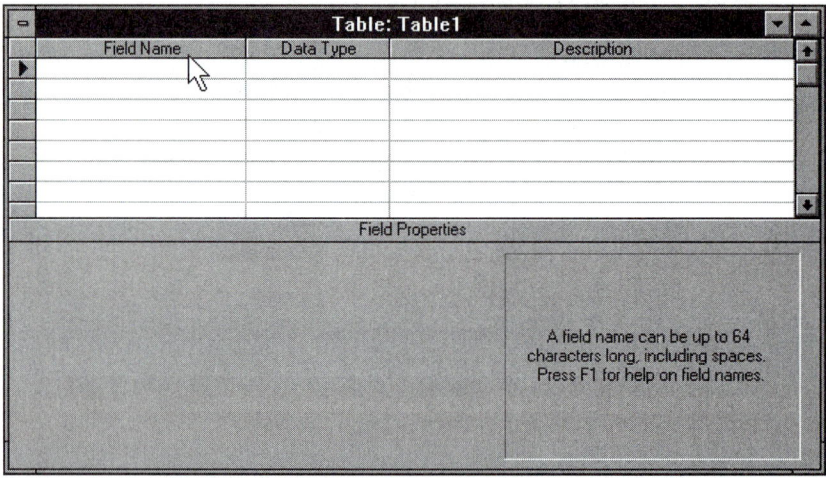

**Figure 5-1**   **New Table Definition window**

4. Type ContactID in the first row of the Field Name column.
5. TAB to the Data Type column. Click the arrow in the box at the right of the column to open a list of data types. Click Number.
6. Press F6 to move down to the Field Properties box.
7. Click the arrow in the box at the right of Field Size to open a list of numeric data types. Click Long Integer.

   You must use the Long Integer data type for this field because you will be relating it to the ContactID in the Contacts table, which is a counter data type. MS-Access uses the Long Integer type internally for all its counter fields.

8. Type Contact ID in the Caption field. Press F6 to return to the Field Definitions.

   Spaces are acceptable in the Caption field, as this is just a label for the field.

9. Move the cursor to the first row of the Description column and type Contact ID. Press ↵ ENTER.
10. Move the cursor to the second row of the Field Name column and type PhoneNumber. Press ↵ ENTER. Leave the data type as Text.
11. Press F6 to move down to the Field Properties box. Move to the Input Mask field and click the button to the right of the field.

12. The Save Table dialog box appears asking to save the table now. Click Yes.

13. When prompted for a table name, type PhoneNumbers. Choose OK.

14. When prompted for a primary key, click No.

    The Input Mask Wizard dialog box appears (Fig. 5-2). The first option listed is phone number.

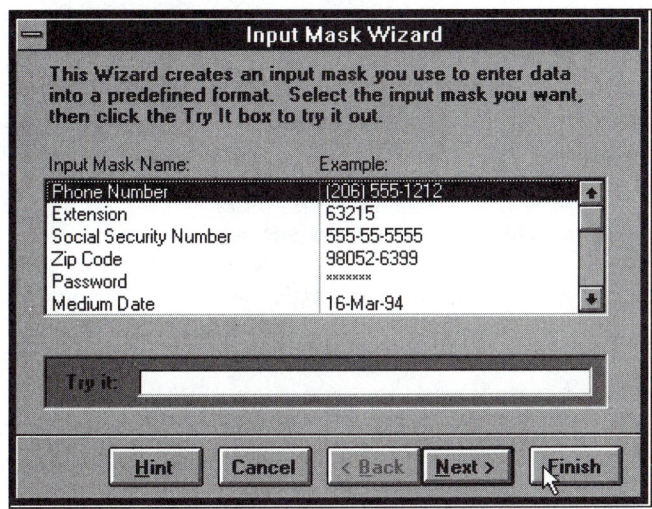

**Figure 5-2**  **Input Mask Wizard dialog box**

15. Phone Number is already highlighted, so click Finish.

    MS-Access builds the input mask for you.

16. Type Phone Number in the Caption field.

17. Press F6 to return to the Field Definition box. Move to the Description field.

18. Type Phone Number and press ↵ ENTER.

19. Move the cursor to the third row of the Field Name column and type PhoneType. Press ↵ ENTER.

20. Leave the field type as Text. Press F6 to move to the Field Properties box. Type Type of Phone Number for the caption.

21. Press F6 to return to the Field Definition box. Type the description Type of Phone Number.

22. Click in the left margin of the Table Definition window, so that the entire first row is highlighted.

23. Hold down SHIFT and click the margin of the PhoneNumber field so that *both* lines are highlighted. Release SHIFT.

24. Click the Set Primary Key icon on the Toolbar to create a two-line primary key.

    Both ContactID and PhoneNumber show key symbols in their left margins (Fig. 5-3).

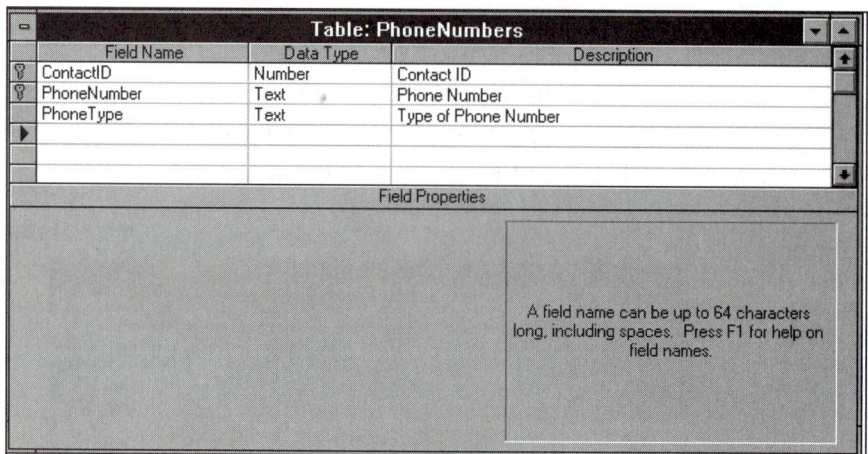

**Figure 5-3   The PhoneNumber table**

25. Choose File/Save to save your new table. Choose File/Close to exit.

## Defining Relationships Between Tables

**referential integrity**

**orphan records**

Now that you have two tables designed to be linked, you can specify how they are related. MS-Access provides help when you are defining relationships between tables. It takes care of important details, including *referential integrity*, which means that MS-Access will not let you delete a record from one table that has related records in another table. Such a deletion would result in *orphan records*—records that were once part of a one-to-many relationship on the many side that have been abandoned because the related record on the one side was deleted.

**database integrity**

Referential integrity is part of database integrity. *Database integrity* is a measure of the accuracy and correctness of the data stored in a database. If there are orphan records in your database, you have inaccurate data.

**cascade update**

MS-Access protects against orphan records by giving you two options after you choose to Enforce Referential Integrity. *Cascade Update* Related Fields modifies related records for you when you change the value of a primary key. For example, if you change an employee number from AB133 to AB103, all records in other tables associated with that employee will have their employee number data values changed from AB133 to AB103.

**cascade delete**

*Cascade Delete* Related Fields deletes related records in other tables when you remove a record from the first table. For example, if you remove an employee's record from the Personnel table, all records in other tables associated with that employee are also removed.

**join**

A connection or link between tables that have related data is known as a *join*. There are several different types of joins, and MS-Access explains each type of join in easy-to-understand language. You select the tables, connect the fields that are common to the two tables, and choose the type of join needed.

## Exercise 2: Creating a relationship between two tables

In this exercise, you will create a relationship between the Contacts and PhoneNumbers tables.

1. At the Database window choose Edit/Relationships from the top menu.

   The Add Table dialog box opens, with the Contacts table highlighted (Fig. 5-4).

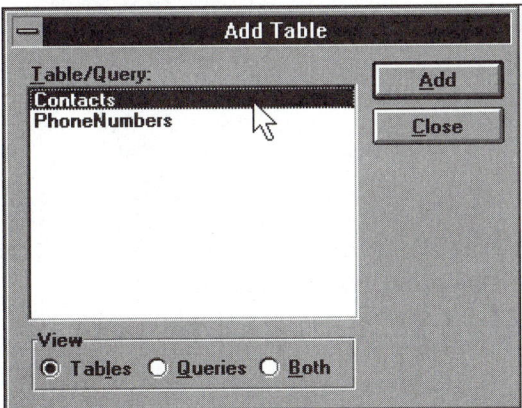

**Figure 5-4**   **The Add Table dialog box**

2. Click the Add button to include the Contacts table in the relationship.
3. Highlight the PhoneNumbers table, add it to the relationship by clicking Add.
4. Close the Add Table dialog box (Fig. 5-5).

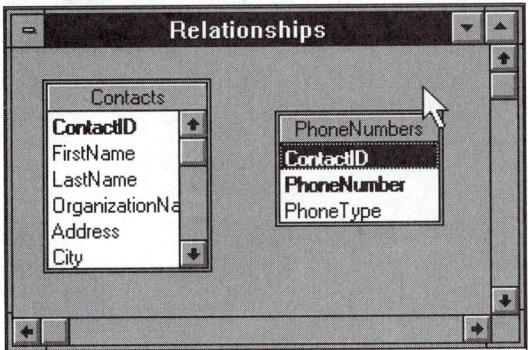

**Figure 5-5**   **The Relationships dialog box with the PhoneNumbers table added**

5. Place the cursor over the ContactID field in the Contacts table and hold down the left mouse button. Drag the cursor to the right until it is over the ContactID field in the PhoneNumbers field. Release the mouse button (Fig. 5-6).

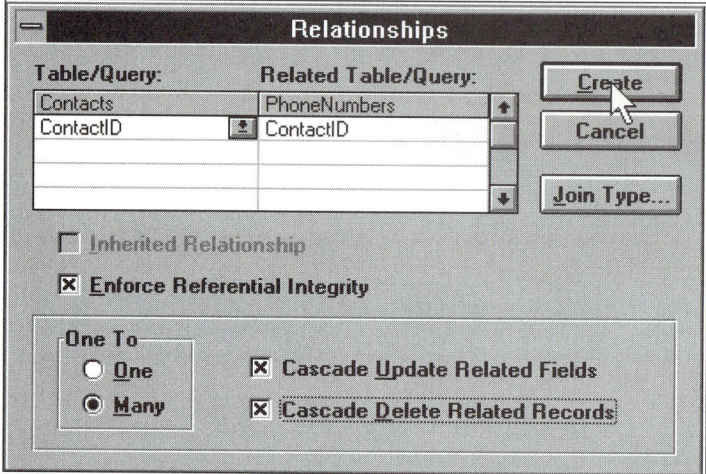

**Figure 5-6** **The Relationships dialog box**

6. In the Relationships dialog box, click Enforce Referential Integrity. Note that the One-To-Many option is chosen for you.

7. Click the option boxes to turn on Cascade Update Related Fields and Cascade Delete Related Fields.

An X appears in each box to show that the option is selected.

8. Click Join Type to open the Join Properties dialog box (Fig. 5-7).

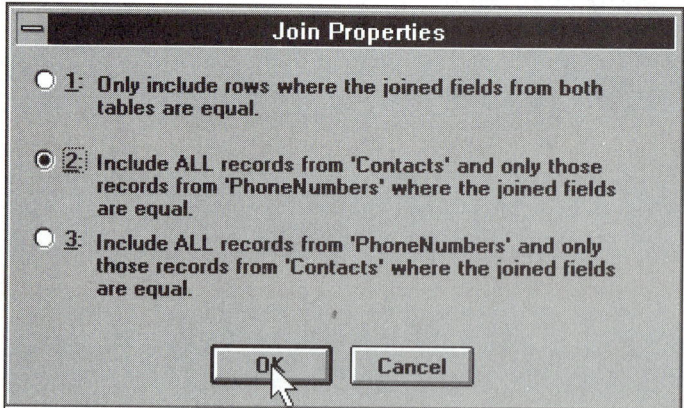

**Figure 5-7** **The Join Properties dialog box**

9. Select the second option from the list of Join Types. Click OK.

The Join Properties dialog box closes and returns you to the Relationships dialog box.

10. Click Create to create the relationship.

11. Click File/Save Layout to save the relationship. Close the Relationship window.

**Using indexes**

MS-Access can retrieve data most rapidly when it is performing the search on an indexed field. As we said before, you want to index the fields you use most often for sorting, such as LastName and PostalCode, and those that link or join two tables together, such as ContactID. However, you do not want to index every field in a table. Each time you enter a new record into the database, the index must be updated to include the new data, thus slowing MS-Access performance.

# Objective 2:  Sorting Records

When you look at or print out data from your database, you want the data to be organized. For example, you might want to list your contacts by last name or by city. Sorting in MS-Access is quick and easy because only the screen display or report is sorted. MS-Access does not actually rearrange the data on the disk. If you close and open the form, it reverts to its original data storage order.

## Exercise 3: Sorting records in the DataSheet view

In this exercise, you will sort records in ascending and descending order.

1. Open the Contacts table in Datasheet view and position the cursor in the Last Name column.

2. Click the Sort Ascending icon on the toolbar.

   The records are sorted in ascending order by the Last Name (Fig. 5-8).

| Contact ID | First Name | Last Name | Organization Name | Address | City | S |
|---|---|---|---|---|---|---|
| 1 | Sam | Adams | Antiques Unlimited | 47 Main Street | Boston | M |
| 8 | Ignacio | Chavez | Precision Surveys, Inc. | 348 Embarcadero | San Francisco | C |
| 7 | Robin H. | Clark | Precision Surveys, Inc. | 270 Butte Meadows | Boise | IID |
| 9 | Hiroshi | Kanzaki | Precision Surveys, Inc. | 897 Green Mountain I | Portland | O |
| 2 | George | Langford | Langford Trucking | 1 Farm Road | Mount vernon | V |
| 10 | Wendy | Monteleone | Monteleone Legal Serv | 1478 27th Avenue S\ | Washington | D |
| 4 | Margaret | Moore | Liberty Shield Insurance | 145 Independence A | Philadelphia | P |
| 6 | Roger S. | O'Leary | Precision Surveys, Inc. | 2525 Forest lane | Walla Walla | W |
| 3 | G. David | Swenson | Swenson Adventure To | 101 Chase Lane | Nashville | T |
| (Counter) | | | | | | |

Table: Contacts

Record: 1  of 9

**Figure 5-8**   **The Contacts table in Datasheet view sorted by last name**

3. Position the cursor in the Organization Name column and click the Sort Ascending icon.

   The records are sorted in ascending order by organization name.

4. Position the cursor in the Contact ID column list and click the Sort Descending icon.

   In descending sort, the most recently entered data is positioned at the top.

5. Close the Datasheet view.

# Objective 3: Changing Field Size and Format

After using the database for a while, you might discover that some fields are too short. You can easily change the length of a field, but think carefully before you reduce the size of a field because long data items may be truncated. For example, if you reduce a field from 30 to 20 characters, data items stored in this field between 21 and 30 characters long will be cut off.

## Exercise 4: Changing field size

The PostalCode field is currently 20 characters long. For longer zip codes, including nine-digit zip codes and Canadian postal codes, a 10-character field will suffice, but we will shorten the field to 12 characters to be safe.

1. At the Database window with the Table list showing, highlight the Contacts table.

2. Open the Contacts table in Table Design mode.

3. Move to the PostalCode field. Press (F6) to switch to the Field Properties box.

4. Change the Field Size from 20 to 12.

5. Click File/Save.

   A dialog box appears warning that you may lose data.

6. Click OK. Click File/Close.

# Objective 4: Adding Validation Rules to Tables

**validation rule**  A *validation rule* is a business rule that becomes part of the database. Validation rules put restrictions on the data you may enter.

The rule you will implement is that all entries in your contact database must have a Last Name. In the language of databases, the LastName field "is not null." A null data value is one that indicates that a field has been left blank intentionally. The validation rule Is Not Null means that the field cannot contain a blank space or null value.

### Exercise 5: Validation rule: every record must have a LastName value

In this exercise, you will create a validation rule.

1. Open the Contacts table in Design mode.
2. Move to the LastName field and press F6 to shift to the Field Properties box.
3. Go to the Validation Rule field and type Is Not Null.

   You should explain validation rules to the user in the Validation Text field.

4. TAB to the Validation Text field and type Please enter a last name (Fig. 5-9).

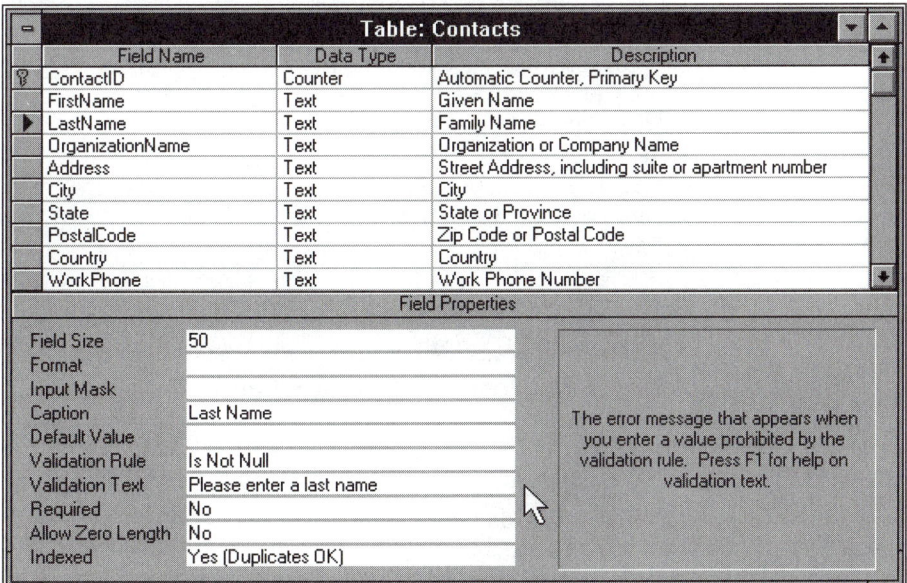

**Figure 5-9**   **The Contacts table in Design view with the LastName validation rule**

5. Click File/Save.

   A message appears on the screen. It offers to check your table for entries that conflict with the new rule. You know that all your records have an entry for LastName, so click No.

6. Click File/Close.

## Objective 5:  Creating Indexes

**index**

To retrieve data from a database efficiently, you should search on an indexed field. An *index* is a database structure built by MS-Access that acts like the index of a book—it tells MS-Access where to look for a piece of information. You want to index the fields that you use most often to sort, such as LastName and PostalCode, as well as those you use to link or join two tables, such as ContactID.

## Exercise 6: Creating an index on the State field

Since you often sort your Contacts database by State, you should build an index for the State field.

1. Open the Contacts table in Table Design mode and click View/Indexes.

    The Index Definition window opens with Indexes: Contacts in the window header (Fig. 5-10).

**Indexes: Contacts**

| Index Name | Field Name | Sort Order |
|---|---|---|
| LastName | LastName | Ascending |
| OrganizationName | OrganizationName | Ascending |
| PostalCode | PostalCode | Ascending |
| PrimaryKey | ContactID | Ascending |

**Index Properties**

| | |
|---|---|
| Primary | No |
| Unique | No |
| Ignore Nulls | No |

The name for this index. Each index can use up to 10 fields.

**Figure 5-10  Index Definition window**

2. Move to the first empty row in the Index Name column and type State.
3. Move to the Field Name column and click the down arrow to show a list of fields (Fig. 5-11).

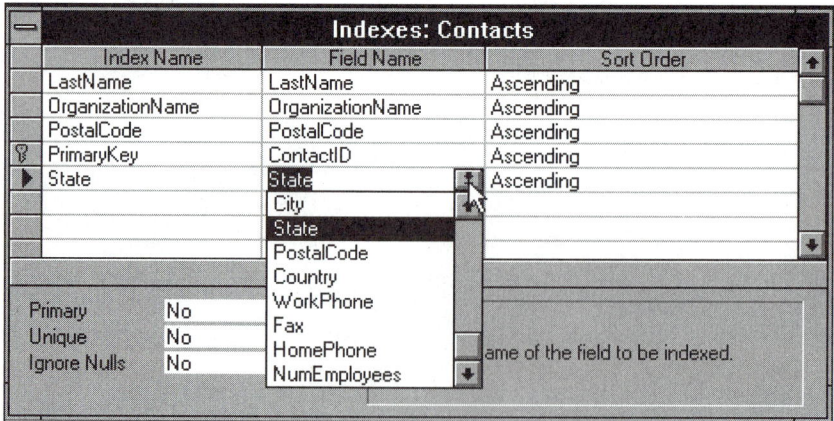

**Indexes: Contacts**

| Index Name | Field Name | Sort Order |
|---|---|---|
| LastName | LastName | Ascending |
| OrganizationName | OrganizationName | Ascending |
| PostalCode | PostalCode | Ascending |
| PrimaryKey | ContactID | Ascending |
| State | State | Ascending |

City
State
PostalCode
Country
WorkPhone
Fax
HomePhone
NumEmployees

| | |
|---|---|
| Primary | No |
| Unique | No |
| Ignore Nulls | No |

ame of the field to be indexed.

**Figure 5-11  Index Definition window showing a list of fields**

**The Term "Computer Bug" Was First Used . . .**

. . . in 1947 when the late Mary Grace Hopper was investigating a problem with an early computer. She could not figure out why the program she had written was not running as it should, so she looked inside the computer's memory, or "core" as it was called then. She found a dead moth lying on the memory assembly. When she removed it, her program worked fine. From then on, computing errors became known as "bugs," and chasing down and fixing errors became known as "debugging."

Mary Grace Hopper taped the moth to her logbook next to that day's entry. The logbook and the moth are on display at the U.S. Naval Museum in Dahlgren, Virginia.

4. Click the State field. Leave the Sort Order column as Ascending.

5. Close the Index Definition window. You have just indexed the State field.

6. Save your changes. Close the Table Design window.

# Objective 6: Making a Backup of the Database

One cannot overemphasize the importance of backup copies for your database. You will come to rely on your databases; if you lose them, it is hard to recover from the loss. The primary copy of your database is on the hard disk. You should always keep a backup copy of your database on a floppy disk. Make backups regularly and store one copy in a different location, away from your hard drive.

There are two ways to make backups of your database. The first is by using MS-Windows File Manager to copy the .mdb file onto a floppy disk or tape. The second way is to use the MS-Access Compact facility.

As you change your database—building forms and reports and making design changes to the tables—MS-Access adds the changes to the database file. When you delete data records, MS-Access reclaims the space that the records occupied but does not reuse it. Gradually, the database grows and becomes disorganized. Compacting it reorganizes and reduces the size of the database file.

When you compact the database, you can compact it into a new database with a new name, or you can compact it into itself. If you compact and save your database into a new database on a floppy disk, the new database can act as your backup copy. Then you can compact the database into itself on your hard disk, recovering some disk space in the process.

## Exercise 7: Making a backup of your database

The following exercise shows you how to use the MS-Windows File Manager to make a backup of your database.

1. Close the Contacts database (File/Close Database). Minimize MS-Access.

2. Use the MS-Windows File Manager to make a copy of the contacts.mdb file, preferably to a different hard disk, floppy disk (if your database is small enough), tape, or different computer on the network.

3. If you have backup software, you can use it to backup to a floppy disk or tape. MS-DOS V6 has a backup program that runs from DOS or Windows and will backup to a floppy disk.

## Exercise 8: Compacting the database

This exercise shows you how to use the MS-Access Compact facility to backup your database. You will compact contacts.mdb into a new database called cont_bak.mdb, which becomes your backup file.

1. Make sure all your databases are closed.
2. Select File/Compact Database. The Compact Database dialog box appears (Fig. 5-12).

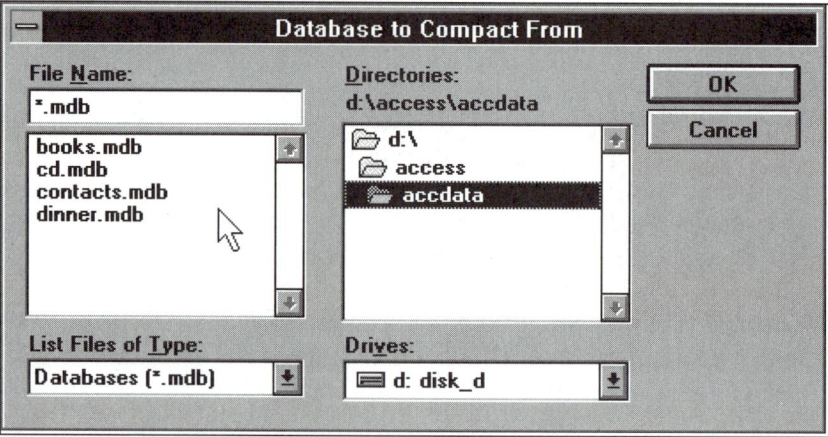

**Figure 5-12** **The Compact Database dialog box**

3. Select contacts.mdb file as the Database to Compact From. Select OK.
   The Database to Compact Into dialog box appears.
4. Type cont_bak.mdb as the new filename. Click OK.
   You may specify a different directory or disk. MS-Access produces a compacted backup of your database. When it finishes, you can open the database and begin using it or exit from MS-Access.

## Chapter Summary

In this chapter you learned how to establish a relationship between two tables, sort data, and adjust field sizes to better fit your needs. You implemented validation rules that define acceptable data for the database. You indexed the State field to improve MS-Access performance when searching that field. After making all these changes, you compacted and made a backup copy of the database.

## Review Questions

### True/False Questions

_____  1. Two tables in a relational database can be associated only in a one-to-one or one-to-many relationship.

_____  2. Violating referential integrity might result in orphan records.

_____  3. The connection between two related tables is known as a *joint*.

_____  4. To make MS-Access run faster, you should index every column in the table.

_____  5. You should make periodic backups of your database to avoid a disastrous loss of data.

### Multiple-Choice Questions

_____  6. During a cascade delete,

A. a record in the table of the many is deleted, which results in all related records in that table being deleted.

B. a record in the table of the many is deleted, which results in the related record in the table of the one being deleted.

C. a record in the table of the one is deleted, which results in all related records in the table of the many being deleted.

D. a record in the table of the one is deleted, which results in all related records in that table being deleted.

_____  7. A database object built from one or more fields of a base table that is used to assist in doing searches for specific data values is called a(n)

A. relational table.

B. index.

C. cascade update.

D. validation rule.

_____  8. If you want to rearrange the order of the records in a datasheet, you perform a

A. join.

B. compact.

C. reformat.

D. sort.

_____ 9. The technique used by MS-Access to retrieve data from a database very rapidly is called

A. Rushmore.

B. Denali.

C. Everest.

D. McKinley.

_____ 10. The procedure used to reclaim space within the database that has been vacated by deleted records is called a database

A. backup.

B. compression.

C. compaction.

D. format.

## Fill-in-the-Blank Questions

11. The kind of relationship in which each record in one table is related or linked to many records in a second table is called a _____ relationship.

12. Database integrity is the measure of the _____ of the data stored in a database.

13. When a data item does not have a value, it is called _____.

14. A format rule, usage rule, or business rule coded into a database table or form is called a _____.

15. You must be careful if you shorten a field of a table because you could _____ the data already stored in the field.

## Acumen-Building Activities

## Quick Projects

### 1. Sorting records in the MyBooks form.

1. Open the Books database. Open the form frmBooks. `TAB` to the Title field.

2. Click the Sort Ascending icon on the top toolbar.

3. Use the controls at the bottom of the form to scroll through the records to verify that they are sorted by book title.

4. `TAB` to the Author field and click on the Sort Ascending icon.

5. Browse the records to verify that they are sorted by author.

6. Click File/Close to close the form.

## 2. Build and test a validation rule for MyBooks.

This exercise is a continuation of Quick Project #1.

1. Open the table MyBooks in Design mode.
2. Move to the Title FieldName and press F6 to shift to the Field Properties box.
3. Go to the ValidationRule field and type is not null.
4. TAB to the ValidationText field and type Please enter a book title.
5. Save your changes (File/Save). Answer Yes when MS-Access asks to test the data in the table with the new validation rule.
6. Choose File/Close to leave Table Design mode. Click the Form tab and Open frmBooks. Click Records/Data Entry from the top menu.
7. Type in the following data, leaving the Title field blank.

| | |
|---|---|
| BOOKCOLLECTIONID | 5 |
| Title | |
| Author | Tony Hillerman |
| ISBNNumber | 0-06-100017-5 |
| PublisherName | Harper |
| DatePurchased | 5/31/94 |
| Pages | 299 |
| Note | A southwest Native American mystery. |

8. Click File/Save Record. Click OK to close the message box warning you not to leave the book Title blank.
9. Return to the Title field and type Skinwalkers.
10. Choose File/Save Record. Close the form.

## 3. Creating an index on the ISBNNumber field.

This exercise is a continuation of Quick Project #2.

1. Open the table MyBooks in Table Design mode. Move the cursor to the FieldName ISBNNumber.
2. Press F6 to move into the Field Properties box and move the cursor to the Indexed field.
3. Click the drop-down list box and select Yes (duplicates OK).
4. Save your changes by selecting File/Save. Close the Table Design window.

## 4. Compacting a database into itself.

This exercise is a continuation of Quick Project #3.

1. Close the Books database. Select File/Compact Database.
2. Select books.mdb as the Database to Compact From and click OK.
3. Type books.mdb as the File Name for the Database to Compact Into and click OK.
4. Click Yes when asked to confirm this action.

## In-Depth Projects

### 1. The CD database.

1. Open the CD database. Create a New table without using the Table Wizard. Use the following field names, data types, descriptions, and field properties.

| FIELD NAME | DATA TYPE | DESCRIPTION | FIELD PROPERTIES |
|---|---|---|---|
| MusicCollectionID | number | Part of primary key; connects this table to CDCollection. | Field size: long integer |
| TrackNbr | number | Second part of the primary key; track number. | Field size: byte |
| TrackTitle | text | Title of the song or track. | Field size: 50 Validation rule: is not null |
| TrackTime | date/time | How long is this track or song? | Format: short time |

2. Highlight the first two lines of the table by holding down SHIFT and clicking each line in the left margin.

3. Click the Primary Key icon to create a two-line primary key. Both MusicCollectionID and TrackNbr will show key symbols in their left margins.

4. Save the table and name it Tracks. Close the Design window for the Tracks table.

5. Open table CDCollection in Table Design mode.

6. Modify Field Name title by changing field size from 20 to 50. Save these changes.

7. Close the Design window for the CDCollection table.

8. Create a relationship (Edit/Relationships) between CDCollection and Tracks. Link the two tables with the MusicCollectionID field. Enforce referential integrity. Indicate that this is a One-To-Many relationship. Turn on Cascade Update Related Fields and Cascade Delete Related Records. Choose Join. Type number 2.

9. Save the layout (File/Save Layout). Close the Relationships window.

10. Create an AutoForm for the table Tracks using the Form Wizard.

11. Save the new form, calling it frmTracks and add data. You may use the data suggested below, which is a continuation from previous chapters, or your own.

| MUSICCOLLECTIONID | TRACKNBR | TRACKTITLE | TRACKTIME |
|---|---|---|---|
| 1 | 1 | Main Title | |
| 1 | 2 | Imperial Attack | |
| 1 | 3 | Princess Leia's Theme | |
| 1 | 4 | The Desert and the Robot Auction | |
| 2 | 1 | Bayou Bay | 4:01 |
| 2 | 2 | If I Had a Heart | 4:06 |
| 2 | 3 | Am I a Fool | 3:51 |
| 2 | 4 | Hey Rene | 3:25 |
| 3 | 1 | Song for the Morning Start | 4:07 |
| 3 | 2 | Daybreak Vision | 1:44 |
| 3 | 3 | Ancestral Home | 4:44 |
| 4 | 1 | Seaplanet | 3:47 |
| 4 | 2 | Australia | 6:07 |
| 4 | 3 | Island Turtles | 3:59 |
| 5 | 1 | Question | |
| 5 | 2 | How Is It (We Are Here) | |
| 5 | 3 | And the Tide Rushes In | |
| 5 | 4 | Don't You Feel Small | |

12. Save your records after you have finished entering the data.

13. Close the Tracks form. Close the CD database.

## 2. The Dinner Party database.

1. Open the Dinner database. Create a New table without using the Table Wizard. Use the following field names, data types, descriptions, and field properties.

| FIELD NAME | DATA TYPE | DESCRIPTION | FIELD PROPERTIES |
|---|---|---|---|
| DinnerID | counter | Primary key. | |
| Place | text | Where is the dinner party held? | Field size: 50 |
| Date | date/time | What day is the dinner party? | Format: short date<br>Input mask: short date<br>Indexed: yes<br>(duplicates OK) |
| Time | date/time | What time is the dinner party? | Format: medium time<br>Input mask: medium time |
| Occasion | text | What, if any, is the occasion? | Field size: 50 |
| Comments | memo | Notes about the dinner party. | |

2. If prompted to save the table during this process, do so. Name it Dinners. Let MS-Access create the primary key. (It will make DinnerID the primary key of the table.)

3. When building the date and time input masks, do not attempt to customize the mask. Accept the default design. Save and close the Dinners table.

4. Create a second New table without using the Table Wizard. Use the following field names, data types, descriptions, and field properties.

| FIELD NAME | DATA TYPE | DESCRIPTION | FIELD PROPERTIES |
|---|---|---|---|
| GuestID | number | Part of the primary key; links to the table DinnerGuests. | Field size: long integer |
| DinnerID | number | Second part of the primary key; links to the table Dinners. | Field size: long integer |

5. Save the table, naming it GuestList. Do not create the primary key when prompted.

6. Highlight both lines of the table by holding down ⟨SHIFT⟩ and clicking each line in the left margin.

7. Click the Primary Key icon to create a two-line primary key. Both GuestID and DinnerID will show key symbols in the left margin.

8. Save the table GuestList and close the Design window for the table Guestlist.

9. To create a set of relationships (Edit/Relationships) for the tables DinnerGuests, GuestList, and Dinners, add these tables to the Relationships window in the order listed.

10. Link DinnerGuests to GuestList using the GuestID field. Enforce referential integrity. Indicate that this is a One-To-Many relationship. Turn on Cascade Update Related Fields and Cascade Delete Related Records. Choose Join. Type number 1.

11. Link Dinners to GuestList using the DinnerID field. Enforce referential integrity. Indicate that this is a One-To-Many relationship. Turn on Cascade Update Related Fields and Cascade Delete Related Records. Choose Join. Type number 1.

12. Save the layout (File/Save Layout) and close the Relationships window.

13. Create an AutoForm for the table Dinners using the Form Wizard.

14. Save the new form and call it frmDinners.

15. Add some data using the Dinners form. You may use the data suggested below, which is a continuation from previous chapters, or your own.

| PLACE | DATE | TIME | OCCASION | COMMENTS |
|-------|------|------|----------|----------|
| Fred's house | 02/13/94 | 02:00 PM | Valentine's Day dinner | Had a lovely time despite the snowstorm. A super seven-layer Valentine's cake. |
| Mary's house | 04/03/94 | 11:00 AM | Easter brunch | A wonderful sampling of Eastern European dishes. |
| Observatory Park | 05/29/94 | 12:00 PM | Memorial Day picnic | Deep southern cooking, Cajun and Creole, fried chicken and all the fixins. |
| Linda's house | 07/19/94 | 04:00 PM | Midsummer BBQ | A feast of smoked ribs and smoked turkey, salads and side dishes. |
| Sue's house | 08/30/94 | 06:00 PM | Linda's birthday | Southeast Asian menu and a big birthday cake. |

16. Save your records after you have finished entering the data. Close the Dinners form.

17. Create an AutoForm for the table GuestList using the Form Wizard. Save the new form, calling it frmGuestList.

18. Add some data using the Dinners form. You may use the data suggested below, which is a continuation from previous chapters, or your own.

| GUESTID | DINNERID |
|---------|----------|
| 1 | 1 |
| 2 | 1 |
| 3 | 1 |
| 4 | 1 |
| 5 | 1 |
| 1 | 2 |
| 2 | 2 |
| 3 | 2 |
| 4 | 2 |
| 3 | 3 |
| 4 | 3 |
| 5 | 3 |
| 1 | 4 |
| 2 | 4 |
| 3 | 4 |
| 4 | 4 |
| 5 | 4 |

**continued**

| GUESTID | DINNERID |
|---------|----------|
| 1 | 5 |
| 2 | 5 |
| 3 | 5 |
| 4 | 5 |
| 5 | 5 |

19. Save your records. Close the GuestList form.

20. Create a new report from the Dinners table using the Report Wizard. It will be an AutoReport.

21. Examine your report on the Print Preview screen and, if you are connected to a printer, print out the report.

22. Save the report, calling it rptDinners. Close the report. Close the Dinner database.

# CASE STUDIES

 **Coffee-On-The-Go:**

## Working with Tables

In this chapter, you learned to create relationships between two tables. You will use the skills you have learned so far to create another table and link it to the Employee table for Coffee-On-The-Go.

1. Create the following table:

| Field | Type | Size |
|-------|------|------|
| Location | Text | 2 |
| Name | Text | 15 |
| Union | Yes/No | 1 |
| Benefits | Text | 20 |

2. Name the table Benefits. Make Location the primary key.

3. Add the following data:

| Location | Name | Union | Benefits |
|----------|------|-------|----------|
| 01 | Portland | Y | Blue Cross |
| 02 | Eugene | N | none |
| 03 | Seattle | Y | Washington HMO |
| 04 | San Diego | N | California HMO |

4. Establish a relationship between the Employee table and the Benefits table. The Location field is used to connect the two.

5. Open the Employee table, and make the following changes:

   Create an index on the LastName field.

   Create an index on the Location field.

Delete the index on the LastName field.

Change the width of the LastName field to 15.

Add a new field and name it Union.

Delete the Union field.

6. Print both tables.

7. Save your changes and close the database.

# CASE STUDIES

 **Videos West:** ### Working with Tables

In this chapter, you learned to create relationships between two tables. You will use the skills you have learned so far to create another table and link it to the Inventory table for Videos West.

1. Create the following table:

| Field | Type | Size |
|-------|------|------|
| Type | Text | 2 |
| Name | Text | 20 |
| Vendor | Text | 20 |

2. Name the table Vendor. Make Type the primary key.

3. Add the following data:

| Type | Name | Vendor |
|------|------|--------|
| 01 | Sports and Outdoors | Outdoor Video Productions |
| 02 | Fitness | Better Bodies Videos |
| 03 | Health and Medicine | Medical Video Corp. |
| 04 | Finances | Financial Video, Inc. |
| 05 | Hobbies | Craft Video Productions |
| 06 | Languages | Language Videos, Inc. |

4. Establish a relationship between the Inventory table and the Vendor table. Use Type as the common field to connect the two.

5. Open the Inventory table, and make the following changes:

Create an index on the Title field.

Create an index on the Type field.

Delete the index on the Title field.

Change the width of the Title field to 35.

Add a new field and name it Number Sold.

Input data into the Number Sold field.

6. Print both tables.

7. Save your changes and close the database.

# Chapter 6

## Creating Forms

*Key Terms*

| TERM | DEFINITION |
| --- | --- |
| **Form** | an interactive screen that connects the user and the database management system; it can be used for both entering and displaying data |
| **Calculated Field** | a field on a form that displays the result of a calculation based on data stored in the database |
| **Reference Table** | a table of static data—that is, data whose values don't change often—such as state abbreviations or zip codes |
| **Properties Sheet** | an MS-Access window in which you can view or modify the properties of a selected object on a form |
| **Handle** | a marked position at a corner or side of a form object in Form Design view that allows you to modify the size of that object |
| **Toolbox** | a set of tools available in Form Design mode that you use to place objects and controls on a form |

| TERM | DEFINITION |
|---|---|
| **Palette** | an MS-Access window available in Form Design mode that contains color choices, box special effects, and border-line styles and widths |
| **Font** | a typeface that can be applied uniformly to all letters, numbers, and symbols within a document; the font style is typeface, while the font size is the size of the typeface are measured in points |
| **Text Box** | an MS-Access object on a form; a control that provides a place to view or update data from the database |
| **Label** | an MS-Access object on a form; a control that displays descriptive characters on a form |

**Forms**    *Forms* are used for data entry or displaying data on the computer screen. Using Forms offers more flexibility than entering data in Datasheet view. With a form, you can select fields from a table to view. You can also combine data from more than one table in a form. You can use the form to check the values of data you enter to ensure that they are within acceptable ranges. You can build a calculated field—that is, a field on a form that displays the result of a calculation based on data stored in the database—such as Totals or Subtotals. We will discuss calculated fields in Chapter 9.

The best way to start designing your form is with the MS-Access Form Wizards. Once you have the form on the screen, you can modify it by adding or deleting fields, moving fields, and adding or changing text. You can add boxes, lines, and color to delineate the various parts of the form. Visual cues guide the user and make the form easier to use. You customize the form **toolbox** using the set of tools in the toolbox and the color palette. The *toolbox* is a **palette** set of tools that places objects and controls on a form. The *palette* is a window that contains color choices, box special effects, and border-line styles and widths.

# Objective 1:  Creating a Form Using the Form Wizards

You have already used the Form Wizards to create a QuickForm for the Contacts table. When you use the Form Wizards this time, you will exert more control over the final product.

## Exercise 1: Creating a form using the Form Wizards

In this exercise, you will build a new form based on the Contacts table.

1. Start at the Contacts database with the Form tab highlighted. Click New (Fig. 6-1).

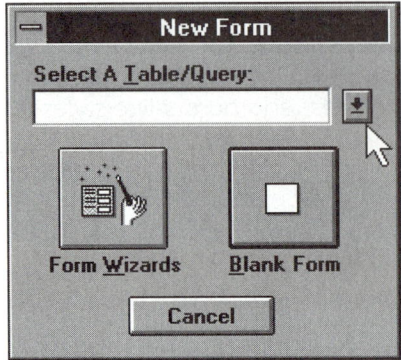

**Figure 6-1    New Form dialog box**

2. In the New Form dialog box select the Contacts table. Click Form Wizards.

3. Select the Single-Column Form Wizard. Click OK (Fig. 6-2).

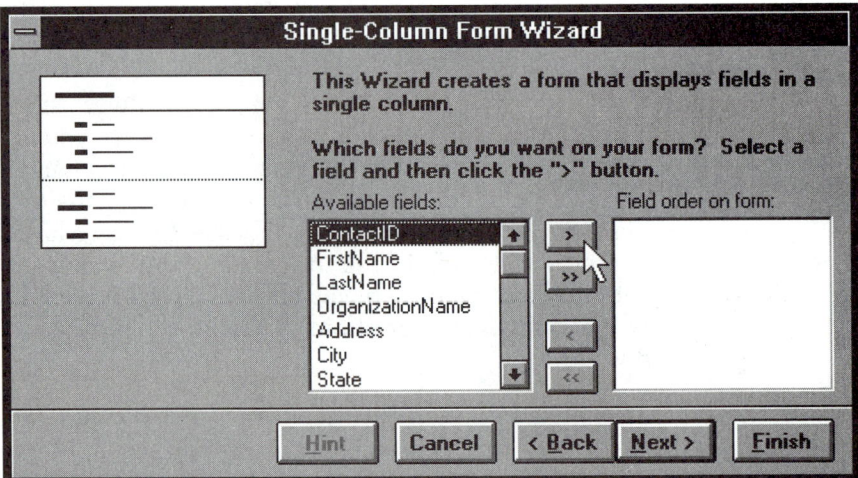

**Figure 6-2    Single-Column Form Wizard dialog box**

4. Move ContactID and FirstName from the list of available fields to the Field Order on Form column by highlighting the field name and then clicking the single right arrow.

5. Move the other fields to the Field Order on Form box by clicking the double right arrow. Click Next.

6. Choose the Embossed style. Click Next (Fig. 6-3).

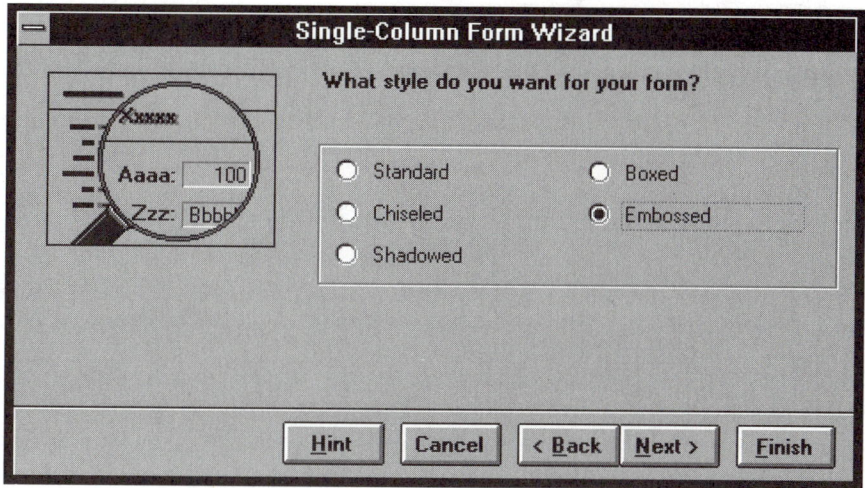

**Figure 6-3**  *Single-Column Form Wizard: styles*

7.  Leave the form title as Contacts and select the option to open the form with data in it. Click Finish to complete building the form and view the results.

8.  Save the form (File/Save Form). Type Contacts for the form name. Click OK (Fig. 6-4).

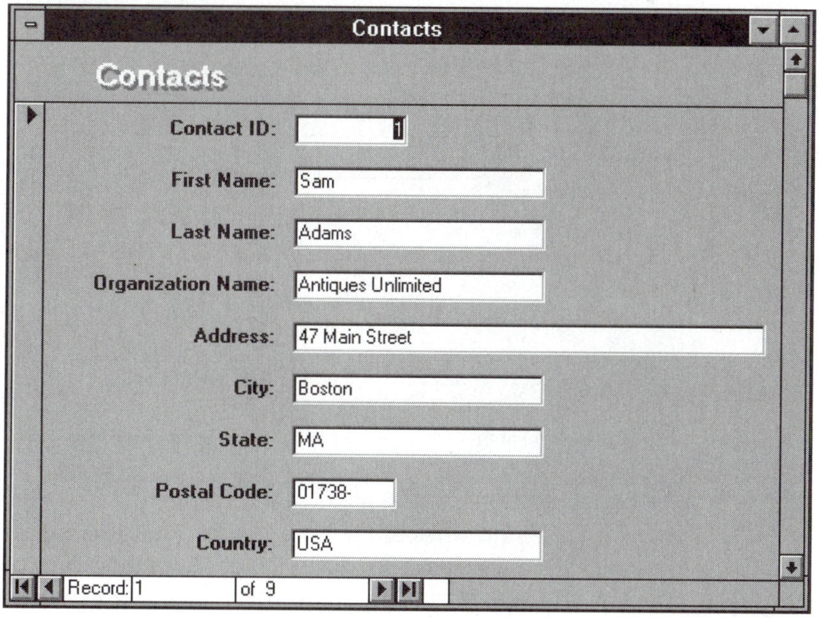

**Figure 6-4**  **Newly-created Contacts form**

# Objective 2:  Editing a Form

To make a form easier to use, you want to adjust the vertical spacing between fields and rearrange objects on the form so everything fits comfortably on a single page. This avoids time-consuming scrolling.

## Editing a Form: Deleting Fields on a Form

To delete a field, you must identify the field and then remove it.

**⚠ WARNING**   MS-Access has a one-level Undo feature. When you delete a field, you can undo the deletion if you act at once. However, if you perform another operation after deleting a field, you can no longer recover the deleted field.

## Exercise 2: Editing a form: deleting fields

In this exercise, you will first delete the NumEmployees field and then undo the deletion.

1. Click View/Form Design.
2. Maximize your form by clicking the up arrow in the upper right corner of the Form window (Fig. 6-5).

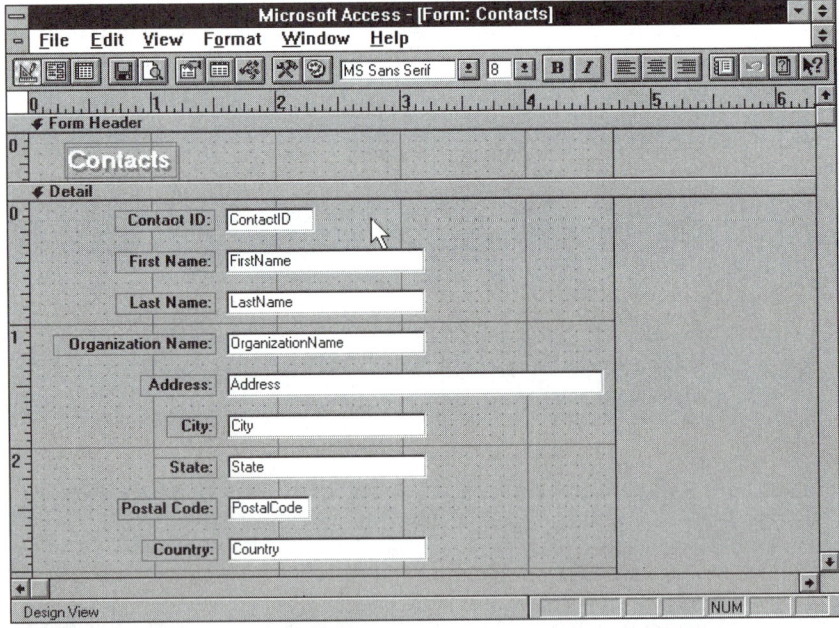

**Figure 6-5    The Contacts form in Design view, maximized**

3. Click anywhere on the NumEmployees field (Fig. 6-6).

**handles**   The corners of the field show handles. The *handles* on an object allow you to resize it.

**Figure 6-6**   **The Contacts form with the NumEmployees field selected**

4. Press ⟨DELETE⟩ to remove the NumEmployees field.

5. Click Edit/Undo Delete to recover the NumEmployees field. Click File/Save.

## Editing a form: moving fields on a form

You can move and resize fields. You can move more than one field at a time by drawing a box around a group of fields with the mouse. MS-Access provides formatting tools that help you space fields evenly on a form.

### Exercise 3: Moving fields manually

You will move several of the fields around the Contact form. Then you will use the MS-Access alignment tools to make the fields align properly.

1. Draw a box around the ContactID and FirstName fields so that both fields and their labels are selected at once. (You accomplish this by drawing a box around these objects. First, position the mouse where you want the upper left corner of the box. Hold down the left mouse button and drag the cursor where you want the the lower right corner of the box. Then release the mouse button.)

2. Position the cursor over one of the selected fields until the cursor changes from an arrow to a hand (Fig. 6-7).

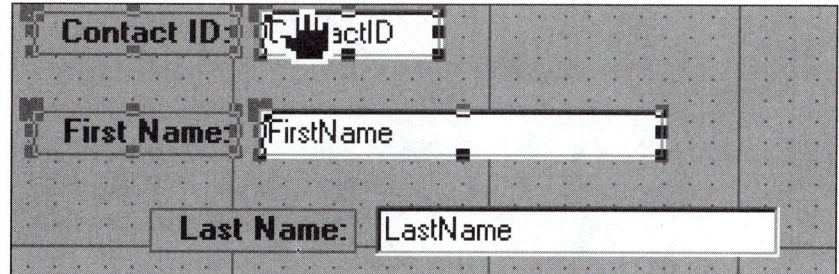

**Figure 6-7**   **Moving fields on the Contacts form**

3. Hold down the left mouse button and move the cursor to the left. The fields move with the cursor. When the labels are 0.75" from the left margin, release the mouse button.

4. Position the cursor over the right margin of the form. The cursor changes from an arrow to a double-headed horizontal arrow with a vertical crossbar. Drag the margin to the 6" line on the top ruler and release the mouse button.

   If the ruler is not visible, click View/Ruler to make it visible.

5. Move the LastName field so that it lines up horizontally to the right of the FirstName field.

6. Click the vertical ruler to the left of the FirstName field.

   The cursor changes to a horizontal arrow, and all objects on a horizontal line to the right are selected.

7. From the top menu, click Format/Align/Top.

   The FirstName and LastName fields and labels are aligned.

8. Draw a box around the remaining fields and labels from OrganizationName to NumEmployees.

9. Press ⌷PAGE UP⌷ so that you can see what you are doing in the next step.

10. Hold down ⌷CTRL⌷ and press the ⌷↑⌷ repeatedly until the fields are positioned closer to the top of the form.

11. Click anywhere on the form background to deselect the fields (Fig. 6-8).

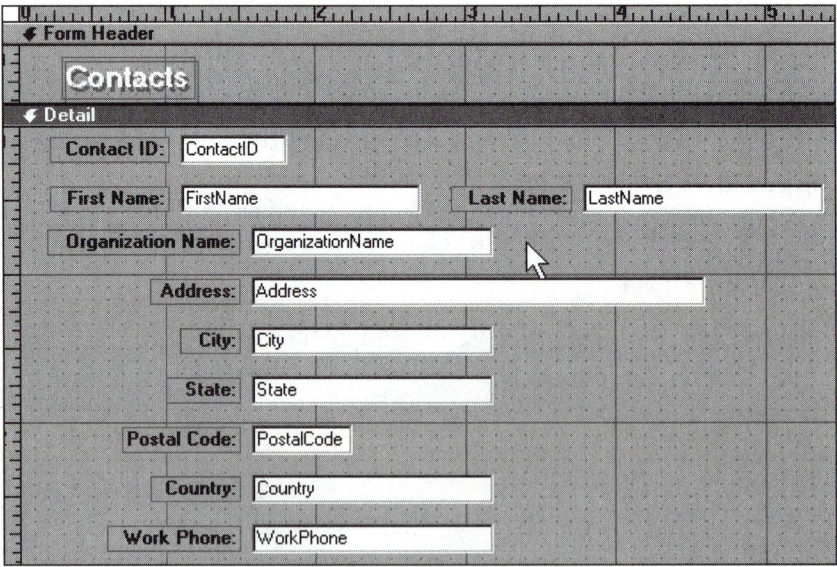

**Figure 6-8   The Contacts form with the fields in their new locations**

12. Click File/Save to save your work.

## Exercise 4: Moving fields with the format tools

In this exercise, you will re-adjust the spacing between fields on a form.

1. Select all the fields in the Detail section by drawing a box around them.
2. Click Format/Vertical Spacing/Make Equal.
3. Click Format/Vertical Spacing/Decrease. Repeat as necessary until all the fields fit on the screen.
4. Deselect the fields by clicking the form background. Click File/Save.
5. Reduce the size of the form by dragging the bottom margin up to just below the NumEmployees field.
6. Click the Form view icon.

   The whole form now fits on the screen (Fig. 6-9).

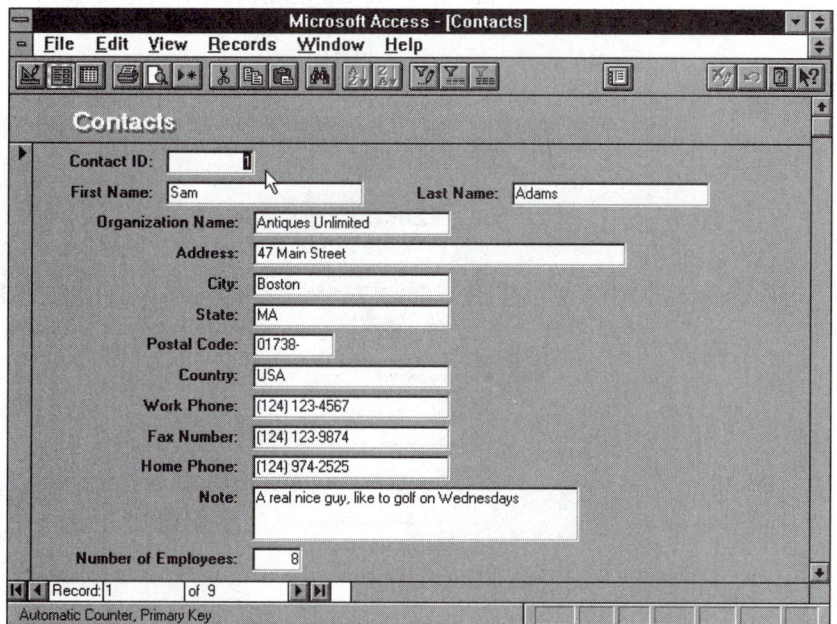

**Figure 6-9**   *The Contacts form with smaller field spacing*

## Editing a Form: Adding and Changing Text

If a field name is not descriptive enough, you can change it. You can add, delete, or modify the text already in place. These labels are derived from the Caption, which you entered when you defined the table and fields. If you did not supply a caption then, the field name is used as a label.

## Exercise 5: Changing the text

In this exercise, you will change the label of a field and reduce the label's size.

1. Switch to Design view. Click the *label* Organization Name to select it. (Don't click the OrganizationName field.)

2. Position the cursor inside the label; it will change from an arrow to an I-beam.

3. Place the I-beam between "Organization" and "Name" and click.

4. Remove the word "Name" from the label.

5. Click the box surrounding the label to select it.

6. Resize the box with the mouse by dragging the handle on the left side of the box.

7. Draw a box around the fields from Organization to NumEmployees and move them to the left, aligning them with the ContactID and FirstName fields (Fig. 6-10).

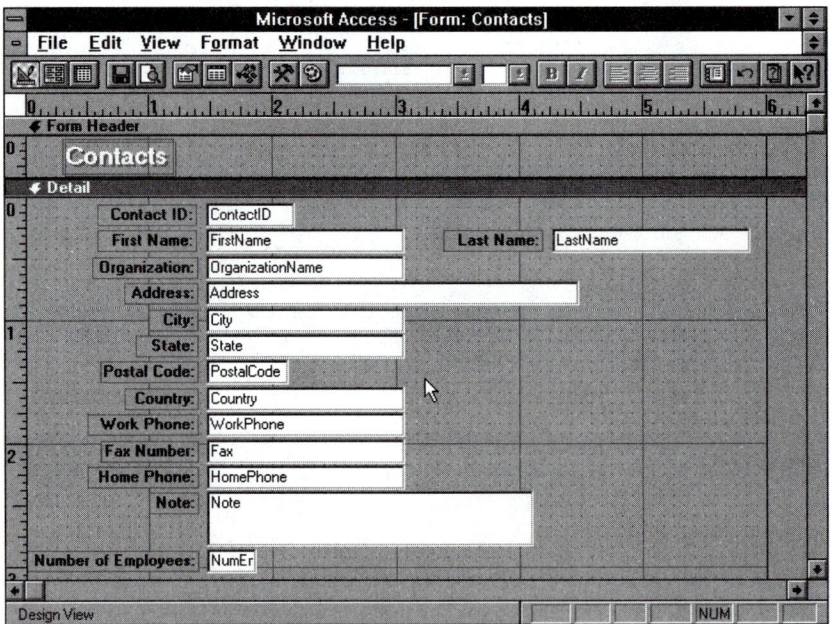

**Figure 6-10  The Contacts form with fields aligned left**

8. Draw a box around the fields, from ContactID to NumEmployees. Do not include the labels.

9. Click Format/Align/Left to align the fields. Click File/Save to save your work.

# Objective 3:  Adding Boxes, Lines, and Color

**text box**   All text added to the form must be in a text box. A *text box* provides a place to view and update data. You use the Toolbox to add a text box to the form. The Toolbox icon looks like a crossed wrench and hammer. When you click it, the toolbox appears on the screen. You can position it anywhere, dragging it to the top, bottom, or either side of the screen. Once you position it, the Toolbox turns into a horizontal or vertical toolbar.

⚠️ **WARNING**   Be careful of MS-Access's terminology: A text box is used to input data values and is associated with a field in the database. In the following exercise, you will add text to a label, which is simply placing text on a form.

## Exercise 6: Adding a label

**font**   In this exercise, you will add a label to the screen to identify the application and its author, then change the *font*, or typeface, and font size to make the text easier to read.

1. Click the Toolbox icon and position the Toolbox along the top of the window.

2. Click the Label button, then move to the open area at the right of the form.

   The cursor changes to an "A" with a plus sign (+) above and to the left of it.

3. Position the plus sign where you want the upper left corner of your label box. Hold down the left mouse button and drag the cursor diagonally down and to the right to create a box about 1.5" deep by 2" wide. Release the left mouse button.

4. Click the cursor in the box and type

   Contact Database ( CTRL + ↵ ENTER )

   by (*your name here*) ( CTRL + ↵ ENTER )

   Copyright (*year*)

   Do not press ( ↵ ENTER ) at the end of each line, or MS-Access will assume that you are finished typing and exit from the label box. Instead, press ( CTRL + ↵ ENTER ) to indicate the end of each line.

5. Click outside the box, then on the outer edge of the box to select it.

   The font name and size information are displayed on the top toolbar.

6. Click the down arrow to the right of the Font Name box and select a font from the list.

7. Click the down arrow to the right of the Font Size box and select a font size.

8. Click the Center-Align Text icon, which is to the right of the Font Size box, to center the text in the box. Adjust the size of the box if necessary (Fig. 6-11).

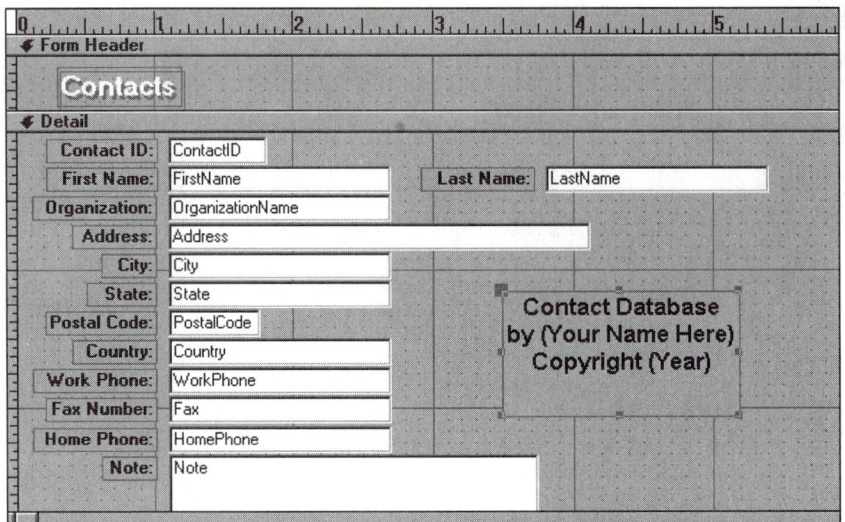

**Figure 6-11    The Contacts form with a copyright label.**

9. Click File/Save.

## Exercise 7: Adding lines

To emphasize the ownership notice, you will place a line under the label box.

1. Click the Line icon on the toolbox.

2. With the mouse, draw a line under the label box. Position the cursor 0.25" below the left edge of your label box. Hold down the left mouse button, drag the cursor horizontally to the right side of the label box, and release the button.

3. Draw another line just below the first.

## Exercise 8: Adding boxes and color

The color of any object on a form can be changed by selecting it and clicking the color palette. In this exercise, you will use the Edit/Undo option to return the object to its previous color.

1. Click the Rectangle icon in the toolbox.

2. Draw a rectangle to cover the copyright notice and the lines below.

   This new box should be slightly larger than the copyright notice box and lines, and it should hide them.

3. Click the Palette icon on the toolbar.

4. Click the Clear option for the Back Color bar on the palette so that you can see your notice again.

5. Click the text of the copyright notice to select it. Click a colored square in the Fore Color bar of the palette.

   The text changes color. Find a color you like.

6. Change the background color. Find a Fore Color/Back Color combination that you like (Fig. 6-12).

7. Close the palette by clicking its icon on the toolbar. Close the Toolbox the same way. Click File/Save.

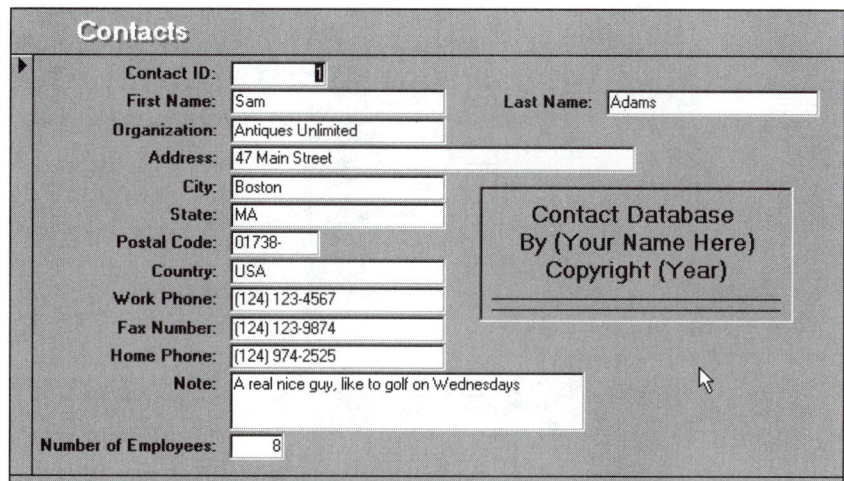

**Figure 6-12** **The Contacts form with a colored copyright box**

# Objective 4: Controlling Numeric Input

As we discussed in Chapter 5, you need to control input data to prevent errors in the data entered into your database. Input masks and validation rules are two forms of control that can be used in forms. But it is better design to place input masks and validation rules in the table field definitions so that these rules apply to every object that uses those fields. Sometimes you will need to control input masks on the data-entry form.

If you modify an input mask in a form, then the change affects only data that is entered through this form. It does not change how the data is stored.

**properties sheet** In the following exercise, you will use a *properties sheet*, which allows you to view and modify the properties of a selected object. Every object on a form has a properties sheet that shows the set of properties specific to that type of object. Even the form itself has a properties sheet.

## Exercise 9: Controlling numeric input

In this exercise, you will modify an input mask to control how the zip code is input.

1. Click the PostalCode field to select it.

2. Click the Properties icon on the toolbar.

3. Move to the Input Mask entry in the properties sheet and change the entry to 00000.

4. Tab out of the Input Mask entry and click File/Save to save your work (Fig. 6-13).

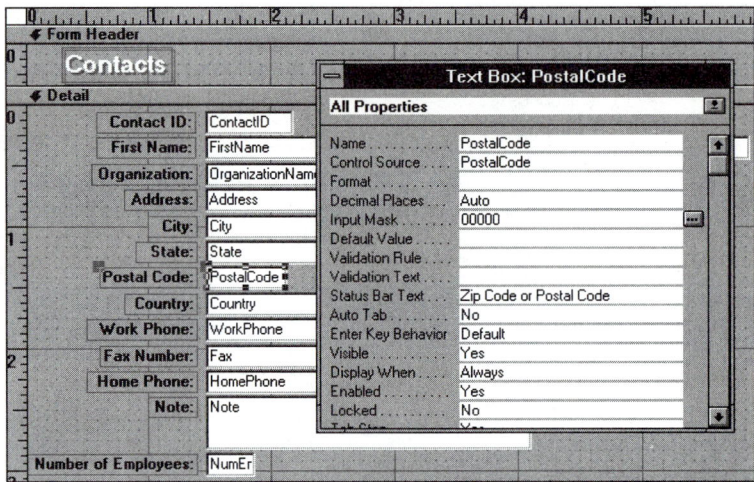

**Figure 6-13    Contacts form with its properties sheet modified**

# Objective 5:  Controlling Character Input

Controlling character input is very similar to controlling numeric input. Validation rules and input masks are used to control text characters input into the database. The Format option is another tool used to control text when it is input. For instance, you can automatically convert lowercase letters to uppercase letters during data entry. However, when you use this feature, the text is stored in the database exactly as typed, even if it is typed in lowercase letters.

## Exercise 10: Controlling the State field

In this exercise, you will control the State field data that is input so that it appears in uppercase letters on the form.

1. Click the State field to select it.

2. Click the Format row in the properties sheet. Type the greater-than symbol (>).

3. ⌨TAB out of the Format row. Click File/Save to save your work.

In this exercise, you changed the State field on the form only. It is a good idea to make this same change at the table level so that the data in the State field will display in uppercase letters wherever it appears. The next time you open the Contacts table in Design mode, make this same change to the State field. This ensures the values are stored throughout the database as uppercase letters.

4. Close the Properties box by clicking the Properties icon on the toolbar.

## FEATURE

**Storing different types of data in MS-Access**

When you created the Contacts database in Chapter 2, you included a field called Photograph. (We later deleted this field in Chapter 4.) This field is an example of MS-Access's ability to store objects in databases. You can store pictures, voice or music recordings, and full-motion video. These stored objects are produced by other software applications and are known as OLE objects. An OLE object is a piece of information created in a Windows application that supports Object Linking and Embedding technology. This technology allows you to store an image generated by a graphics design package, a scanned photograph, or a video clip from a video capture program. You can edit movies that you record with your camcorder and use segments in other applications. The applications for OLE objects are limitless: Imagine selecting a destination in a travel database and being able to view a short movie about that place in a window on your computer screen, or storing employee photographs along with personnel records.

Over the next few years, OLE technology will become more prevalent as the traditional report gives way to multimedia presentations.

## Objective 6:  Using the Form

From the Database window, with the Forms tab selected, you should see a list that includes the Contacts form that you built and the quick form you created in Chapter 3. Now you can open the form, browse the records, and add records.

### Exercise 11: Browsing Records

1. Open the Contacts form. Maximize the form.
2. Browse the records using PAGE UP and PAGE DOWN.
3. Browse the records using the controls at the bottom of the form.

### Exercise 12: Adding Records

In this exercise, you will place the form in Data-Entry mode and add a record.

1. Click the New button on the toolbar.
2. Enter the following data:

   Tom Lincoln

   Lincoln Log Homes, Inc.

   1278 Acadia Avenue

   Peoria, IL 37482 USA

WorkPhone: 282-383-1193 Fax 282-383-1195 HomePhone 282-384-1914

Note: This company has lots of potential for growth with the recent surge in homebuilding and the back-to-nature movement that seems so strong in many parts of the country.

NumEmployees 37

**NOTE**   When typing text into a memo field, pressing (↵ ENTER) is interpreted as the end of your data entry in this field. At the end of a line, continue typing, and the text will wrap around. If you want to start a new line while entering text, press (CTRL)+(↵ ENTER).

3. Click File/Save Record.

4. Close the database and exit from MS-Access.

## Chapter Summary

In this chapter, you learned how to make forms work for you. You started with a form generated by the Form Wizard and then customized it. You learned how to remove unnecessary fields, the difference between a text box and a label, and how to modify static text and labels on a form. You rearranged the fields on the form to make the form easier to use, then added text, lines, and boxes to give the user visual clues. You investigated the use of color on a form and how it can add to the form's functionality. Using a properties sheet, you added numeric and character controls to the form to assist with data entry.

## Review Questions

### True/False Questions

_____ 1. You should wait until all editing changes are completed before saving a new form.

_____ 2. Forms are used only for data entry.

_____ 3. A field on a form will use the input mask defined for that field in the underlying table if you have not changed the input mask in the form's properties sheet.

_____ 4. Changing the color of one field on a form changes the color of the other fields on that form.

_____ 5. A form can show data from more than one table.

## Multiple-Choice Questions

_____ 6. The spacing between fields on a form can be adjusted by using:

A. Ctrl+arrow keys.

B. the mouse.

C. the Format/Horizontal (or Vertical) Spacing command.

D. Any of the above.

_____ 7. The default label that is used for a field on a form is

A. the field name as defined in the table.

B. the caption as defined in the table.

C. the caption as defined in the table unless it is blank in which case the field name is used.

D. blank. The Form Designer must add the label.

_____ 8. Which of the following zip codes would be rejected by an input mask of 00000\-9999 ?

A. 12345-2829

B. 12345-28

C. 1234

D. 12345

_____ 9. To add color, special effects, and border-line styles to your form, you would use the

A. pallete in Design view.

B. toolbox in Design view.

C. properties sheet in Design view.

D. properties sheet in Form view.

_____ 10. To control numeric input when using your form, you would use a feature called

A. a control mask.

B. a data-entry mask.

C. an edit mask.

D. an input mask.

## Fill-in-the-Blank Questions

11. _____ are a major component of the interface between user and database.

12. A _____ is a table of static data that is used to assist data-entry operations by offering a list of values from which the operator can choose.

13. The entries in a field on a form can be automatically modified so that they will be displayed in all uppercase letters by entering a _____ character in the Format row of the properties sheet.

14. In Form Design view, the colors of a field can be changed using the
    _____ .

15. In order to delete a field in Form Design view, you would select the
    field and press _____ .

## Acumen-Building Activities

### Quick Projects

### 1. Creating a form using the Form Wizards

1. Open the Books database and move to the Forms listing. Begin building a New form.
2. Select the table MyBooks and use the Form Wizards.
3. Select the Single-Column Form Wizard. Click OK.
4. Click the double right-arrow button to move all fields from Available
   Fields to Field Order on Form. Click Next.
5. Select the Embossed style. Click Next.
6. Name the form Books. Select Open the form with data in it.
   Select Finish.
7. Click File/Save Form. Name the form Books and click OK.

### 2. Moving fields around the Books form.

This exercise is a continuation of Quick Project #1.

1. Switch to Form Design mode and maximize the form.
2. Draw a box around the Pages text box and label to select both and reposition the Pages field 0.5" to the right of the DatePurchased field.
3. Select both fields and click Format/Align/Bottom.
4. Select both the text field and the label for Note. Press CTRL+↑ to
   move the note up, closing the gap in the form.
5. Position the cursor over the right edge of the form until it changes
   shape. Drag the right margin line to the 6" position on the top ruler to
   widen the form.
6. Click File/Save to save your work.

### 3. Resizing fields on the Books form.

This exercise is a continuation of Quick Project #2.

1. Click and select the BookCollectionID text box.
2. Shorten the box. Position the cursor on the right vertical edge of the
   box until it changes to a horizontal arrow. Drag the edge to the left to
   the 2.5" position on the top ruler.

3. Resize the Title text box. Drag the right side of the box to the right to the 4" position on the top ruler.

4. Click File/Save to save your work.

## 4.  Drawing boxes and using color on the Books form.

This exercise is a continuation of Quick Project #3.

1. Open the toolbox by clicking its icon on the top toolbar.

2. Click the Rectangle icon in the toolbox and draw a rectangular box to cover the bottom three fields of the form (DatePurchased, Pages, and Note).

3. Click the Palette icon on the upper toolbar.

4. With the rectangular box still selected, click the BackColor/Clear button.

5. Adjust the size of the rectangular box to fit comfortably around the three fields.

6. Select the labels of the three fields in the box and change the color of the text from black to dark blue by selecting Fore Color on the palette.

7. Change the background color of the labels by selecting Back Color on the palette from pale grey to a color of your choice.

8. Click the form background and change the color to aqua.

9. Close the palette by clicking its icon on the toolbar.

10. Close the toolbar by clicking its icon on the toolbar. Click File/Save.

11. Return your form to normal size by clicking the lower double-headed arrow in the upper right corner. Widen the window by dragging the right side to the right.

12. View your finished design by clicking View/Form.

13. Close the form (File/Close). Close the Book database.

## In-Depth Projects

## 1.  The CD database.

1. Open the CD database and create a New form from the table CDCollection using the Single-Column Form Wizard. Add the fields to the new form in the following order:

MusicCollectionID

Title

GroupName

RecordingLabel

PurchasePrice

Length

YearReleased

Classification

2. Select a Shadowed style, name the form CDCollection, and select Open the form with data in it.

3. Save your new design and name it frmCDCollection.

4. Switch to Form Design mode and maximize the form to make it easier to work with.

5. Widen the form by moving the right edge to the 5" position on the top ruler.

6. Draw a box around YearReleased, selecting the label, text box, and underlying shadow.

7. Reposition YearReleased 0.5" to the right of LengthInMinutes and align the two fields along the bottom.

8. Reposition Classification by moving it up, closing the gap between it and the above line.

9. Save your work.

10. Lengthen the Title text box by moving the right edge to the 4" position on the top ruler.

    *Hint:* Use (SHIFT) to carefully select both layers of the text box (the active display and the underlying shadow) and enlarge both at the same time.

11. Enlarge the text boxes for GroupName, RecordingLabel, and Classification by dragging all three to the 4" position on the top ruler.

12. Save your work.

13. Click the Palette icon to open it.

14. Click the form background. Choose a back color and modify the color of the background. Modify the color of the other objects (labels and text boxes) if you want to. Your goal is to make the form easy to use and pleasant to look at.

15. Close the palette. Close the Toolbox.

16. Return your form to normal size, resizing the window if necessary.

17. Save your work. View your finished design.

18. Close the form. Close the CD database.

## 2. The Dinner Party database.

1. Open the Dinner database and create a New form from the table DinnerGuests using the Single-Column Form Wizard. Add the fields to the new form in the following order:

   GuestID

   FirstName

   LastName

   HomePhone

   Likes

   Dislikes

   HealthProblems

Address

City

State

PostalCode

2. Choose a style, name the form DinnerGuestList, and select Open the form with data in it.

3. Save your new design and name it frmDinnerGuest2.

4. Switch to Form Design mode and maximize the form to make it easier to work with.

5. Widen the form by moving the right edge to the 6" position on the top ruler.

6. Reposition LastName so that it is on the same line as FirstName and align the two.

7. Reposition Dislikes so that it is on the same line as Likes and align the two.

8. Move HomePhone, Likes, and Dislikes up to close the gap in the form.

9. Move HealthProblems, Address, City, State, and PostalCode up to close the gap in the form.

10. Delete the State label. Shorten the State text field. Reposition it so that it is on the same line as City.

11. Reposition the PostalCode field so that it is on the same line as City and State. Align the three fields (City, State, and PostalCode).

12. Shorten the form by dragging the bottom of the form up to just below the City, State, and PostalCode fields.

13. Save your work.

14. Draw a box around Likes, Dislikes, and Health Problems. Click the Palette icon.

15. Make the back color of the newly drawn box clear.

16. Select all the fields and labels inside the box. Click Format/Bring to Front.

17. Select the box and choose a back color for the box that contrasts with the form. Experiment with color combinations.

18. Close the palette.

19. Return your form to normal size and resize the window if necessary so that you can see your modifications.

20. Save your work. View your finished design.

21. Close the form. Close the Dinner database.

# CASE STUDIES

 **Coffee-On-The-Go:** **Creating Forms**

In this chapter, you learned to create forms. You will use those skills to create an on-line data entry form for the Coffee-On-The-Go Coffee database.

1. Open the Coffee database.
2. Create a data entry form for the Employee table.
3. Move fields and change the text to make the screen easy for data entry.
4. Enhance the screen form with lines or boxes.
5. Allow only F or M in the Sex field.
6. Allow only numbers greater than 8,000 in the Salary field.
7. Add two records using the form.
8. Save the form and close the database.

# CASE STUDIES

 **Videos West:** **Creating Forms**

In this chapter, you learned to create forms. You will use those skills to create an on-line data entry form for the Videos West Video database.

1. Open the Video database.
2. Create a data entry form for the Inventory table.
3. Move fields and change the text to make the screen easy for data entry.
4. Enhance the screen form with lines or boxes.
5. Allow only PG or R in the Rating field.
6. Allow only numbers greater than 1.00 in the Retail field.
7. Add two more videos to the database using the form.
8. Save the form and close the database.

# Chapter 7

## Querying a Database

**Objectives**

- Setting Up Queries
- Specifying Criteria
- Using Operators
- Matching Approximate Values
- Using the Query Wizard
- Selecting Unique Values
- Saving a Query

**Key Terms**

| TERM | DEFINITION |
|------|------------|
| Query | a question about data stored in database tables or a request to perform an action on data |
| Criteria | conditions and restrictions imposed on data in order to limit the information presented in the results of a query |
| Query Wizard | a predefined set of instructions built into MS-Access that assists in building a query by asking questions and then constructing a query |
| Recordset | the list of records that result from running a query |
| Operator | the means used to set conditions and compare values |

**query**   A *query* is a question about data stored in a database. You use a query whenever you want to extract specific information from database tables. For example. a query might ask for a list of all the people from the Contacts database who live in the state of Colorado.

In a previous chapter, you learned how to find a particular record in a table, searching, for example, on a specific zip code. When you perform this type of search, MS-Access takes you to the record you want, but still shows all other data in the table. Suppose that you want to make a list of all your contacts in a specific zip code. You could do so by repeating your MS-Access search until you find all entries in the table with that zip code. Even then, you would have to keep a handwritten list of each record. What you really want is for MS-Access to list *only* the records that meet your criteria. *Criteria* are conditions and restrictions imposed on data to limit the information presented by a query. That is exactly what a query can do: It provides a list of specified records, sorts them in whatever order you wish, and then allows you to print out the list in a report.

**criteria**

A simple query might be, "List all contacts with LastName of Smith." This query has to match only one condition: Last name is Smith. A query can match many conditions or selection criteria, such as "Show me all customers in the state of Oregon who have placed orders this month and have an outstanding balance of more than $1000."

A query can combine data from more than one table. As an example, suppose you are in charge of information systems for a mail-order company. Your Inventory table contains information about back-ordered items. The Orders table contains information about customer orders. The Customers table contains address information for each customer. The sales manager decides to send a discount coupon to all customers who are waiting for back-ordered products. To do this, she needs a set of mailing labels. So you build a query that says, "Get the name and address (from the Customers table) for each customer who has an outstanding order (from the Orders table) for a back-ordered item (from the Inventory table)." In a later chapter, you will build a multitable query. For now, just use the Contacts table.

In a previous chapter, you built forms using a table as the foundation. In many cases, you will build forms and reports that use a query rather than a table for the underlying data. This is especially true if you want to combine data from more than one table on the form or report. The order-entry form, or an invoice, combines the customer data and shipping information with a list of items ordered.

A query is not always built to extract information directly from the database tables. It can be constructed to use the output from another query as the starting point.

**Query Wizard**

Queries can be constructed using the Query Wizard. The *Query Wizard* is a predefined set of instructions built into MS-Access that assists in building a query. It differs from the Form and Table Wizards in that it contains four specific Wizards; each is used for generating a special-purpose query. In most cases, you will design the query yourself rather than use the Query Wizard.

Queries can also be used to perform actions on the database, such as deleting selected records or adding data from one table to another.

**recordset**  The list of records that results from running a query is called a *recordset*. A recordset can be thought of as a virtual table. It is not written to your hard disk and disappears as soon as you close the results window. If you want to see the list again, you need to run the query again. When you open a form or a report built on a query, the query retrieves the information. This is beneficial because the form or report always shows current information. If the query results were stored, you would run the risk of looking at old data.

# Objective 1:  Setting Up Queries

Begin with MS-Access running and the Database window open. You will set up a new query and define which table the query will use. Next, you will select some fields from the table for the query. You can do this by double-clicking the field name or dragging and dropping the field name from the list to the query. Finally, you will run the query to see the resulting recordset. In the recordset, the fields appear in the same order in which they appear in the query—that is, the order in which you choose them. This might be different from the order in which they appear in the original table.

### Exercise 1: Setting up a simple query

You will build a simple query to select FirstName, LastName, OrganizationName, and State from the Contacts table.

1. Click the Query tab in the Database window. Click New to build a new query.
2. Click New Query.

   The Select Query Design window opens with the Add Table dialog box (Fig. 7-1).

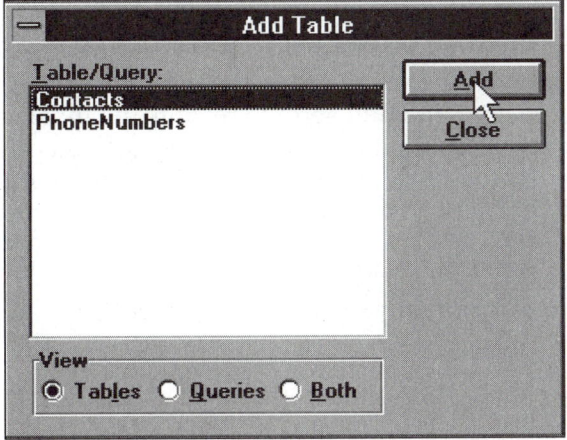

**Figure 7-1**  **The Add Table dialog box**

3. Double-click Contacts to select the Contacts table and click Close.

   The table, with a list of fields, appears in the Query Design window. Note that at the top of the list is an asterisk. This means that all fields in the table are included.

4. Double-click FirstName to add this to the list of fields in the query.
5. Double-click LastName, OrganizationName, and State to add them to the list of fields in the query.

   (Alternatively, you can drag and drop the field name from the table to the query list.)

6. Click the Run icon (which shows an exclamation point) to see the results of your query (Fig. 7-2).

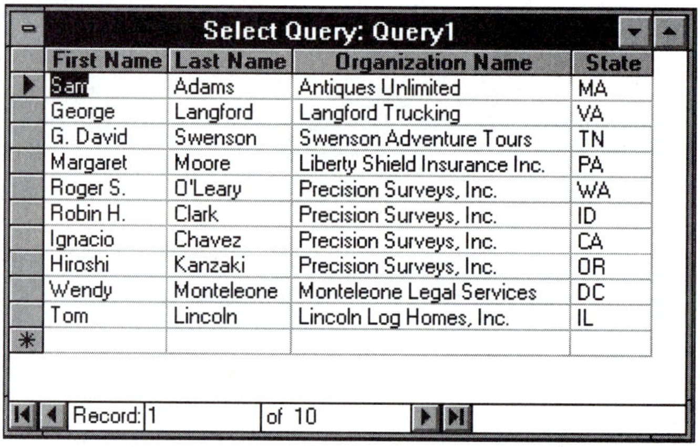

Select Query: Query1

| First Name | Last Name | Organization Name | State |
|---|---|---|---|
| Sam | Adams | Antiques Unlimited | MA |
| George | Langford | Langford Trucking | VA |
| G. David | Swenson | Swenson Adventure Tours | TN |
| Margaret | Moore | Liberty Shield Insurance Inc. | PA |
| Roger S. | O'Leary | Precision Surveys, Inc. | WA |
| Robin H. | Clark | Precision Surveys, Inc. | ID |
| Ignacio | Chavez | Precision Surveys, Inc. | CA |
| Hiroshi | Kanzaki | Precision Surveys, Inc. | OR |
| Wendy | Monteleone | Monteleone Legal Services | DC |
| Tom | Lincoln | Lincoln Log Homes, Inc. | IL |

Record: 1 of 10

**Figure 7-2 Query results**

## Objective 2: Specifying Criteria

The resulting recordset shows four fields: FirstName, LastName, OrganizationName, and State. The records are shown in the order in which they are stored in the database. It would make more sense to specify criteria to sort the records in alphabetical order by last name. In addition to sorting the results, you can specify criteria that restrict the output to a limited set of records. For example, you might want to see only the contacts at Precision Surveys, Inc.

### Exercise 2: Specifying sort criteria

In this exercise, you will sort the results of the previous query by last name.

1. Return to Design mode by clicking the Design View icon on the toolbar.
2. In the Query Design window, click the Sort row under the Last Name column.

**Database Marketing: Did You Know That . . .**

. . . marketers can target smaller and more specialized segments of the population as a result of newer, faster, more powerful computers and database management systems? This new business enterprise, called database marketing, is becoming critical to the success of many companies in the United States and thoughout the world. According to a survey by Donnelly Marketing, Inc., 56% of manufacturers and retailers are currently building marketing databases, and 85% believe they will need marketing databases if they are to stay competitive into the next decade. It is one of the most important marketing developments of the 1990s (*Business Week*, September 5, 1994).

Massive parallel processing, which can be done easily by supercomputers, is being used to divine which customers are likely to buy what products and when. Big credit-card companies, airlines, and insurance companies are jumping on the data-mining bandwagon in an effort to get an edge on the competition. A Gartner Group vice president predicts that sales of parallel-processing computers could expand tenfold, to $5 billion by the end of 1998, as a result of this explosion in database marketing. While marketing types are plunging ahead, academics are warning of possible problems. One business professor warned that "the fallout could be nasty if companies start abusing their new found information. The companies doing this have a big responsibility. Otherwise there will be an information Chernobyl" (*The Wall Street Journal*, August 16, 1994).

3. Click the down arrow and choose Ascending from the list.

4. Click the Run icon to see the results of your query (Fig. 7-3).

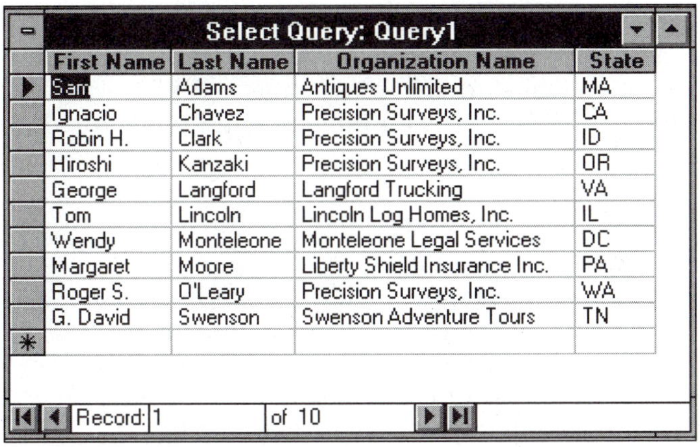

| First Name | Last Name | Organization Name | State |
|---|---|---|---|
| Sam | Adams | Antiques Unlimited | MA |
| Ignacio | Chavez | Precision Surveys, Inc. | CA |
| Robin H. | Clark | Precision Surveys, Inc. | ID |
| Hiroshi | Kanzaki | Precision Surveys, Inc. | OR |
| George | Langford | Langford Trucking | VA |
| Tom | Lincoln | Lincoln Log Homes, Inc. | IL |
| Wendy | Monteleone | Monteleone Legal Services | DC |
| Margaret | Moore | Liberty Shield Insurance Inc. | PA |
| Roger S. | O'Leary | Precision Surveys, Inc. | WA |
| G. David | Swenson | Swenson Adventure Tours | TN |

Record: 1 of 10

**Figure 7-3** **Query results, sorted by LastName**

## Exercise 3: Specifying selection criteria

You will now limit the results of the previous query by OrganizationName.

1. Return to Design mode by clicking the Design View icon on the toolbar.

2. In the Query Design window, click the Criteria row, under the Organization Name Column.

3. Type ="Precision Surveys, Inc." Be sure to include the quotation marks.

**WARNING** You must enclose the name of the company in quotation marks because there are spaces in the name. If you do not, you will see a dialog box on the screen telling you that there is a syntax error in the query.

4. Click the Run icon to see the results of your query (Fig. 7-4).

The results include only those contacts who work for Precision Surveys. The records are still sorted by last name because you did not modify the sort instruction from the previous exercise.

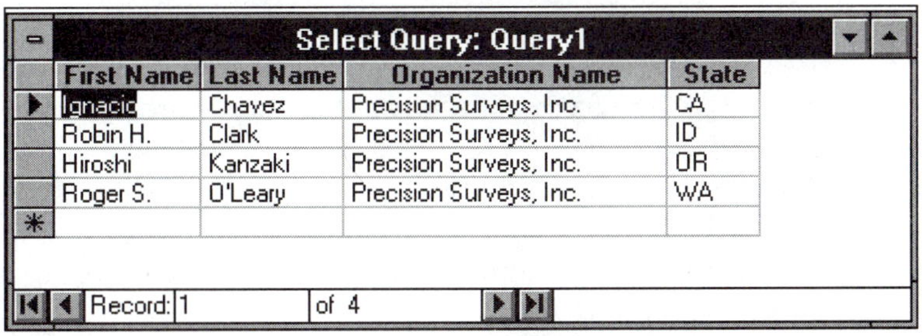

| First Name | Last Name | Organization Name | State |
|---|---|---|---|
| Ignacio | Chavez | Precision Surveys, Inc. | CA |
| Robin H. | Clark | Precision Surveys, Inc. | ID |
| Hiroshi | Kanzaki | Precision Surveys, Inc. | OR |
| Roger S. | O'Leary | Precision Surveys, Inc. | WA |

Record: 1 of 4

**Figure 7-4** **Query results, sorted by LastName with only Precision Surveys, Inc. contacts**

# Objective 3: Using Operators

**operators**  To specify more complex criteria, you use operators. *Operators* set conditions and compare values. For example, operators such as less than (<) or greater than (>) are normally used with numeric fields—for example, credit limits or number of employees. Operators such as Like are used with text fields—for example, names and addresses. It is possible to set criteria on fields which do *not* show in the results. You will see an example of this in Exercise 4.

## Exercise 4: Using operators

You have a training class that you offer to companies who want to improve their employees' computer skills. Normally you teach this class at a computer lab, and people come to you. But for companies with 50 or more employees, it is more cost-effective for you to go to their office. You want a listing of all the companies in your contact database with 50 or more employees. Modify the existing query to produce the list. Run the query. Then modify the query so that the NumEmployees field does not show in the recordset, as you might if you were producing mailing labels from this list.

1. Return to Design mode by clicking the Design View icon on the toolbar.

2. Double-click on NumEmployees in the list of fields to add it to the query.

3. Delete the condition from the OrganizationName field.

4. Move to the Criteria row under the NumEmployees column. Type >49.

   The > symbol means greater than. You could type >=50 , meaning greater than or equal to 50, but it is more efficient to specify greater than 49.

5. Run the query (Fig. 7-5).

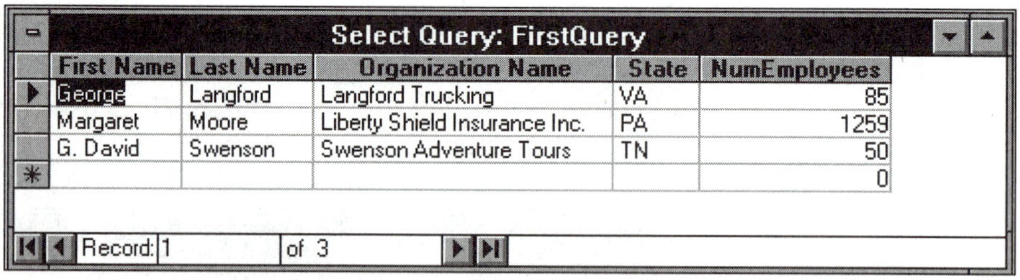

| First Name | Last Name | Organization Name | State | NumEmployees |
|---|---|---|---|---|
| George | Langford | Langford Trucking | VA | 85 |
| Margaret | Moore | Liberty Shield Insurance Inc. | PA | 1259 |
| G. David | Swenson | Swenson Adventure Tours | TN | 50 |
| * | | | | 0 |

Record: 1 of 3

**Figure 7.5  Query results with NumEmployees greater than 49**

6. Return to Design mode by clicking the Design View icon on the toolbar.

7. Click the box in the Show row under NumEmployees to remove the X.

8. Run the query again.

   The list looks the same as last time except that the NumEmployees field is *not* shown in the results.

# Objective 4:  Matching Approximate Values

Sometimes, you do not want to search for an exact match, as you did in Exercise 4. For example, let's say you cannot remember the exact name of Precision Surveys, Inc. You remember only "Precision *something*." In this case, you use the Like operator and give the query a pattern to search for.

The Like operator searches for records that are similar to the values you type in the query. You specify what you want to match and then add an asterisk. The asterisk indicates that any characters are acceptable. Suppose you specify that you want to search for records where State Like Mi*. (Assume that you are using complete state names rather than two-letter state codes.) This query results in records from Minnesota, Mississippi, and Missouri because the first two letters match. Now you change the requirement to State Like Mis*. Now only records from Mississippi and Missouri will be listed. What would the results be for the query State Like M*?

## Exercise 5: Approximate searches

In this exercise, you will use the pattern-matching capabilities of the Like operator to find a match.

1. Return to Design mode by clicking the Design View icon on the toolbar.

2. Delete the >49 condition in the NumEmployees column.

3. In the Query Design window, click the Criteria row under the Organization Name Column.

4. Type Like Prec*.

   MS-Access adds quotation marks when you move the cursor out of the cell.

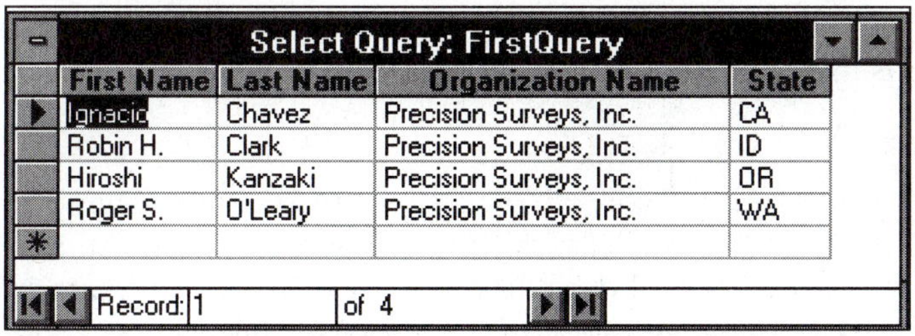

| First Name | Last Name | Organization Name | State |
|---|---|---|---|
| Ignacio | Chavez | Precision Surveys, Inc. | CA |
| Robin H. | Clark | Precision Surveys, Inc. | ID |
| Hiroshi | Kanzaki | Precision Surveys, Inc. | OR |
| Roger S. | O'Leary | Precision Surveys, Inc. | WA |

Select Query: FirstQuery — Record: 1 of 4

**Figure 7-6  Query results, sorted by LastName with only Precision Surveys, Inc. contacts**

5. Click the Run icon to see the results of your query (Fig. 7-6).

6. Close the query by clicking File/Close.

7. When asked if you want to save changes to the query, save it as FirstQuery.

FEATURE

**MS-Access naming conventions**

MS-Access allows you to use embedded spaces when naming objects—such as tables, forms, and queries—but this is not a good practice for two reasons: (1) A space in a table or form name is considered a character. If, from a form or report, you reference a table that has an embedded space in its name and accidentally type two spaces instead of one, the form or report will not recognize the table name. This kind of error is easy to make but hard to track down, making it very frustrating to deal with. (2) Compatibility with other database management systems is another issue. At the time of this writing, no other database management system allows embedded spaces in the names of tables, fields, forms, or reports. The power and purpose of MS-Access is to allow quick and easy connectivity to other database management systems. But to do so, MS-Access object names must conform to industry-standard naming conventions. You may think now that you will never need to integrate an MS-Access application with that of another database management system. But think of the hundreds of thousands of Paradox and dBase databases already in place in front offices across the country. Think of the millions of Oracle, Ingres, Sybase, Informix, and DB/2 databases in back offices. It makes sense to follow prevalent naming conventions for database objects today, so that you can take advantage of existing database resources tomorrow.

# Objective 5:  Using the Query Wizard

There are certain situations in which the Query Wizard can help you. One such situation is finding duplicate records in your database. This is not an overwhelming task when your database is small. But as your database grows, you will find that the number of duplicate records grows. (How many times have you received multiple copies of the same catalog from a company?) Once you know how to build a query to find duplicate records, you can prevent this mistake from annoying *your* contacts.

## Exercise 6: Using the Query Wizard to find duplicate records

In this exercise, you will look for duplicate company names. These are not true duplicate records, because they refer to different people. But this exercise will illustrate the technique of finding duplicate information. Start at the Database window with the Queries tab selected.

1.  Click New. Click Query Wizards (Fig. 7-7).

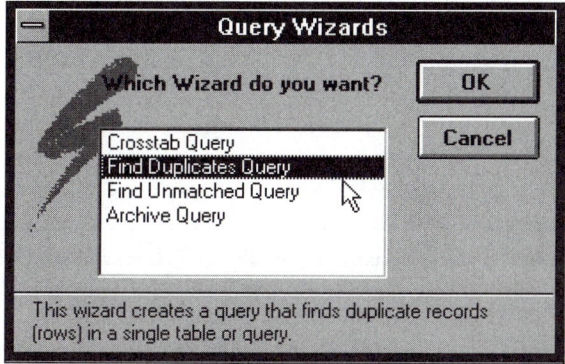

**Figure 7-7** **Query Wizards dialog box**

2. Double-click the Find Duplicates Query field (Fig. 7-8).

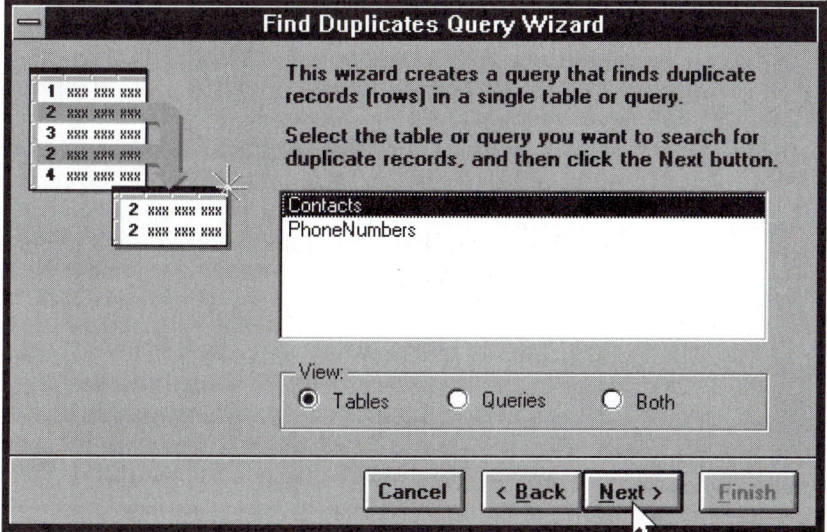

**Figure 7-8** **Find Duplicates Query Wizard dialog box**

3. Highlight the Contacts table and click Next.

4. Double-click the OrganizationName field to select it as the field in which to look for duplicate values. Click Next.

5. Select the following additional fields for the output results by double-clicking each: FirstName, LastName, City, and State.

6. Click Next.

7. At the checkered flag screen, accept the default values and click Finish (Fig. 7-9).

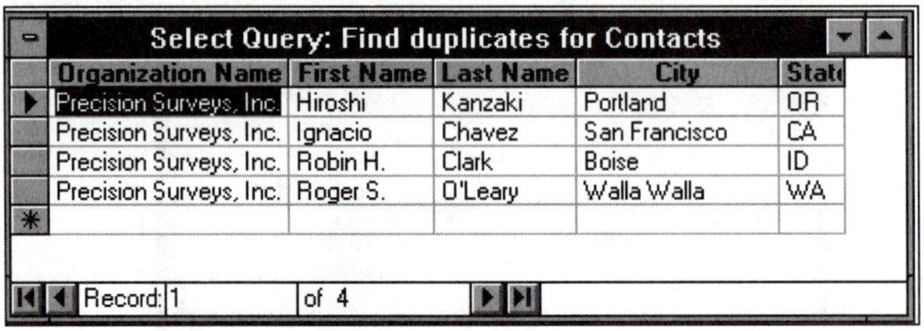

**Figure 7-9** **List of duplicate records**

8. Save your query. If prompted for a name, accept the MS-Access suggestion.
9. Close the query (File/Close).

# Objective 6: Selecting Unique Values

Normally, a query returns all records that meet the specified criteria. But there are times when you do not want all the records; instead, you need a list of unique values from a field or fields. For example, suppose you wonder if you have at least one person from every state in your contact database, which contains thousands of records. A simple query on the state field produces a list of the state values for all the records but does not answer your question. If you tell the query that you want only unique values, then the output list will show only the first occurrence of each state value. If you look at the status bar at the bottom of the screen, the total number of records is shown. If this number is less than 50, then you know that you do not have a contact in every state.

## Exercise 7: Selecting Unique Values

Every object in MS-Access—whether a form, field, report, or query—has associated properties. By changing a setting in the Query properties, you can request only unique values in the results.

1. At the Database window click New to begin building a new query.
2. In the New Query dialog box, click New Query.
3. Double-click Contacts to select the Contacts table.
4. Click Close to close the Add Table dialog box.
5. Double-click State in the list of fields to add it to the query.
6. Click anywhere on the background of the query window, then click the Properties icon on the toolbar to open the Query Properties window (Fig. 7-10).

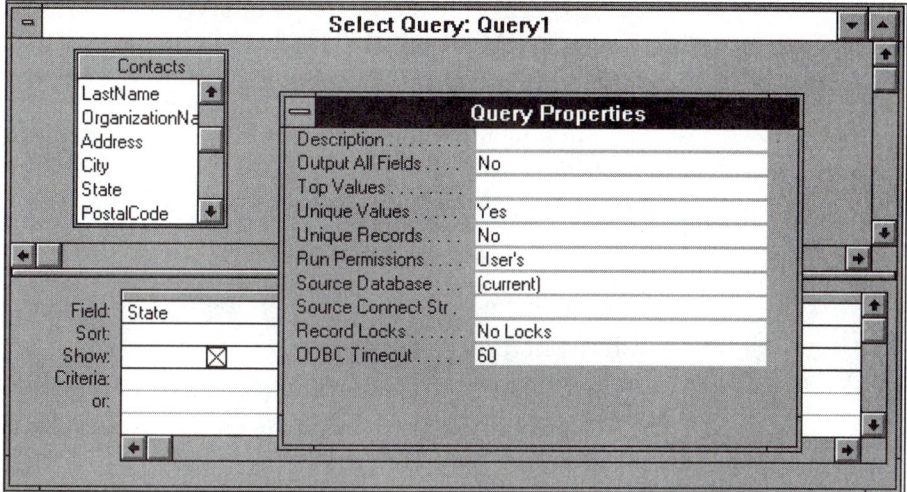

**Figure 7-10** **The Query Design window with the Query Properties dialog box open**

7. Change the setting for Unique Values to Yes and run the query.

A list of states in which you have contacts appears (Fig. 7-11).

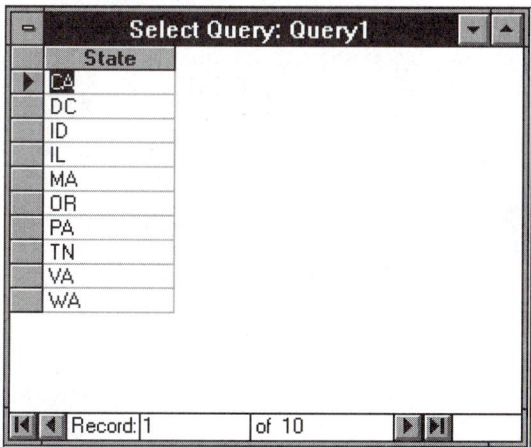

**Figure 7-11** **List of states in which you have contacts**

# Objective 7: Saving the Query

Save the query you have built so that you can use it as the basis for forms and reports. You can modify it and extend it. If you make copies of this query under different names, you can modify the copies to perform other queries.

Many MS-Access developers start query names with the lowercase letters "qry," as in qryMailingList. This helps identify the file as a query, which has two benefits: (1) When you build forms and reports, you can easily distinguish a table from a query and (2) when you modify a form or report, it will be obvious how you built it—with a table or query. You can extend this naming convention to tables, forms, and reports by beginning the filenames with tbl, frm, or rpt, respectively.

### Exercise 8: Save the query

Save the query with an appropriate name.

1. Click File/Save Query As.
2. Type qryUniqueState for the query name and click OK.
3. Click File/Close to close the query design window.
4. Click File/Close Database to close the database. Exit from MS-Access.

## Chapter Summary

Queries are used to extract information from the database. A query can show information that meets certain conditions. The results can be sorted and the fields displayed in a desired order. Approximate searches simplify matching data. Special-purpose queries, generated by the Query Wizard, simplify tasks such as finding duplicate records in a table.

Remember: The main purpose of a database is information retrieval. To do this well, a database must be able to store and manage data efficiently. The query is the real key to turning raw data into useful information. It harnesses the power of the relational database to give you precisely the information that you want to see.

## Review Questions

### True/False Questions

_____ 1. A query can contain only fields from one table.

_____ 2. A form or report can be based on the results of a query instead of a table.

_____ 3. You can set selection conditions on one field and sort the results of the query on a different field.

_____ 4. You always build queries using the Query Wizard.

_____ 5. The results of a query are stored on disk in a recordset.

## Multiple-Choice Questions

_____ 6. To find all records in the Contacts table with a state value of AZ, you would use the following criterion for the state code:

A. =AZ.

B. ="AZ".

C. Like "AZ".

D. Any of the above.

_____ 7. To find duplicate records in a table,

A. print out the table and look for similar records on the printout.

B. build a query to list the records in the table and run the query twice.

C. use the Query Wizard to build a query to find duplicate records.

D. None of the above. There is no way to find duplicate records in a table.

_____ 8. To list only companies with more than 100 employees, you would set the NumEmployees criterion to

A. <100.

B. >100.

C. >99.

D. >=99.

_____ 9. Which of the following statements about sorting in a query is incorrect:

A. The records may be sorted in ascending or descending order.

B. The sort can be done only on an indexed field.

C. The records must be sorted on a field that appears in the output recordset.

D. The sort can be done in addition to other selection criteria.

_____ 10. To set criteria on a field, but exclude the field from the results of the query, you would

A. set the criterion for that field to =NULL.

B. click the box in the Show row to remove the X.

C. not include the field in the query.

D. set the criterion for this field to "invisible."

## Fill-in-the-Blank Questions

11. To set conditions such as greater than, less than, or like, you use comparison _____.

12. The output from a query is called a _____.

13. Conditions that you set to limit output data are known as _____.

14. A form or report can be built on either a _____ or _____.

15. You want to find your contacts at a company whose name you recall is "*something* Surveys" but you forget what that *something* is. So you build a query where the criterion for OrganizationName is Like "_____".

## Acumen-Building Activities

### Quick Projects

### 1. Setting up a simple query for MyBooks.

1. Open the Books database. Click the Query tab in the Database window.
2. Create a New Query without using the Query Wizard.
3. Add MyBooks to the Query Design window. Click Close.
4. Double-click Title, Author, and Pages to add them to the query.
5. Click the Run icon to run the query.
6. Return to Query Design mode.
7. In the Query Design window, in the Title column, click the Sort row and choose Ascending from the list.
8. Run the query.

### 2. Specifying selection criteria in the MyBooks query.

This exercise is a continuation of Quick Project #1.

1. Return to Query Design mode.
2. In the Query Design window, in the Title column, click the Criteria row and type Friday.
3. Run the query and check the results.

### 3. Using operators in the MyBooks query.

This exercise is a continuation of Quick Project #2.

1. Return to Query Design mode.
2. Delete the criteria from the Title column.
3. In the Pages column of the Criteria row, type >= 300.

4. Run the query and check the results. Return to Query Design mode.

5. Click the box in the Show row of the Pages column to remove the X so that this field will not appear in the query output.

6. Run the query again and compare the results to the previous query.

### 4. Doing approximate searches in the MyBooks query.

This exercise is a continuation of Quick Project #3.

1. Return to Query Design mode.

2. Delete the criteria in the Pages column and turn Show back on.

3. In the Author column of the Criteria row, type like *peter*.

4. Click the Run icon and check the results.

5. Save the query by clicking File/Save Query and name it qryFirst.

6. Close the query by clicking File/Close.

7. Close the Books database.

## In-Depth Projects

### 1. Querying the CD database

1. Open the CD database.

2. Create a New query without using the Query Wizard.

3. Add the table CDCollection to the Query Design screen.

4. Choose Title, GroupName, RecordingLabel, and Length for the query.

5. Sort the query in ascending order by Title and run the query.

6. Return to Query Design mode.

7. Modify the query to find those CDs with length greater than or equal to 45 minutes, run the query.

8. Return to query design mode.

9. Delete the condition in the Length column.

10. Modify the query to find those CDs recorded by M*B* and run the query.

11. Return to Query Design mode.

12. Delete the condition in the GroupName column.

13. Save the query and name it qryFirst.

14. Close the query.

15. Close the CD database.

### 2. Querying the Dinner Party database.

1. Open the Dinner database.

2. Create a New query without using the Query Wizard.

3. Add the table DinnerGuests to the Query Design screen.

4. Choose FirstName, LastName, City, Likes, and Dislikes for the query and run the query.

5. Return to Query Design mode.

6. Modify the query to sort the output in ascending order by City and run the query.

7. Return to Query Design mode.

8. Save this query and name it qryGuestByCity.

9. Close this query.

10. Create a New query without using the Query Wizard.

11. Add the table Dinners to the Query Design screen.

12. Choose Date, Time, Place, and Occasion for the query.

13. Sort the query by Date in descending order and run the query.

14. Return to Query Design mode.

15. Modify the query to find the Valentine's Day dinner and run the query.

16. Return to Query Design mode.

17. Delete the previous search condition.

18. Modify the query to find those dinners held after 5:00 P.M. and run the query.

**⚠ WARNING** This is a tricky one. When searching a date or time data type, use the pound symbol (#) as you would the quotation mark (") for a search of a text field. For example, to find those dinners that started at noon, your search criteria would look like =#12:00PM#.

19. Save the query and name it qryDinnerDates.

20. Close the query.

21. Close the Dinner database.

# CASE STUDIES

**Coffee-On-The-Go:**

## Querying a Database

In this chapter, you learned to set up queries to a database. You will use those skills to select records from the Coffee-On-The-Go Employee table based on a query.

1. Open the Coffee database.

2. Open the Employee table.

3. Set up a query to see all employees who work in location 01. Print the results.

4. Set up a query to see all employees who make more than $15,000. Print the results.

5. Set up a query to see all current employees. Print the results.

6. Set up a query to see all employees who started working for the company before 1990. Print the results.

7. Set up a query to see all female employees. Print the results.

8. Save the query and close the Coffee database.

# CASE STUDIES

**Videos West:**

## Querying the Database

In this chapter, you learned to set up queries to a database. You will use those skills to select videos from the Videos West Inventory table based on a query.

1. Open the Video database.

2. Open the Inventory table.

3. Find all the videos which cost $5.99. Print the results.

4. Find all the videos with a retail price of $14.99. Print the results.

5. Find all the videos in the 01 category. Print the results.

6. Find any videos which have Tennis in the title. Print the results.

7. Find all the videos produced before 1992. Print the results.

8. Save the query and close the Video database.

# Chapter 8

## Creating Reports

**Objectives**

- Understanding the Report Wizard
- Using the Report Wizard
- Modifying the Report—Removing and Moving Fields
- Adding and Changing Fields
- Modifying the Page Footer
- Modifying the Page Header and Report Header
- Adding Lines and Boxes
- Formatting Data in a Report
- Saving a Report
- Previewing a Report
- Printing a Report

**Key Terms**

| TERM | DEFINITION |
|------|------------|
| Report | information output from a database on paper or in electronic form |
| Formatting | establishing a pattern for the display, storage, or printing of data |
| Report Header | a section of a report that appears before the page header on the first page of the report, often containing a title, logo or picture |
| Report Footer | a section of a report containing report summary information that appears after the page footer at the end of the report |
| Page Header | a section of a report that appears at the top of every printed page of the report, often containing the title and date of the report |
| Page Footer | a section of a report that appears at the bottom of every printed page of the report, often containing the page number |

**report**　　A *report*, whether printed or on the screen, is used to distribute information from the database. Printed documents, e-mail messages, and mailing labels are all reports. A report extracts current data from the database each time you run it and acts as a snapshot of the information in the database as it exists at the time the report is run.

When you build a report in MS-Access, you are actually building a template or pattern. You define how you want the data to appear in the report—the fonts, spacing, organization of the data on the page, and page numbering.

**formatting**　　These specifications are called the *formatting* of the report. Once you have the report saved on your hard disk, you may run it as often as needed.

## Objective 1:  Understanding the Report Wizard

You have the choice of building a new report from scratch or using a Report Wizard. The Report Wizard, like the Form Wizard, ensures that the information you want appears on the report. Like the Form Wizard, the layout of that information is very simple. The Report Wizard is a good starting point from which you can customize the appearance of the report.

## Objective 2:  Using the Report Wizard

The Report Wizard offers a selection of reports, some of them fairly complex. In the Quick Preview, you were introduced to the Mailing Label report. This time you will use the Single-Column report.

### Exercise 1: Using the Report Wizard to generate a default report

In this exercise, you will use the Report Wizard to generate a report of your contacts. Begin with the Contacts database window open and the Reports tab selected.

1. Click New.
2. Select the Contacts table, then click Report Wizards (Fig. 8-1).

**Figure 8-1**　*The Report Wizards dialog box*

3. Double-click Single-Column in the Report Wizard dialog box.

   The Single-Column Report Wizard dialog box opens (Fig. 8-2).

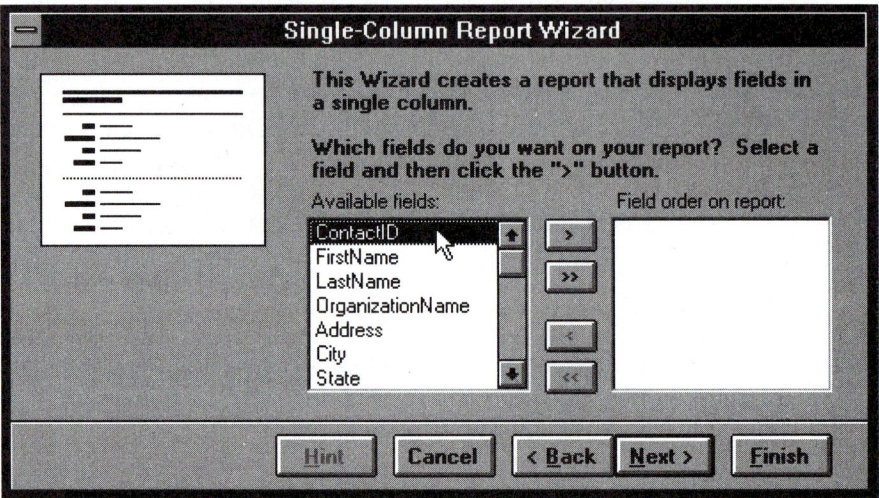

**Figure 8-2** **The Single-Column Report Wizard dialog box**

4. Move the following fields from the List of Available fields to the Field order on report list: FirstName, LastName, OrganizationName, Address, City, State, PostalCode, and WorkPhone.

5. Click Next.

6. Move the LastName field then the FirstName field to the sort order list. Click Next.

7. Choose a style. Click Next.

8. When the checkered flag screen appears, click Finish.

   The report appears in Preview mode (Fig. 8-3).

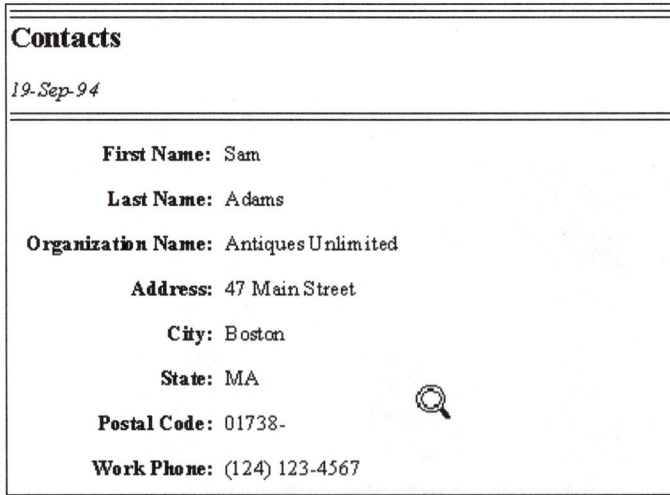

**Figure 8-3** **The Single-Column report in Preview mode**

# Objective 3:  Modifying the Report— Removing and Moving Fields

The report produced by the Single-Column Report Wizard shows the data you requested, but not necessarily as you might like it arranged. You can move fields, change labels, and reduce the amount of space allotted to each record. To modify a report, you must switch to Design mode. In Design mode, the report is divided into sections: the report header, page header, detail, page footer, and report footer.

In the next exercise, you will remove some field labels. The label on a report is like the label on a form—it is static text taken from either the field name in the table or the caption in the Field Properties box. Removing a data field is similar to removing a report label.

### Exercise 2: Modifying the report: removing fields

In this exercise, modify the report layout by deleting some field labels.

1. From Print Preview, click the Close Window icon to switch to Design mode (Fig. 8-4).

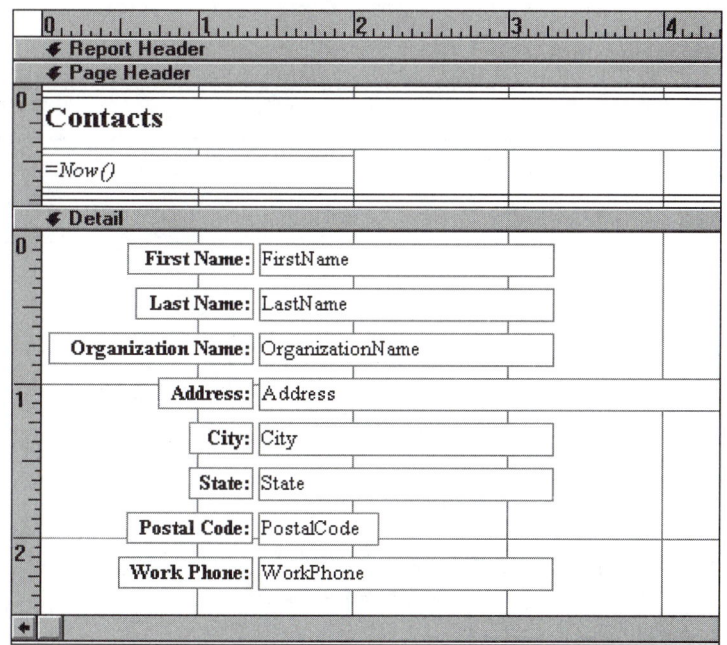

**Figure 8-4   The report in Design mode**

2. Drag the right edge of the report to widen it to 6".

   It may help to maximize the report window so that you can see more of the report.

**WARNING** A common problem encountered when printing reports is that every other printed page is blank. This occurs when the report is too wide for the page. If this happens, check your margin settings and decrease the width of the page.

3. Click the label Last Name, then press ⟨DELETE⟩.

Do not delete the data field. The label is the text in bold characters to the left of the field.

4. Repeat Step 3 for the State and Postal Code labels.

## Exercise 3: Modifying the report: moving fields

1. Drag the LastName field and position it to the right of the FirstName field.

2. Drag the State field to position it to the right of the City field.

3. Reduce the size of the State field to allow for two character state codes.

4. Drag the PostalCode field to position it to the right of the State field.

5. With the mouse, draw a box around the OrganizationName, Address, City, State, and PostalCode fields. Drag this box up to move the fields closer to the name fields.

6. Move up the WorkPhone field to just below the City field.

7. Drag the bottom border of the Detail section to just below the WorkPhone field.

8. Click the Print Preview icon to see what the report looks like (Fig. 8-5).

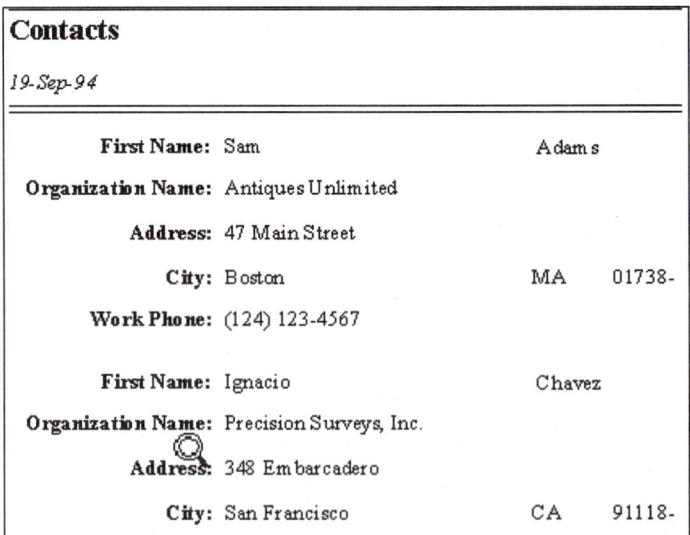

**Contacts**

*19-Sep-94*

| | | | |
|---|---|---|---|
| **First Name:** | Sam | Adams | |
| **Organization Name:** | Antiques Unlimited | | |
| **Address:** | 47 Main Street | | |
| **City:** | Boston | MA | 01738- |
| **Work Phone:** | (124) 123-4567 | | |
| | | | |
| **First Name:** | Ignacio | Chavez | |
| **Organization Name:** | Precision Surveys, Inc. | | |
| **Address:** | 348 Embarcadero | | |
| **City:** | San Francisco | CA | 91118- |

**Figure 8-5  The modified report**

9. Click the Close Window icon to return to Design mode.

# Objective 4:  Adding and Changing Fields

After reviewing the report, you decide that the fax number ought to appear as well. This is also a good time to modify the label for the name field.

The toolbar at the top of the screen contains a Field List icon. When you click this icon, you see a list of the fields in the table or query upon which you built the report. To add a field to the report, drag it from the field list and drop it on the report.

## Exercise 4: Adding a field

1.  Click the Field List icon.
2.  Drag the Fax field from the list and drop it on the report to the right of the WorkPhone field.
3.  Click the Field List icon to close the Field List window.
4.  Adjust the position and size of the Fax field so that it aligns with the surrounding fields.
5.  Click the Print Preview icon to see what the report looks like with the fax numbers added.
6.  Click the Close Window icon to return to Design mode.

# FEATURE

### Concatenating names in MS-Access

How many times have you received mail that is meant to appear as if it is addressed to you personally but is obviously a mass mailing? The giveaway is the space between the first and last names. In order to allow for long first names, the FirstName field on the report has to be larger than needed for the average name. Here is how to make such mailings look better by eliminating that space.

1.  Delete the LastName field completely.
2.  In the FirstName field, change the entry to read
    = [FirstName] & " " & [LastName]

Make sure you include the equals sign and use the square brackets. The space between the quotation marks is the amount of space you will see between the first and last names on your report.

To do the same for the city, state, and zip code, eliminate the State and PostalCode fields and change the entry in the City field to read

=[City] & " " & [State] & " " & [PostalCode]

You may need to enlarge the Name and City fields since they now show more information than before.

## Exercise 5: Changing a field

The label on the line that contains the names currently reads First Name:.
You want it to read Name:.

1. Position the cursor over the First Name label (*not* the data field) and click. The field is selected, and the cursor turns into an I-beam.
2. Position the cursor between the words First and Name and click again. The cursor changes to a vertical line.
3. Use the ( ← BACKSPACE ) to delete First.
4. Click anywhere outside this label to complete the edit (Fig. 8-6).

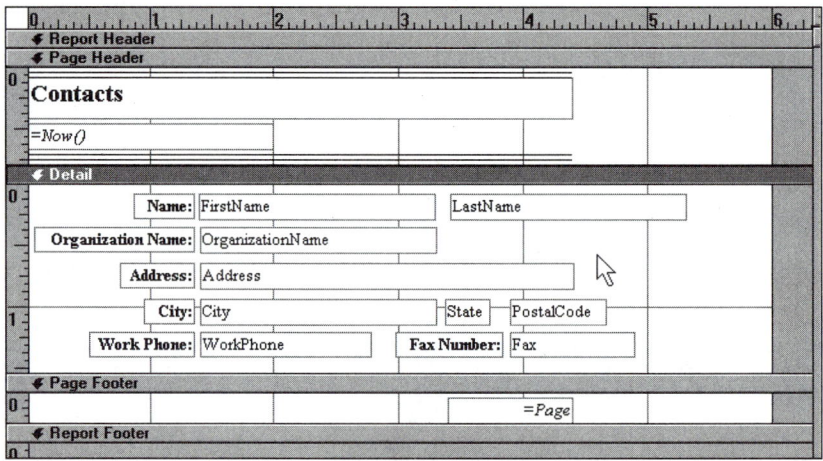

**Figure 8-6   The report with modified labels**

5. Click PrintPreview to see what the report looks like.
6. Click the Close Window icon.

# Objective 5:  Modifying the Page Footer

**page footer**     The *page footer* is a section of the report that appears at the bottom of every page and often contains the page number. Anything in the page footer will show on every page of a report. The Report Wizard builds a page footer that is very plain. You can change the page footer to include more information—for example, "Page 1 of 12" or however many pages are in your report.

## Exercise 6: Modifying the page footer

1. Scroll down the report until you see the Page Footer section (Fig. 8-7).

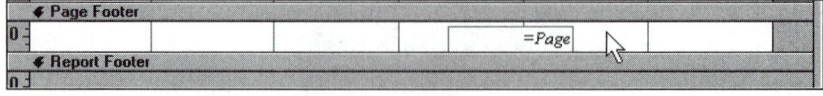

**Figure 8-7   The Page Footer section**

2. Double-click the PageNumber field to open the Properties box.

3. Click the Control Source line in the Properties box.

4. Use ( ← BACKSPACE ) or ( DELETE ) to remove the entry for Control Source.

5. Click the button with the three dots to the right of the Control Source line to open the Expression Builder (Fig. 8-8).

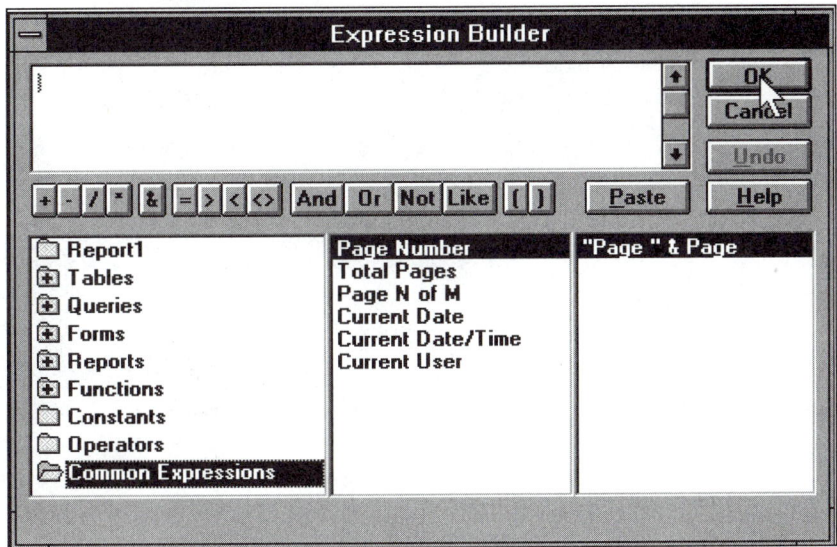

**Figure 8-8** **The Expression Builder window**

6. Click Common Expressions at the bottom of the list of objects.

7. Double-click Page N of M in the list of Common Expressions. Click OK.

8. Click the Properties Box icon to close the Properties box.

9. Click PrintPreview to review the changes to the report.

10. Click CloseWindow to return to Design mode.

# Objective 6:  Modifying the Page Header and Report Header

**page header**  The *page header* is a section of the report that can contain information such as the report title or date. It appears at the top of every page of the report. You will modify the page header to use the space more efficiently. The Report Wizard includes lines in the page header. Now that the report is wider, you need to lengthen those lines for a more balanced look.

**report header**  The *report header* is a section of the report that may contain a title, picture, or logo that appears on the first page of the report. The Wizard did not build a report header, so you will add one, including your name so you can easily identify your report as it comes off the printer. The report header can be used to create a cover or title page for the report.

**report footer** The *report footer* is a section of the report that may contain summary information. It appears at the end of the report. Report footer information follows page footer information.

## Exercise 7: Modifying the page header

First you need to shorten the space for the title. Then you will move the date up to the same line as the title. The current date is automatically put on the report using the =Now() command.

1. Click the Contacts title box in the page header (Fig. 8-9).

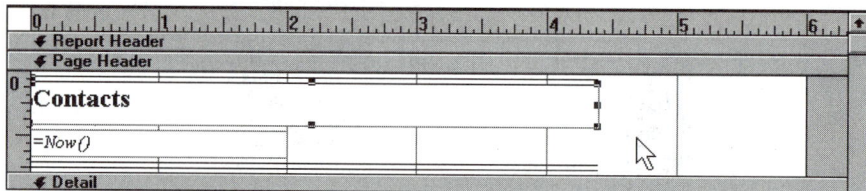

**Figure 8-9    The Page Header section**

2. Use the right handle to decrease the size of the box to 3".
3. Reduce the size of the Date field to about 1.25".
4. Move the Date field box to the right of the Contacts title box.
5. Click the top horizontal line.
6. Hold down SHIFT and carefully click the other three lines.
   All four lines are now selected.
7. Press SHIFT + → repeatedly to extend the line to about 5.8".
8. Select the two lower lines and move them up to just under the title box.
9. Drag the bottom margin of the Page Header section to just below the lower of the two lines (Fig. 8-10).

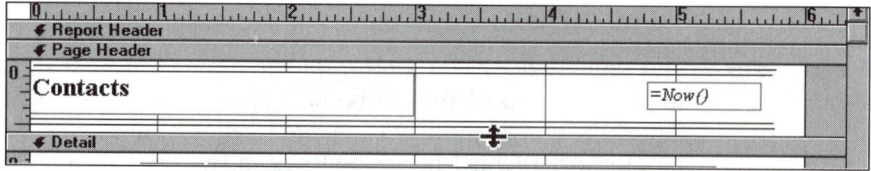

**Figure 8-10    The Page Header section with changes**

10. Use PrintPreview to see the effects of your changes. Return to Design mode.

### Exercise 8: Adding a report header and title

In this exercise, you will add a report header with a report title.

1. Place the cursor on the line that divides the report header from the page header and drag it down about 1".
2. Click the Label button in the Toolbox.

   (If the Toolbox is not already open, you will need to open it.)
3. Move the cursor to the Report Header section.

   The cursor changes to a cross-hair with the letter A below it.
4. Use the mouse to draw a box about 4" wide by 0.5" deep in the Report Header section.

   When you release the mouse button, you will see a blinking vertical line at the right side of the box. The line indicates that you can type text into the box.
5. Type *your name* in the box.

   The text is small because it uses the default font, which is small. You will enlarge the font in a later exercise.

## Objective 7:  Adding Lines and Boxes

You can add visual impact to your report with lines and boxes.

### Exercise 9: Adding lines

To separate your new report header from the page header, draw lines above and below the text box you just created. Then modify the properties of the lines to make them thicker.

1. Click the Line icon in the toolbox. Draw a horizontal line above the report title.
2. Repeat Step 1 to draw a horizontal line below the report title.
3. Select both lines.
4. Click the Properties icon on the toolbar to open the Properties box.

   The title of the Properties box reads Multiple selection. This indicates that you have selected more than one object.
5. Click the Border Width entry in the Properties box.
6. Click the arrow that appears on the right of the Border Width entry.
7. Click the 2 pt value and close the Properties box.
8. If necessary, reduce the size of your Report Header area.
9. Use PrintPreview to see the effects of your changes (Fig. 8-11), then return to Report Design mode.

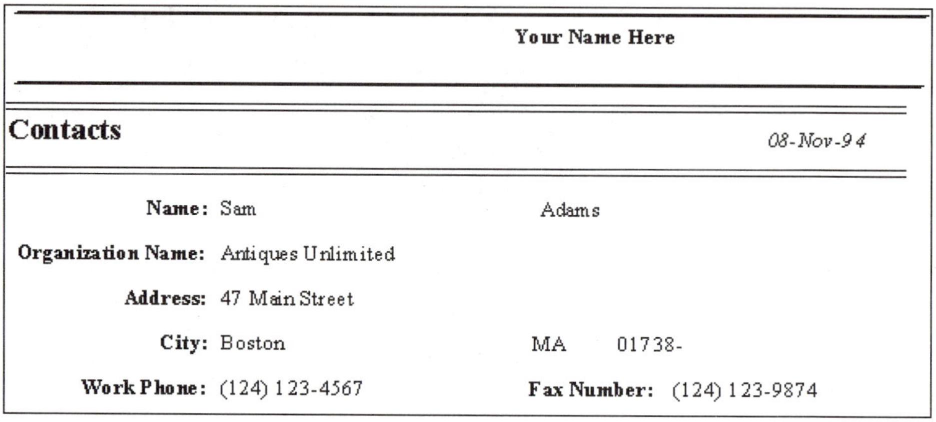

Your Name Here

Contacts 08-Nov-94

Name: Sam Adams

Organization Name: Antiques Unlimited

Address: 47 Main Street

City: Boston MA 01738-

Work Phone: (124) 123-4567 Fax Number: (124) 123-9874

**Figure 8-11 The report with lines added**

## Exercise 10: Adding boxes

To visually separate each record from the surrounding records on the page, add a box around the whole record in the Detail section. It will seem as though all your data disappears because you have placed the box on *top* of the fields. All you have to do is position the box *behind* your fields, and your data will reappear.

1. Click the Rectangle button in the Toolbox.
2. Using the mouse, draw a box around all the fields in the Detail section.
3. Click Format/Send to Back on the menu bar to make the fields visible.

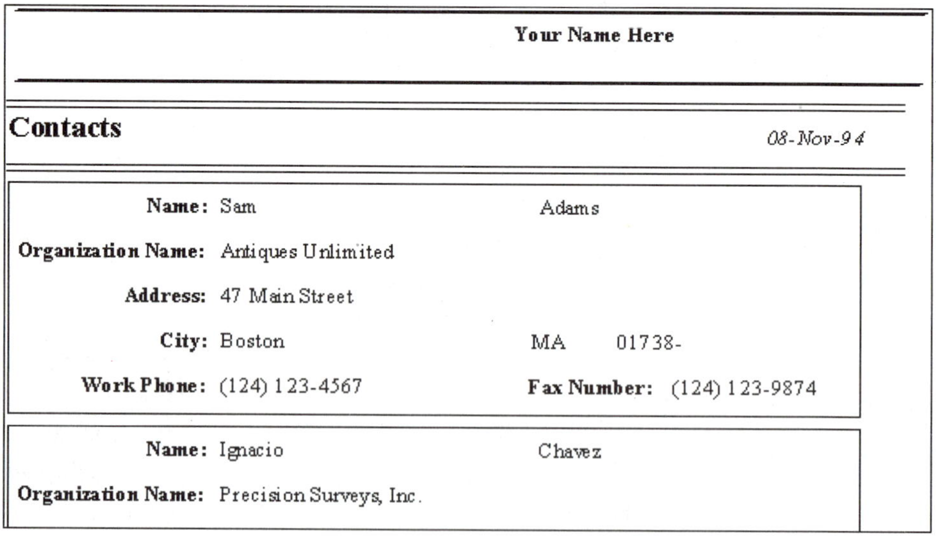

Your Name Here

Contacts 08-Nov-94

Name: Sam Adams

Organization Name: Antiques Unlimited

Address: 47 Main Street

City: Boston MA 01738-

Work Phone: (124) 123-4567 Fax Number: (124) 123-9874

Name: Ignacio Chavez

Organization Name: Precision Surveys, Inc.

**Figure 8-12 The report with a box added**

4. Use PrintPreview to see the effects of your changes (Fig. 8-12), then return to Design mode.

# Objective 8:  Formatting Data in a Report

Formatting a report includes changing font types and sizes, rearranging items on the screen, changing the spacing between lines, and modifying the appearance of the printed report. All the fonts on your computer that are available to MS-Windows applications are available in MS-Access. The fonts on your computer may vary from those available on another computer depending on the fonts installed on each and the printer connected to each. If you are in doubt as to which font to use, Arial comes with MS-Windows and is a plain font suitable for titles and headlines.

## Exercise 11: Changing fonts

The name you typed into the report title is still displayed in the default font. In this exercise, you will make the name larger and change the font style of the title in the page header to italic.

1. Click the box that surrounds your name on the report title.

    On the top toolbar, a font name and size are listed in the viewing areas of two drop-down list boxes (Fig. 8-13).

**Figure 8-13   Fonts on the toolbar**

2. Click the arrow on the font-name drop-down box to show a list of available fonts.
3. Select a font.
4. Click the arrow on the font-size drop-down box.
5. Select a font size from the list or type a value.

    (Try 24-point type and adjust this value up or down, as necessary.)

6. Click the Center-Align Text icon on the toolbar.

    This centers the text within the text box, not the report. To center the text on the report, move the box or enlarge the box so that it is as wide as the report.

7. Click the Contacts title in the page header to select it.
8. Click the Italic icon on the toolbar (Fig. 8-14).

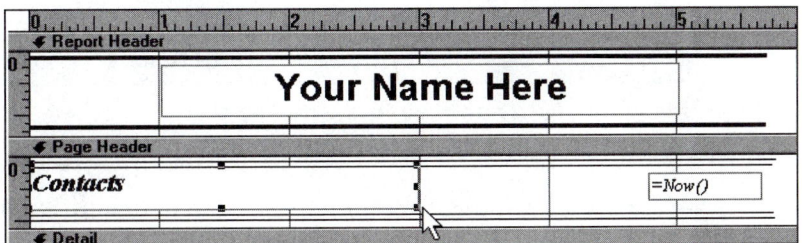

**Figure 8-14   Modified report header**

9. Use PrintPreview to see the effects of your changes. Return to Design mode.

# Objective 9: Saving the report

If you have not already done so, save the report.

### Exercise 12: Saving the report

1. Click File/Save As on the menu bar.
2. When prompted for a report name, type rptContactList. Click OK.

# Objective 10: Previewing the Report

When you use Print Preview, the screen changes. The button bar is considerably different. It shows a restricted set of options—those that you need while in Print Preview. Even the cursor changes; it looks like a magnifying glass. This is a visual reminder that by clicking once you can zoom in to magnify a section of a report or zoom out to see the full page.

### Exercise 13: Print Preview mode

1. Click the Print Preview icon on the toolbar.
2. Use the balloon help to examine the function performed by each icon on the button bar.
3. Use the zoom feature, clicking the mouse button to zoom in and out. Move around the page and examine the report.
4. Click the Print Setup icon.

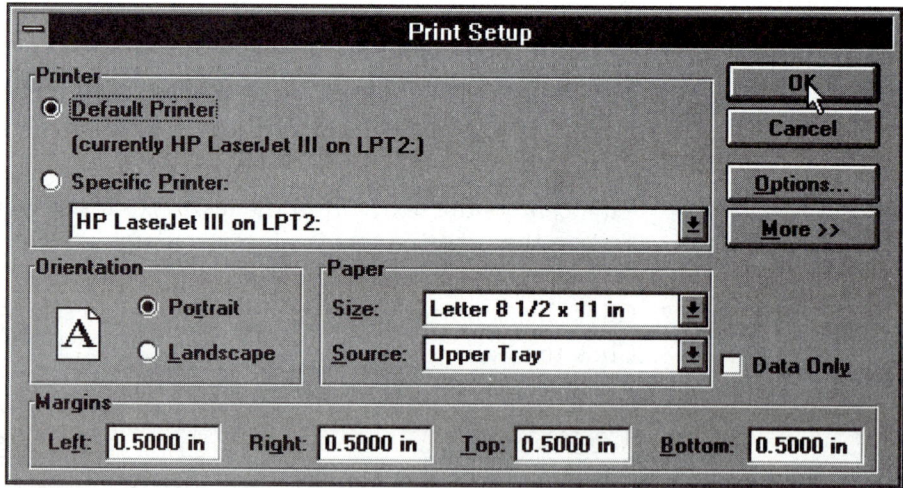

**Figure 8-15** *The Print Setup dialog box*

The Print Setup dialog box opens (Fig. 8-15). This is where you can set the margins of the report or change to a different printer. Leave the default values unless you are told to change them.

5. Click Cancel to exit from the Print Setup dialog box.

# Objective 11: Printing a Report

Print out the first page of your report. Take a minute to look over this first page; if it looks the way you want it to, print the entire report. The report header contains your name, so you can identify your report even if it is printed along with someone else's.

### Exercise 14: Printing the report

1. Click the Print icon to open the Print dialog box.
2. In the Print Range From: and To: boxes, type 1. Click OK.
3. Check the report. Make sure it looks the way you want it to. If it does not, go back to Design mode and correct any problems.
4. If all is well, click the Print icon. Select All for the Print Range. Click OK.
5. Exit from Print Preview mode.
6. Exit from Report Design mode.
7. Close the database and exit from MS-Access.

## Chapter Summary

In this chapter, you used the Report Wizard to generate a report, which you then modified by moving, deleting, and adding fields. You changed the page header and footer and added a report header. You added visual accents such as lines and boxes. You changed the formatting of the report. Once you were satisfied with the report, you previewed it and then printed it.

## Review Questions

### True/False Questions

_____ 1. The Today() function is used to put the current date on a report.

_____ 2. The width of the report generated by the Report Wizard can be changed later.

_____ 3. MS-Access can use any fonts on your computer that are recognized by MS-Windows.

_____ 4. The report header appears on every page of the report.

_____ 5. The Print Preview option prints out only the first page of the report.

## Multiple-Choice Questions

_____ 6. To provide visual clues about important items on a report, you can use

    A. fonts.

    B. boxes.

    C. lines.

    D. Any of the above.

_____ 7. To add lines and boxes to a report, you use the

    A. toolkit.

    B. toolbox.

    C. toolbar.

    D. tollbooth.

_____ 8. The title that appears at the top of each page in a report is called the

    A. title bar.

    B. report header.

    C. page header.

    D. page footer.

_____ 9. If every other page of your report prints out blank, you should

    A. check the width of your report page.

    B. print only every other page.

    C. check the margin settings.

    D. A and C

_____ 10. The report header can be used to

    A. identify the author of the report.

    B. specify the title of the report.

    C. show when the report was generated.

    D. All of the above.

## Fill-in-the-Blank Questions

11. The _____ section of the report contains the line-by-line listing of the database records.

12. To add a text data field to a report, you would begin by clicking the _____ icon on the toolbar.

13. The margins of a report can be changed using the File/_____ option.

14. Changing the appearance of a report by modifying fonts, layout, and spacing is known as _____ the report.

15. To make the page number appear near the bottom edge of each page, you would place the page () in the _____ section of the report.

## Acumen-Building Activities

### Quick Projects

### 1. Using the Report Wizard for MyBooks.

1. Open the Books database. Click the Reports tab. Click New for a new report.
2. Select the table MyBooks. Click Report Wizards. Double-click Single-Column.
3. Move the following fields from the List of available fields to the Field order on report list: Title, Author, PublisherName, ISBNNumber, and Note. Click Next.
4. Sort by Title. Click Next.
5. Choose the Executive style and Portrait orientation. Click Next.
6. Accept the default title and options. Click Finish.

### 2. Modifying the detail area of the MyBooks report.

This exercise is a continuation of Quick Project #1.

1. Click the Close Window icon to return to Report Design mode. Maximize the screen.
2. Drag the right edge of the report to the 6" mark on the ruler.
3. Lengthen the Title field by drawing it out to the 3" mark on the ruler.
4. Reposition the Author field and label so that they are on the same line as Title.
5. Modify the label of ISBNNumber to read ISBN. Resize the label.
6. Reposition the ISBN label so that it is on the same line as Publisher. Align both and move them up closer to the line that contains Author and Title.
7. Lengthen the Note field so that it stretches across the page. Move it up closer to the line that contains Publisher and ISBN.
8. Preview the results.

### 3. Modifying the title area of the MyBooks report.

This exercise is a continuation of Quick Project #2.

1. Return to Design mode. Click the MyBooks title box in the page header.
2. Use the right handle to decrease the size of the box to 3".
3. Change the font style to italic and the font size to 18 point.
4. Reduce the size of the date field to about 1.5". Right-align the text.
5. Position the Date field box on the right side of the report.
6. Hold down (SHIFT) and carefully select the two lower horizontal lines. Move them up to just below the Title field.
7. Press (SHIFT)+(→) to extend these lines to the right margin of the report.
8. Hold down (SHIFT) and carefully select the top two lines. Press (SHIFT)+(→) to extend these lines to the right margin of the report.

9. Adjust the size of the page header to make it smaller.

10. Preview your work.

## 4. Adding visual impact to the MyBooks report.

This exercise is a continuation of Quick Project #3.

1. Return to Design mode.

2. Click the Rectangle button in the toolbox.

3. Using the mouse, draw a box around all the fields in the Detail section.

4. Click the Format/Send to Back option on the menu bar.

5. Adjust the size of the Detail area leaving 0.25" of space below the lowest box.

6. Preview your work. Return to Report Design mode.

7. Save your report (File/Save As) and name it rptBookList.

8. Close the Report Design screen.

9. Close the Books database.

## In-Depth Projects

## 1. Building a report for the CD database.

1. Open the CD database and go to the Reports window.

2. Build a New single-column report from the table CDCollection using the Report Wizards.

3. Include the following fields in the report: Title, GroupName, RecordingLabel, Length, YearReleased, and Classification.

4. Sort first by Classification, then by Title. Select your own style and use Portrait orientation. Accept the default title and options and click Finish. Preview the results.

5. Return to Report Design mode. Make the report 6" wide.

6. Position GroupName and RecordingLabel so they are on the same line and aligned along the top.

7. Position LengthInMinutes and YearReleased so they are on the same line and aligned along the top. Move them closer to the line above.

8. Reduce the size of both LengthInMinutes and YearReleased to a little over 0.5" each.

9. Position Classification directly beneath LengthInMinutes.

10. Adjust and refine the position of the fields as appropriate.

11. Drag the border of the Detail section to within 0.25" of the bottom of Classification.

12. Preview your work. Return to Report Design mode.

13. Decrease the size of the CDCollection title box in the page header to 3" and change the font style to italic.

14. Reduce the size of the date field to 1.5" and right-align the text.

15. Move the Date field box to the right side of the report, aligning it and the title field along the top.

16. Move the two lower horizontal lines up to just below the title field and extend all four lines to the right margin of the report.
17. Adjust the size of the page header to make it smaller.
18. Preview your changes. Return to Report Design mode.
19. Using the Toolbox, draw a rectangle around all the fields in the Detail section of the report and send it to the back so that the fields are superimposed on the rectangle.
20. Preview the effects of your changes. Return to Report Design mode.
21. In the page footer, move the page number to the right margin of the report.
22. Create a label box on the left side of the page footer, type *your name*, and left-align it within the label box.
23. Save your report and call it rptCDList. Print the report after previewing it.
24. Close the Report Design screen. Close the CD database.

## 2. Building a report for the Dinner Party database.

1. Open the Dinner database and go to the Report window.
2. Build a New single-column report from the table Dinners using the Report Wizards.
3. Include the following fields in the report: Place, Date, Time, and Occasion.
4. Sort by Date. Select your own style and use Portrait orientation.
5. Name this report Dinner List. Accept the other defaults and click Finish.
6. Widen the report to 6".
7. Position Date, Time, and Occasion on the same line.
8. Adjust the size of the Detail section.
9. In the page header, position the Date field near the right margin and right-align it.
10. Italicize the Dinners title field.
11. Adjust the position and length of the horizontal lines in the page header.
12. Adjust the size of the page header.
13. Draw a box around all the fields in the Detail section of the report and send it to the back so that the fields are superimposed on the rectangle.
14. Move the page number in the page footer close to the right margin of the report.
15. Create a label box on the left side of the page footer, type *your name*, and left-align it within the label box.
16. Preview your report, then print it out.
17. Save your report and call it rptDinnerList. Close the Report Design screen.
18. Build a second New report from the table DinnerGuests. Make it the same type of report as rptDinnerList. Include the following fields: FirstName, LastName, Address, City, State, and PostalCode.
19. Sort by LastName, then FirstName.
20. Modify this report as you did rptDinnerList.

21. Preview your work and print it out. Save the report and call it rptDinnerGuestList.

22. Close the Report Design screen. Close the Dinner database.

# CASE STUDIES

**Coffee-On-The-Go:**

### Creating Reports

In this chapter, you learned to create reports. You will use those skills to create reports for Coffee-On-The-Go.

1. Open the Coffee database.

2. Create a report that includes only the following fields from the Employee table:
   Last
   First
   Salary
   Current

3. Enhance the report to include a title, formatting, and lines.

4. Preview the report.

5. When you are pleased with the report, print it.

6. Save the report and close the Coffee database.

# CASE STUDIES

**Videos West:**

### Creating Reports

In this chapter, you learned to create reports. You will use those skills to create reports for Videos West.

1. Open the Video database.

2. Create a report that includes only the following fields from the Inventory table:
   Title
   Retail
   Quantity
   Rating

3. Enhance the report to include a title, formatting, and lines.

4. Preview the report.

5. When you are pleased with the report, print it.

6. Save the report and close the Video database.

# Acumen Critical Thinking Milestone

## the Scouts Cookie Sale Database

It occurs to Mrs. Wilson that, in addition to the home phone number, she needs to record the work number for each customer, so she decides to add that number to the Customer table. She also decides to add some validation rules—like not being able to leave the customer's name or address blank.

After working on the data-entry form to make it more visually appealing and entering this week's cookie sales, she decides to build some queries and generate reports to see who is selling the most cookies and what is the best-selling variety. Then Mrs. Wilson makes a backup of the database.

1. Add WorkPhone to the Customer table. Insert some validation rules to avoid nulls in CustomerName and Address. Enter this week's cookie sales.
2. Modify the data-entry form. Adjust the fields so that all can be viewed on the screen without scrolling. Add features (lines, boxes, color) to make the form visually appealing and easy to use.
3. Build a query to determine how cookie sales are going and who is selling how much. Build another query to determine the best-selling cookie type.
4. Create reports on the previous two queries. Make a database backup.

## the Community Rec Center Database

The Forms Designer in your project group has decided to make the forms more useful by adding visual clues to facilitate data entry and repositioning the fields on the forms to avoid scrolling. Also, the type of membership field on the Members form should not be left empty. The Forms Designer and the Database Administrator must confer to decide where to insert this validation rule: in the form or Members table.

The Report Designer has decided to generate more informative listings, such as which members are using the facilities, which members are checking out equipment, and how much equipment is currently on loan.

The entire project team will work together to enroll this week's new members into the Rec Center database and record reservations and equipment issue. Then the Database Administrator will make a backup of the Rec Center database.

## The Full Project Team

Confer on the best place to position the validation rule regarding the Type of Membership field. Insert the rule. Record this week's new members, reservations, and equipment issues.

## The Database Administrator

If appropriate, add the validation rule for Type of Membership to the Members table. Confer with project team members to ensure that all data items they need to capture have corresponding fields in a table of the Rec Center database. Make a backup of the database.

## The Forms Designer

Enhance the quick forms. Reposition the fields to eliminate scrolling and add visual appeal to enhance data entry. Add any validation rules or input masks that you deem appropriate. Confer with your colleagues before making these changes to make sure they agree with you.

## The Report Designer

Create the following reports: (1) which members are using the facilities, (2) which members are checking out equipment, and (3) how much equipment is currently on loan.

# Part 3

# Advanced Features

# Chapter 9

## Advanced Query Operations

*Objectives*
- ■ **Using Compound Conditions**
- ■ **Specifying Ranges**
- ■ **Using the Not Operator**
- ■ **Prompting for Criteria**
- ■ **Calculated Values in Queries**
- ■ **Creating Multitable Queries**

*Key Terms*

| TERM | DEFINITION |
|------|------------|
| **Compound Condition** | a set of criteria that are combined within a query |

Building a simple query with one condition is not the only type of query you can construct. You can combine several conditions within one query. If your database contains thousands or hundreds of thousands of records, you can use queries to extract a subset of the data by specifying ranges of values.

## Objective 1: Using Compound Conditions

**compound query**

When we first studied queries in this book, we said that if a query were written in English, it would read, "Show me only data where . . . " If you were to write a compound condition in English, it might read, "Show me only data where . . . *and* . . ." A *compound query* is a set of criteria that are combined within a single query. For example, you could query, "Show me all records where the City is Burlington *and* the State is Colorado," because you want data from Burlington, Colorado, but not from Burlington, Vermont. Another type of compound query might read, "Show me only data where . . . *or* . . . ," as in "Show me all the orders we have received from Washington *or* Oregon."

When designing a compound condition, take time to consider how the criteria will be interpreted by MS-Access. If your queries are producing unexpected results, then the combination of criteria you used is incorrect. An example will clarify this point.

Suppose you want to send a letter to all your contacts in Florida who work at companies with more than 50 people. In English, the query would read, "Show me a list of contacts where the state is Florida and the number of employees is greater than or equal to 50." This is interpreted by MS-Access to read, "Show me a list of contacts where (state *equals* Florida) *and* (the number of employees *is greater than or equal to* 50)." The conditions are compounded, so the second condition further restricts the limits imposed by the first condition.

You should have an idea of the type of results you expect from a query. If you are running a report based on a query, run the query first or use Print Preview to make sure you have the records you are getting the results you expect.

How would you write the query to include all your contacts in Florida and Georgia? If you write, "Show me a list of contacts where the state equals Florida and Georgia," you will not see any names in the results. Why? Think about what the query is really saying. Nobody lives in *both* Florida and Georgia—they live in one state or the other. Your query asked for names where both conditions were met—no contacts matched, so no names appeared in the output list. What you really meant was, "Show me a list of contacts where the state equals Florida *or* the state equals Georgia."

The distinction between And compound conditions and Or compound conditions is very important to understand. MS-Access provides considerable help in building queries, but you still have to be very careful to say exactly what you mean.

### Exercise 1: Compound conditions: And

Write a query that uses two conditions connected by And. The two conditions combine to restrict the output recordset and act on two different fields. Your starting point is at the Contacts Database window with the Query tab selected.

1. Open the query FirstQuery in Design mode.

   The query should include only the fields FirstName, LastName, OrganizationName, State, and NumEmployees.

2. Delete the condition for OrganizationName and set the condition for NumEmployees to >49. Make sure that the Show box for NumEmployees is checked (Fig. 9-1).

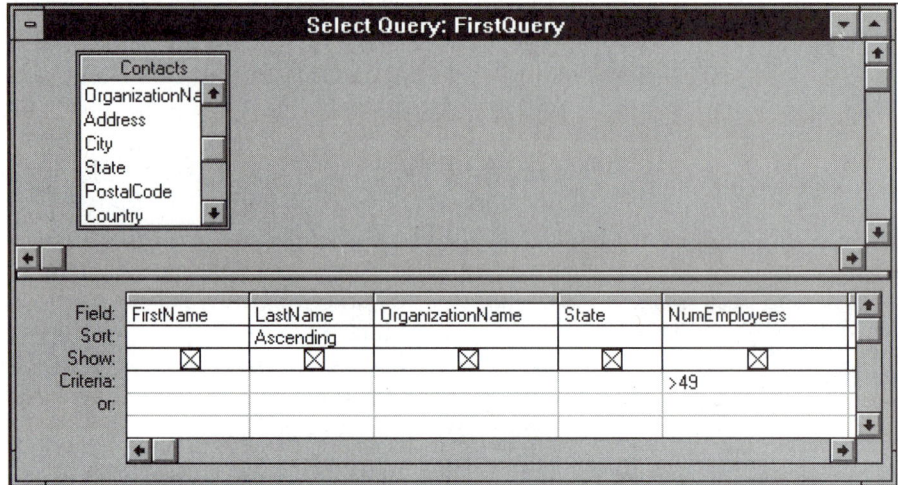

**Figure 9-1** **Initial query criteria**

3. Run the query by clicking the exclamation point on the toolbar.

   The results show all your contacts in companies with 50 or more employees.

   The list includes Moore, Langford, and Swenson.

4. Return to Design mode.

5. In the State column on the Criteria line, type = VA.

   It is important that this goes on the same line as the >49 in the NumEmployees column. Criteria on the same line are combined using the And operator.

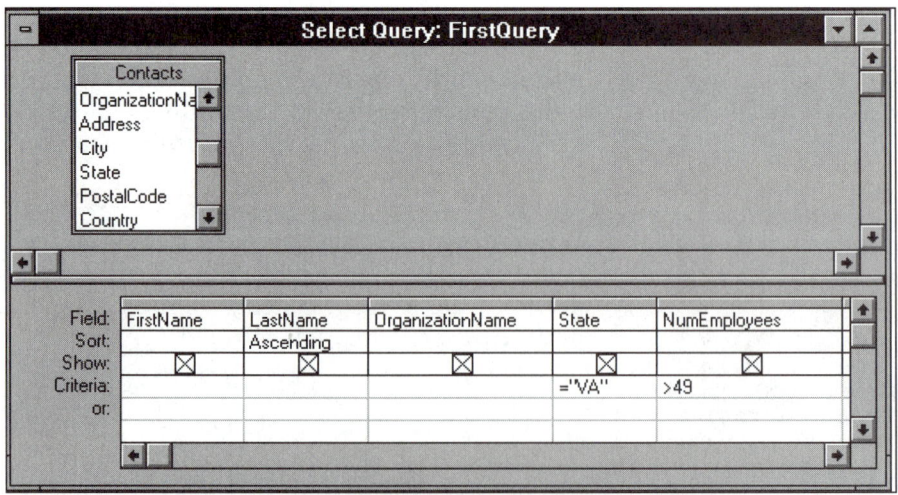

**Figure 9-2** **Compound conditions with the And operator**

6. Run the query again.

   Now you will see only the contacts where both conditions are met. The list shows only Langford.

7. Return to Design mode.

## Exercise 2: Compound conditions: Or

Write a query that uses two conditions connected by the Or operator. Records that meet either condition are returned.

1. Delete the =VA from the Criteria line.

2. Type =ID on the next line.

   This row is labeled or:. The two criteria are combined using the Or operator (Fig. 9-3).

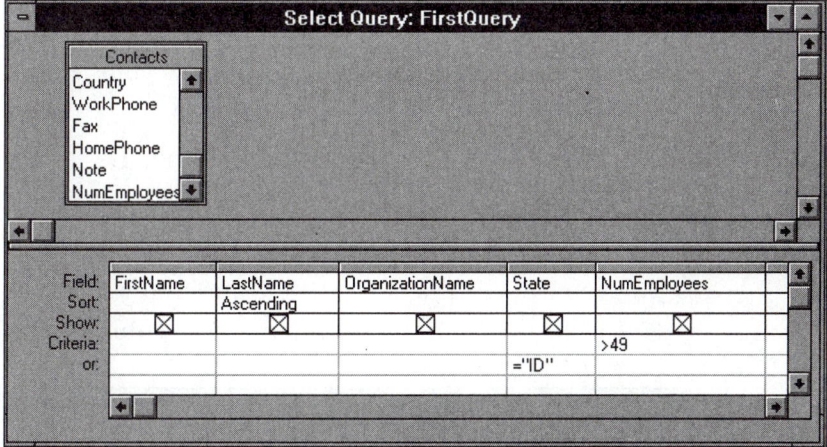

**Figure 9-3  Compound conditions with the Or operator**

3. Run the query.

   You will see a list of contacts in companies with 50 or more employees, and also any contacts in Idaho, without regard to the number of employees.

4. Return to Design mode.

## Exercise 3: Compound conditions on the same field

How would you construct a query that retrieves data from two or more states? One way is to list the states.

1. Delete the =ID condition from the Or line and type = VA or PA on the Criteria line.

2. Run the query.

   The results show your contacts in Virginia and Pennsylvania for companies with 50 or more employees.

3. Return to Design mode.

# Objective 2: Specifying Ranges

Often you will need to extract records from a database where some field has a value that falls within a specified range of values. What if you want contacts from a group of states? You can use the In operator to list the State names. Then you search for records where the State name is in the list.

The Between operator can be used to find, for example, a list of companies with 20 to 200 employees or orders dated between January 1 and July 4. The Between operator is inclusive: Your order list will include orders placed on New Year's Day and the Fourth of July.

If you ask for a list from the Contacts database with last names between A and M, you will see names from Adams to Kanzaki on the list. But you will not see Monteleone or Moore. Why not? Because Mo comes after M when you sort alphabetically. There are two solutions to this possible problem. You can look for names between A and MZZ. Or you could search between A and N. You must know your data in order to specify the correct search criteria.

## Exercise 4: Compound conditions: In

Look for people in Virginia, Pennsylvania, or Washington, DC.

1. Delete = VA or PA from the Criteria row.
2. Type IN (VA, PA, DC) in the Criteria row.
3. Delete >49 from the NumEmployees column (Fig. 9-4).

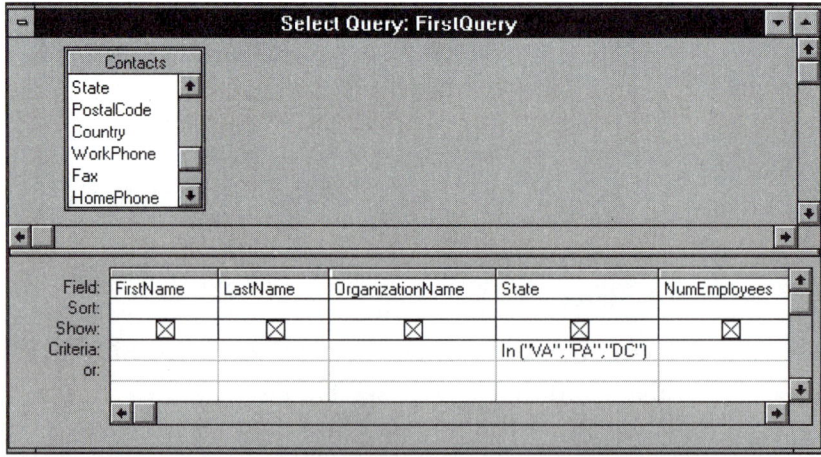

**Figure 9-4   Compound conditions with the In operator**

4. Run the query.

   You will see the records for Langford, Moore, and Monteleone. These are people in the two states that you specified and the District of Columbia.

5. Return to Design mode.

## Exercise 5: Compound conditions: Between

Look for last names that start with letters between A and M.

1. Clear the In condition from the State column.

2. In the LastName column of the Criteria row, type between A and M (Fig. 9-5).

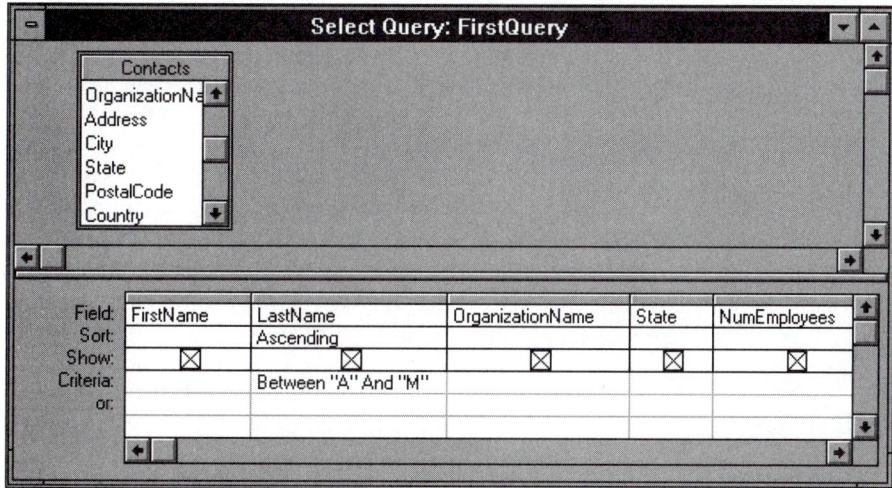

**Figure 9-5  Compound Conditions with the Between operator.**

3. Run the query.

   Monteleone and Moore are not on the list because Mo sorts alphabetically after M.

4. Return to Design mode.

5. Change the Criteria condition to between A and MZZ. Run the query.

   Monteleone and Moore are now on the list.

## FEATURE

### Queries and security

Even when you are building a form based on only one table, you may want to think about using a query instead of a table. One reason for doing so is security. Take the example of employee records. They usually contain sensitive information, such as pay level and performance reviews. You want to design a form so that the clerical staff in the personnel department can enter routine information without having access to confidential data. First, you build a query, selecting only the open information fields. You set permissions so that the query cannot be changed. Then you build the form on that query. Even if a staff member has the Form Design mode available, he or she can modify only the display of the fields selected in the query. The staff member cannot get to the confidential data in the table.

# Objective 3: Using the Not Operator

Not is a special compound condition. It reverses or inverts the effects of other conditions. Records that would have been selected in a regular query are excluded. Records that would have been omitted now make up the output recordset. Sometimes it is easier to specify what you do *not* want than to describe what you *do* want.

To search for all the contacts in Arkansas you use the query Like AK. How do you find all the contacts *not* in Arkansas? Simply change the condition to Not Like AK. It is easier to exclude one state than to create a query that includes 49 states.

There is one potential pitfall when using the Not operator. If a State field is not filled in, it has a value of Null. This record shows up in the out-of-state list because the null value is indeed Not Like AK. To circumvent this situation, add a validation rule to the table that makes State a required field, as you did with the LastName field. You might consider imposing the same rule on any field that you plan to use as the basis for a query.

## Exercise 6: Using the Not operator to reverse the selection criteria

When you ran the query in Exercise 1 with no restrictions on The State field, you saw three records. When you restricted the state to VA, you saw only one record. If you reverse the state condition, the other two records will be listed.

1. Delete the Between condition from the Criteria row in the LastName column.
2. Type <>VA on the Criteria row in the State column.

    <> means "not equal to."
3. Type >49 under NumEmployees on the Criteria row (Fig. 9-6).

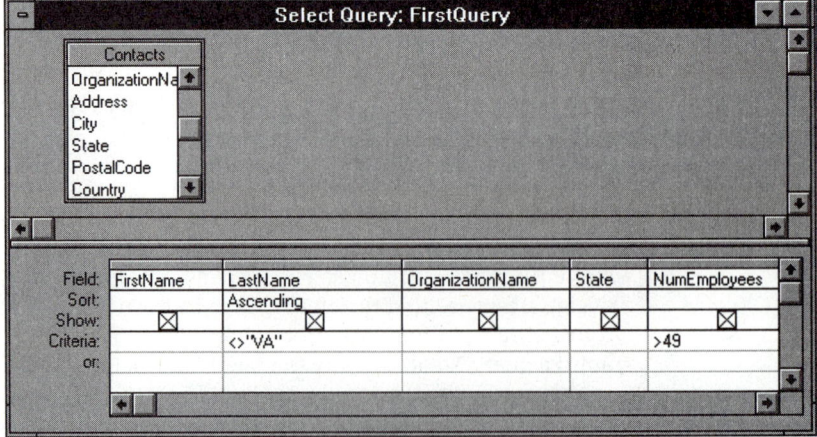

**Figure 9-6  Compound conditions with the Not operator**

4. Run the query.

   Moore and Swenson are listed, and Langford, from Virginia, is not shown.

5. Return to Design mode.

6. Type Not in front of the >49 in the NumEmployees column. Run the query.

   Now the list shows all the contacts who are not in Virginia and who work at companies with less than 50 employees. There's another way to do this.

7. Return to Design mode.

8. Change the Not >49 entry to <50. Run the query. The results are the same as the previous query. Return to Design mode.

# Objective 4: Prompting for Criteria

The previous queries used criteria coded into the query. If you want to look at a list of contacts for each state, you could build fifty queries with each specifying one state in the Criteria row. This is not a good technique. A better way is to build one query with a prompt that asks you which state you want. You can build prompt queries that use approximate matches to the data, or you can build prompt queries that require exact matches. You can combine prompts and normal criteria or even prompt for input values on more than one field.

## Exercise 7: Prompting for criteria

Modify the query so that it prompts you for the state code in which you want to see contacts. Then change the prompt so that you can search for a specific last name.

1. Clear all the criteria from the query.

2. In the criteria row of the State column, type [Enter a two-letter State code]. Make sure you include the square brackets.

3. Run the query. When prompted for a State code, type PA and click OK (Fig. 9-7).

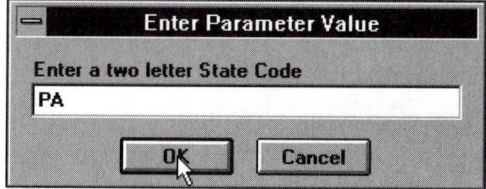

**Figure 9-7** **The Prompt dialog box**

You will see a list of your contacts in Pennsylvania.

4. Switch back to Design mode.

5. Run the query again. When prompted for a State code, type ID and click OK.

   You will see a list of your contacts in Idaho.

6. Switch back to Design mode.

7. Delete the prompt from the Criteria row of the State column.

8. In the Criteria row under LastName, type Like [Enter a Last Name].

9. Run the query. When prompted for a last name, type Lan*.

   The record for Langford is shown. Here you combined the Like operator with the prompt, so you can search for names when you know only part of the spelling.

**⚠ WARNING** You can combine a prompt and the Between operator—you will be prompted for a range of values. This does not work with the In operator. If you execute a prompt using the In operator, MS-Access will crash without warning, and you may lose data.

10. Return to Design mode.

11. Click File/Save As and save the query as qryPromptLastName.

12. Close the query.

# Objective 5: Calculated Values in Queries

We mentioned before that you should not store computed data in a table. The better approach is to compute the data as necessary so that it is always current and correct. Some typical examples of computed data are totals, subtotals, and averages. Often it is useful to know the count of the number of records in a table or the number of records that match the criteria in a query.

## Exercise 8: Calculated totals in queries

First, find the total number of records in your database. Then determine how many records you have in each state. Finally, calculate the average number of people employed by your contact companies in each state.

1. Start at the Database window with the Query tab selected.

2. Click New, then New Query.

3. At the Add Table dialog box, select Contacts. Click Add. Close the dialog box.

4. Double-click ContactID to add it to the query.

5. On the menu bar, click View/Totals.

   A new line appears in the query specification. This line is labeled Total:. The default value is Group By.

6. Click the Group By value to show a list of options (Fig. 9-8).

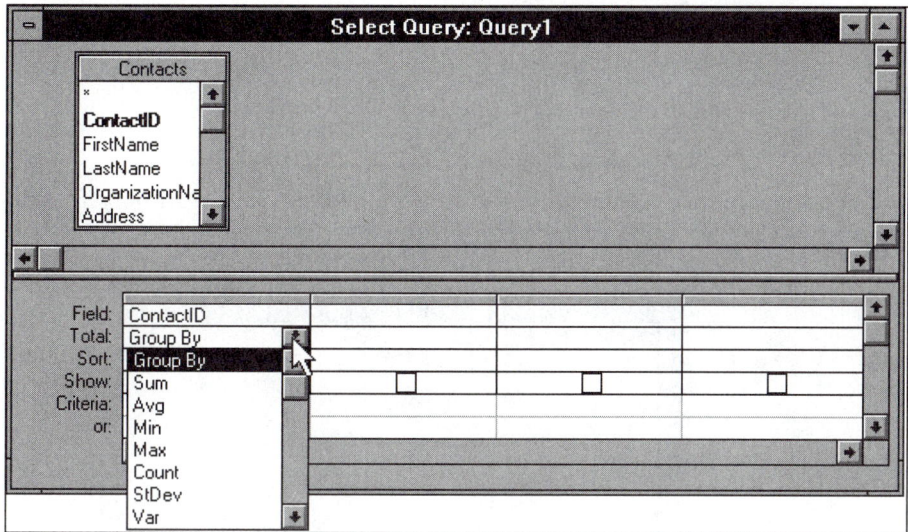

**Figure 9-8 Total Option menu**

7. Select Count from the list and run the query.

   You will see that you have ten records in the database.

8. Return to Design mode.

9. Double-click State in the list of fields for the Contacts table to add it to the query. Leave the Group By value in the Total row. Run the query.

   You have a list of the number of contacts in each state (Fig. 9-9). Because your Contact database is small, this table is not very revealing. It would be more informational if you had a large number of records in the database.

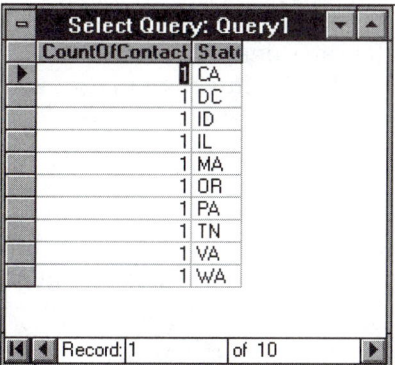

**Figure 9-9 Contacts by state**

10. Return to Design mode.

11. Click the ContactID entry in the Field row and select NumEmployees from the list that appears.

12. Click the Count value in the Total row and change it to Avg. Run the query (Fig. 9-10).

    This query shows you the average number of people employed by your contact companies, grouped by state.

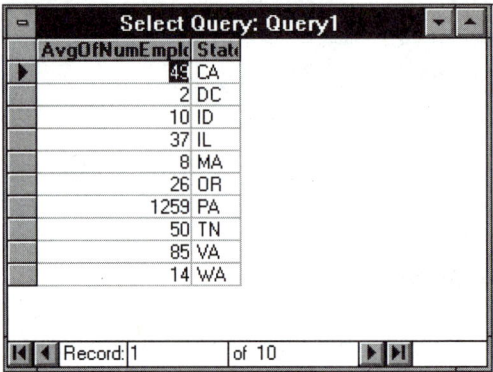

**Figure 9-10** **Average number of employees, grouped by state**

13. Save the query as qryAvgNumEmp. Close the query.

# Objective 6: Creating Multitable Queries

The most common reason for using queries is to extract related data from two or more tables at the same time. This capability is unique to relational databases, and you do it with a query.

It is recommended that the relationships between the tables be established before you create the query. While this is not absolutely necessary (MS-Access generally can deduce the relationships as it runs the query), there is a chance that you may see unexpected results if MS-Access deduces the relationships incorrectly. Also the query will run faster if the relationships are predefined. The relationships between the tables used in the following exercises were established in Chapter 5. But you will have to add some data to the second table before you can use it in a query.

## Exercise 9: Adding data to a second, related table

Begin this exercise at the Database window.

1. Open the PhoneNumbers table in Datasheet view.

2. Add the following values to the table:

| CONTACT ID | PHONE NUMBER | PHONETYPE |
|:---:|:---:|:---|
| 1 | (124) 123-4567 | Work |
| 2 | (703) 234-1234 | Work |
| 3 | (615) 232-4505 | Pager |
| 3 | (615) 459-5245 | Home |
| 3 | (615) 666-7070 | Fax |
| 4 | (215) 222-1111 | Work |
| 6 | (509) 989-1000 | Work |
| 7 | (208) 544-1111 | Work |
| 8 | (415) 222-8880 | Work |
| 9 | (503) 565-7878 | Work |
| 10 | (202) 344-1212 | Work |
| 11 | (282) 383-1193 | Work |

## Exercise 10: Multitable Queries

You have two tables in your Contacts database: the main Contacts table and the secondary PhoneNumbers table. You want to print a telephone directory that shows each contact's name, company, and phone numbers. Construct a query to list the required information. Start at the Database window with the Queries tab selected.

1. Click New, then New Query.

   The Query Design window opens with the Add Table dialog box on top.

2. Double-click the Contacts table to add it to the query.

3. Double-click the PhoneNumbers table to add it to the query.

4. Click Close to close the dialog box (Fig. 9-11).

   The line between the two tables represents the relationship defined in Chapter 5. There is a 1 next to the Contacts table and the infinity symbol next to the PhoneNumbers table. This indicates that between the Contacts and PhoneNumbers tables there is a one-to-many relationship.

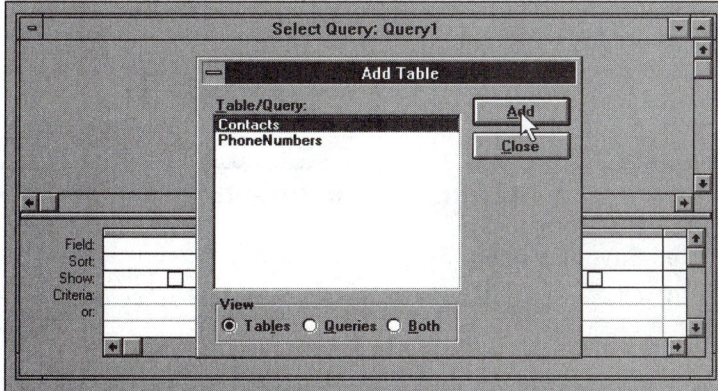

**Figure 9-11  Query Design window with multiple tables**

5. Double-click the LastName, FirstName, and OrganizationName fields from the Contacts table to add them to the query.

6. Double-click the PhoneNumber and PhoneType fields from the PhoneNumbers table to add them to the query.

7. Click View/Table Names to show the table names in the Query Design window (Fig. 9-12).

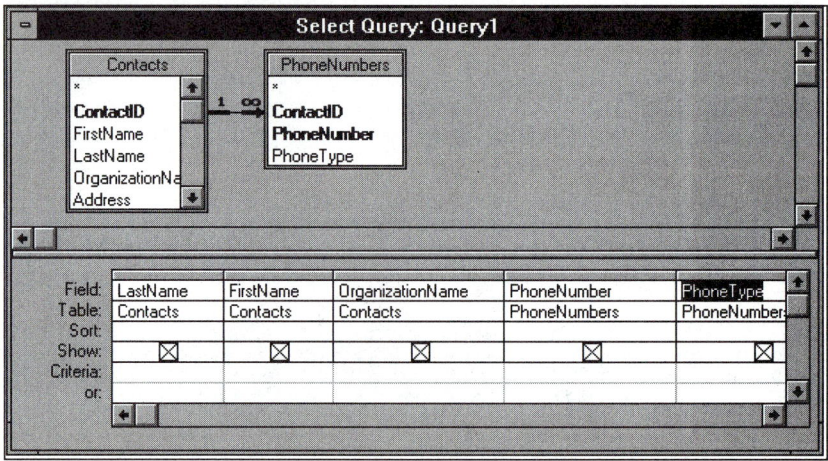

**Figure 9-12   Multitable query**

8. Under LastName, click in the Sort row and select Ascending. Run the query.

| Last Name | First Name | Organization Name | Phone Number | Type of Phone Number |
|-----------|------------|-------------------|--------------|----------------------|
| Adams | Sam | Antiques Unlimited | (124) 123-4567 | Work |
| Chavez | Ignacio | Precision Surveys, Inc. | (415) 222-8880 | Work |
| Clark | Robin | Precision Surveys, Inc. | (208) 544-1111 | Work |
| Kanzaki | Hiroshi | Precision Surveys, Inc. | (503) 565-7878 | Work |
| Langford | George | Langford Trucking | (703) 234-1234 | Work |
| Lincoln | Tom | Lincoln Log Homes, Inc | (282) 383-1193 | Work |
| Monteleone | Wendy | Monteleone Legal Serv | (202) 344-1212 | Work |
| Moore | Margaret | Liberty Shield Insuranc | (215) 222-1111 | Work |
| O'Leary | Roger S. | Precision Surveys, Inc. | (509) 989-1000 | Work |
| Swenson | G. David | Swenson Adventure To | (615) 666-7070 | Fax |
| Swenson | G. David | Swenson Adventure To | (615) 459-5245 | Home |
| Swenson | G. David | Swenson Adventure To | (615) 232-4505 | Pager |

Record: 1    of 12

**Figure 9-13   Results of a multitable query**

9. Save the query as qryPhoneList.

10. Close the database and exit from MS-Access.

# Chapter Summary

In this chapter, you built complex queries using compound conditions to specify multiple criteria. You learned how to use operators to combine criteria and the difference between the And operator and Or operator. You used the In and Between operators to specify ranges of data values. You made your queries more flexible by prompting for criteria instead of building them into the query. You saw how to compute values in a query. The concept of multitable queries was introduced, and you built a query using two tables from your Contacts database.

# Review Questions

## True/False Questions

_____ 1. It is a good idea to define relationships between tables before using them in a multitable query.

_____ 2. Requesting records from one state Or another will result in only those records from the first state being returned.

_____ 3. The Between operator returns records that are between the values you specify, but not those that are equal to the values you specify.

_____ 4. A query can show data that is not in the database tables but is computed from stored data.

_____ 5. The In operator returns the same data as the Or operator.

## Multiple-Choice Questions

_____ 6. To match a list of specific values for a selection condition, you would use the
A. Between operator.
B. Like operator.
C. In operator.
D. Inclusive operator.

_____ 7. To find records for all states except New Hampshire, you would set the criterion on the state field to
A. Unlike "NH".
B. Not Like "NH".
C. Like "NH" Not!
D. Except "NH".

_____ 8. If you have not defined a relationship between two tables before building a query, MS-Access will

    A. deduce the relationship automatically.

    B. show an error message on the screen.

    C. run the query, but give the wrong results.

    D. ask for the relationship to be specified.

_____ 9. Which of the following statements about MS-Access queries is untrue?

    A. You can set multiple conditions on one field.

    B. A query can be used as the basis for a form or report.

    C. The values for the selection criteria can be specified when the query is run.

    D. A query run every week will show the same data.

_____ 10. If you want to find the contacts who live in New Mexico and work for companies with fewer than twelve people, you would

    A. set the criterion in the State column to "NM".

    B. set the criterion in the NumEmployees column to "<12".

    C. set the criterion in the State column to "NM" and set the criterion in the NumEmployees column to "<= 12".

    D. set the criterion in the State column State to "NM" and set the criterion in the NumEmployees column to "< 12".

## Fill-in-the-Blank Questions

11. When you store a field that is computed from other fields, you endanger the _____ of the database.

12. The Not condition is used to _____ the effects of the specified criteria.

13. To select records with a last name of White, Whittle, or Whitton, but not Whyte or Whistler, you would specify LastName Like

_____.

14. To perform computations, such as totals and averages, in a query, click on the _____ / _____ (*two words*) menu option.

15. It is possible for MS-Access to _____ the user for a value for a criterion whenever the query is run.

## Acumen-Building Activities

### Quick Projects

### 1. Compound queries of MyBooks using And.

1. Open the Books database and create a New Query without using the Query Wizard.
2. Add the table MyBooks to the Query Design screen.
3. Include in the query the following fields in the following order: Title, Author, ISBNNumber, PublisherName, Pages, and Note.
4. Sort by Title in ascending order.
5. Run the query. Check the contents and return to the Query Design window.
6. In the Title column of the Criteria row, type like *walk*.
7. In the Note column of the Criteria row, type like *mystery*. Run the query.

   The output from the query is restricted to one row, if you are using the data set provided by the authors. The single record returned contains the value Skinwalkers in the Title field and mystery in the Note field.

### 2. Compound queries of MyBooks using Or.

This exercise is a continuation of Quick Project #1.

1. Return to Query Design mode and delete the criterion from the Title column.
2. Modify the criterion in the Note column so that it reads like *market*.
3. In the next line down, which is labeled or:, type like *relativity*. Run the query.

   The output from the query is restricted to two rows, if you are using the data set provided by the authors. One of the records returned contains the value market in the Note column; the other contains the value relativity.

### 3. Querying for a range of values with MyBooks.

This exercise is a continuation of Quick Project #2.

1. Return to Query Design mode. Delete the criterion from the Note column.
2. In the Pages column of the Criteria row, type between 300 and 350. Run the query.

   The output from the query shows two rows, if you are using the data set provided by the authors. Each of these books has between 300 and 350 pages.

## 4. Using Between to exclude a set of records in MyBooks.

This exercise is a continuation of Quick Project #3.

1. Return to Design mode.
2. Modify the criterion in the Pages column by typing not between 300 and 350. Run the query.

   Three rows are output, if you are using the data set provided by the authors. The first book has 164 pages, the second has 299, and the third has 368. None of the three has between 300 and 350 pages.
3. Save the query by clicking File/Save Query and call it qryCompound. Click OK.
4. Close the Query Display screen. Close the Books database.

## In-Depth Projects

## 1. Advanced queries in the CD database.

1. Open the CD database and go to the Query window.
2. Create a New query without using the Query Wizard. Use only the table CDCollection. Include in the query the following fields in the following order: Title, YearReleased, and Classification.
3. Sort by Title in ascending order.
4. Run the query. Check the contents and return to the Design Mode window.
5. Find those CDs that are classified as rock or country. Run the query.
6. If you are using the data set provided by the authors you will have two rows returned: Evangeline (Cajun/Country) and Question of Balance (Symphonic Rock).
7. Return to Query Design mode. Remove the criterion from the Classification column.
8. Find those CDs that were released between 1970 and 1990. Run the query.
9. If you are using the data set provided by the authors you will have three rows returned: Canyon Trilogy (1989), Question of Balance (1970), and Star Wars (1977).
10. Return to Query Design mode. Remove the criterion from the YearReleased column.
11. Find those CDs that have the values Wars or 2002 in their Title field. Run the query.
12. If you are using the data set provided by the authors, you will have two rows returned: Star Wars and Cusco 2002.
13. Save the query and name it qryCompound. Close the query.
14. Create a New query without using the Query Wizard. Use the tables CDCollection and Tracks for the query.
15. Include in the query the following fields in the following order: from table CDCollection: Title and GroupName; from table Tracks: TrackTitle and TrackTime.
16. Sort by Title in ascending order. Run the query.

17. If you are using the data set provided by the authors, you will have 18 rows returned.

18. Save this query and name it qryJoin.

19. Close the query. Close the CD database.

## 2. Advanced queries in the Dinner database.

1. Open the Dinner database and go to the Query window.

2. Create a New query without using the Query Wizard. Use the table Dinners.

3. Include in the query the following fields in the following order: Date, Time, Occasion, and Place.

4. Sort by Date in ascending order.

5. Run the query. Check the contents and return to the Design Mode window.

6. Find those Dinners that were held between 02/01/94 and 06/01/94. Run the query.

7. If you are using the data set provided by the authors, you will have three rows returned: 02/13/94, 04/03/94, and 05/29/94.

8. Return to Query Design mode. Remove the criterion from the Date column.

9. Find those dinners that were either birthdays or BBQs. Run the query.

10. If you are using the data set provided by the authors, you will have two rows returned: 07/19/94 (midsummer BBQ) and 08/30/94 (Linda's birthday).

11. Save this query and name it qryComplexDinner. Close the query.

12. Create a New query without using the Query Wizard. Use the table DinnerGuests for the query.

13. Include in the query the following fields in the following order: FirstName, LastName, and HomePhone.

14. Sort by LastName in ascending order. Check the contents and return to the Design Mode window.

15. Find those DinnerGuests who live in the 757 phone exchange. Run the query.

16. If you are using the data set provided by the authors, you will have one row returned: John Baccus ((303) 757-9976).

17. Save this query and name it qryComplexGuest. Close the query.

18. Create a New query without using the Query Wizard. Use the tables DinnerGuests, GuestList, and Dinners—in that order—for the query.

19. Include in the query the following fields in the following order: from table Dinners: Date and Place; from table DinnerGuests: FirstName and LastName.

20. Sort by Date in ascending order. Run the query.

21. If you are using the data set provided by the authors, you will have 22 rows returned.

22. Save the query and name it qryTripleJoin.

23. Close the query. Close the Dinner database.

# CASE STUDIES

## Coffee-On-The-Go: Using Advanced Queries

In this chapter, you learned to create advanced queries. You will use those skills to create queries for the Coffee database for Coffee-On-The-Go. You may, if you wish, save each query.

1. Open the Coffee database.
2. Set up a query to find only the employees Smith and Smyth. Print the results.
3. Set up a query to find the employees Smith, Smyth, and Smithsonian. Print the results.
4. Find all female employees who make $15,000 or more. Print the results.
5. Find all male employees who no longer work for the company. Print the results.
6. Find all male employees who work for location 01 and make more than $14,000. Print the results.
7. Find all female employees who started working for the company after 1991. Print the results.
8. Close the database.

# CASE STUDIES

## Videos West: Using Advanced Queries

In this chapter, you learned to create advanced queries. You will use those skills to create queries for the Video database for Videos West. You may, if you wish, save each query.

1. Open the Video database.
2. Find all videos which cost $9.99 and have a retail price of $14.99. Print the results.
3. Find all videos released after 1993 which sell for $9.99. Print the results.
4. Find all the videos in the 01 category with a retail price of $9.99. Print the results.
5. Find all the 02 videos with a PG rating. Print the results.
6. Find all the videos in the 03 or the 04 category. Print the results.
7. Find all the videos which are not in the 01 category. Print the results.
8. Close the database.

# Chapter 10

## Advanced Forms

*Key Terms*

| TERM | DEFINITION |
| --- | --- |
| **Command Button** | a button, icon, or control placed on a form that performs a predefined action when the user clicks it |
| **List Box** | a box on a form that shows a list of acceptable values |
| **Combo Box** | a box on a form that accepts text input or shows a list of acceptable values |
| **Auto Expand** | a feature of the combo box that completes the data entry for you after you type the first few letters of an item in the list of allowed values |
| **Check Box** | a box on a form used to display a Yes/No value; the box contains an X if the value is Yes or True and is empty if the value is No or False |
| **Option Button** | a control on a form used to make one choice among several items |
| **Toggle Button** | a control on a form that shows normal for a No value and depressed for a Yes value |
| **Subform** | a form that shows data inside a main form; the subform is built from a table that is related to another table used to build the main form |

Forms can be used for browsing through the database, but they can do more than serve as a backdrop for your data. They can actively assist with data entry. They can show lists of items from which you can choose a value rather than having to type it. Forms can also include *command buttons*, which are buttons, icons, and controls on a form that perform predefined actions when you select them. They speed movement around and between forms. You can build forms that display data from more than one table.

**command buttons**

# Objective 1: Providing a List of Choices

In earlier chapters, you learned to put restrictions on some data fields. You made sure that State codes were shown as uppercase characters and that telephone numbers were entered according to an input mask. These techniques help avoid confusion and inconsistency in data entry. With these goals in mind, how would you handle a field like the PhoneType field? How would you prevent one person entering "Office" and someone else entering "Work" as the value in your database's PhoneType field? The answer is to provide a standard list of values, which everyone in the organization must use. You do this with a combo box or a list box. The *combo box* displays a list from which you can either choose or type a value. The *list box* is more restrictive; it shows a list of acceptable values from which you can choose one. The combo box has a really nice feature called *Auto Expand:* You type in the first few letters of the value you want and the combo box finishes entering the data for you. Depending on your needs, you would use either the combo or list box.

**combo box**

**list box**

**Auto Expand**

When creating a combo box, you can incorporate the list of values into the combo box and form. This is a good scheme for a short list that does not change often. For longer lists of values or lists with values that change constantly, you can design the combo box to refer to a table in the database. Another feature of the combo box is that it can be restricted like a list box; you can limit the data entered to just those values in the combo box list.

### Exercise 1: Building a combo box

In this exercise, you will build a form for the PhoneNumbers field. Then you will replace the PhoneType field with a combo box. Start by opening the Contacts database and selecting the Form tab.

1. Click New to build a form for the PhoneNumber table.
2. Select the PhoneNumbers table and click Form Wizards.
3. Use the Autoform Wizard.

   Now that you have the PhoneNumbers form (Fig. 10-1), you can begin to modify it.

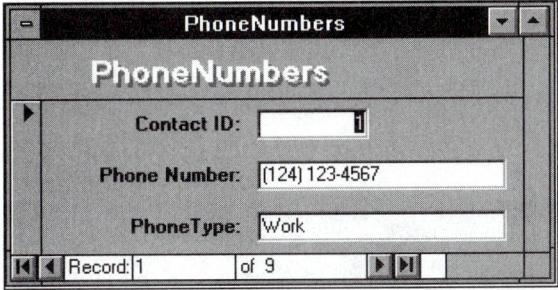

**Figure 10-1   PhoneNumbers form**

4. Switch to Form Design mode and maximize the Form window. Be sure the Toolbox is open and the Control Wizards button in the Toolbox is depressed.

5. Delete the PhoneType Field and its label.

6. Click the Combo Box button in the Toolbox.

   The button will stay depressed and the cursor will change as you move it to the Detail section of the form.

7. Draw a box approximately where the PhoneType box used to be.

   The Combo Box Wizard dialog box opens (Fig. 10-2).

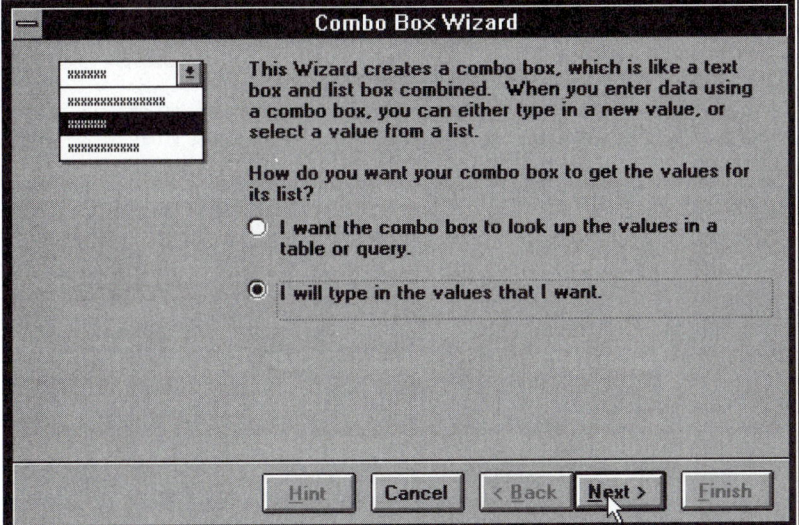

**Figure 10-2   Combo Box Wizard dialog box**

8. Select the option: I will type in the values that I want. Click Next.

9. Tell the Wizard that you only want one column in the box. Use ⌶TAB⌷ to move to the column to begin data entry.

10. Type the following values, one per line, and press `↵ ENTER` after each value: Work, Home, Fax, Pager, Cellular, Direct, 800 line, Data line, and 2nd line.

The items appear in the list in the order in which you type them (Fig. 10-3).

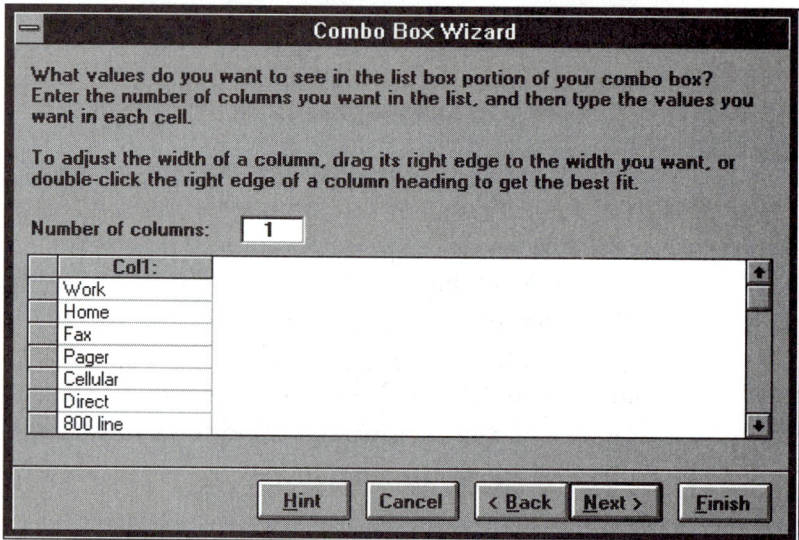

**Figure 10-3**   **Combo Box Wizard, entering the list of values**

11. Click Next.

12. Click the option: Store that value in this field. Select the PhoneType field, then click Next.

13. Type Type of Phone Number for the name of the combo box. Click Finish.

14. Adjust the size and placement of the combo box and label.

15. Switch to Form view to test your changes (Fig. 10-4).

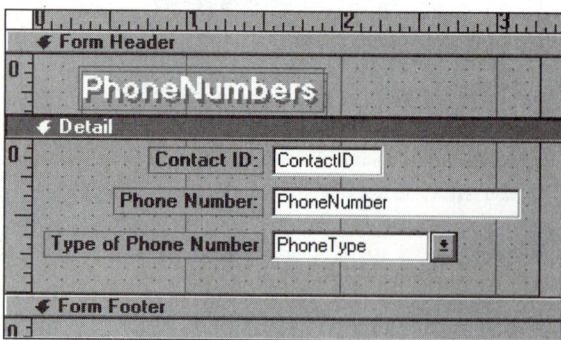

**Figure 10-4**   **Form with combo box**

16. Click the arrow to the right of the combo box to see the list of allowed values. Select Cellular.

17. Now type direct in the box. Notice that you do not need to type the entire word; MS-Access fills in the value using its Auto Expand feature.

18. Enter values for Home and Work. Watch Auto Expand in action.

## Exercise 2: Limiting input values

You want to limit the values entered to those listed in the combo box. You must go back to Design mode to change the properties of the combo box.

1. Return to Design mode and click the combo box to select it.

2. Click the Properties icon to open the Properties box (Fig. 10-5).

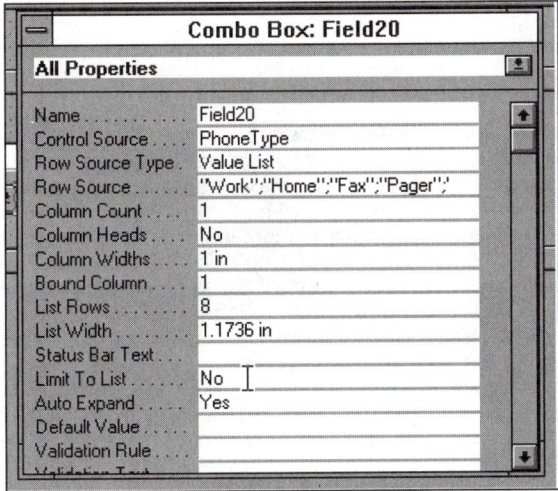

**Figure 10-5**   **Properties box for the combo box**

Notice the fourth item from the top of the box: the Row Source, which lists values. This is where you edit the list.

**TIP**   You can give yourself more space to work by pressing SHIFT + F2 to zoom the box to a larger size. Make your edits and click OK to close the zoom box.

3. Scroll down the properties list until you see the entry Limit to List. Change this value to Yes.

4. Close the Properties box and return to Form view.

5. Type Office in the combo box. Press ← ENTER.

You see a message telling you that what you typed is not a valid entry and you must match a value in the list (Fig. 10-6). Once you close the message box, MS-Access helpfully pops up the list of choices for you.

**Figure 10-6  Message box following an invalid data entry**

6. Select Work, which is a valid entry from the list.

7. Click File/Save Form As. When prompted for a name, type frmPhoneNumbers.

8. Click File/Close.

---

**Telecommuting, Boom or Bust?**

The number of virtual offices is swelling and more and more people are opting to telecommute to their jobs. Integrated Services Digital Network (ISDN) connections, which are used for high-speed data communications and are necessary to connect to corporate networks, are increasing dramatically. There are estimates that the number of basic-rate ISDN lines will double from 1993 to 1994.

At the same time, the companies that are moving their workers into telecommuting positions are facing some very real problems. An office in the home means there is no clear definition between work hours and off hours, which can lead to employee burnout. One vice-president has been trying to figure out how to stop her home-office staff from sending faxes in the middle of the night. "People are now thinking and working on the job 12 to 18 hours a day." Other companies tend to misuse the situation, expecting their employees to produce more than what could normally be done in an eight-hour day.

Some companies have had great success with telecommuting. Following the Los Angeles earthquake in January of 1994, Pacific Bell made a special effort to offer telecommuting opportunities to its workers. Nine months later, 90% of the people who took advantage of the "telecommuting relief package" are still working from home, 50% of whom are working five days per week. Almost half of those who started telecommuting in January had never considered it before, and more than half have managerial responsibilities (*Investor's Business Daily*, September 29, 1994).

But despite Pacific Bell's success, the Conference Board reports that fewer than 1% of employees at 155 businesses nationwide are telecommuters. "Some 75% of those surveyed say their greatest hurdle is convincing managers that employees can be productive and properly supervised when they work from home," says the report (*The Tampa Tribune*, October 2, 1994).

---

## Objective 2:  Displaying Yes/No Values

As you use your database, you will refine it to make it more useful. You might add a Christmas card field to the Contacts table. For such a field, a simple Yes/No value would suffice. Either the contact is on your Christmas card list or is not. On the form, all you need is a check box. A *check box* is a small square box that contains an X for a Yes value and is blank for a No value. You click the box to turn the checkmark on or off for yes or no.

**check box**

Alternatively, you could use an option button or toggle button for this field. An *option button* is round and shows a black center for a Yes value and a white center for a No value. Normally, option buttons are grouped

**option button**

**toggle button**

together and are used to select one of several options. They are also known as radio buttons. A *toggle button* appears pressed down for a Yes value and raised up for a No value. It is used to trigger some action inside the form and is not often used for a simple Yes/No selection.

## FEATURE

### Dialing out from MS-Access

If your computer has a modem, you can have MS-Access dial telephone numbers for you. It's easy to add an autodialer command button to your form. Follow the steps below:

1. Open the form in Design mode.

2. Place a command button on the form.

3. When the Wizard opens, select the Miscellaneous category and choose the autodialer option. Leave the Telephone icon in place.

4. For the button's name, type cmdAutodial.

5. Size and position the button. Switch to Form view and test.

The autodial feature is simple to use. In Form view, click a telephone number field and click the autodial command button. The autodialer shows you which number it will dial. It even has an option to include a prefix, like a 9, for an outside line. It will dial the number and tell you when to pick up the phone.

## Exercise 3: Displaying Yes/No values with a check box

In this exercise, you will add a Yes/No field and values to the Contacts table. Then open the Contacts form and add a check box.

1. Start at the Database window, with the Table tab selected.

2. Select the Contacts table and click Design.

3. Add a new field at the end of the table. Name the field ChristmasCard.

4. Make the field type Yes/No and set the default value in the properties box to No.

5. Switch to Datasheet view, saving the table when prompted.

6. Change the ChristmasCard value to Yes for the following names: Clark, Kanzaki, Monteleone, Moore, and Swenson.

7. Close the table, return to the Database window, and click the Form tab.

8. Select Contacts, click Design, and maximize the window.

9. Click the Check Box icon in the toolbox.

10. Position the cursor in the Detail section, and draw a box for the control. (Place this box to the right of the Address field.)

11. Open the Properties box (Fig. 10-7).

    At the top of the Properties box, you will see Check Box.

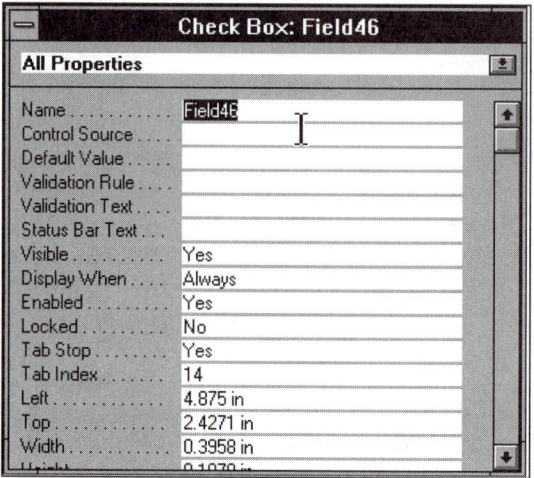

**Figure 10-7** **Properties box for Check Box**

12. Click the Control Source line of the box, then click the down arrow.

    A list of fields in the Contacts table appears.

13. Select the ChristmasCard Field.

14. Click the label for the check box.

15. Type Christmas Card: in the Caption field and close the Properties box.

16. Position and size the label and check box appropriately.

17. Switch to Form view and browse through the records (Fig. 10-8).

    Note that there is an X in the check box for only those contacts for whom you changed the option to Yes—that is, Clark, Kanzaki, Monteleone, Moore, and Swenson.

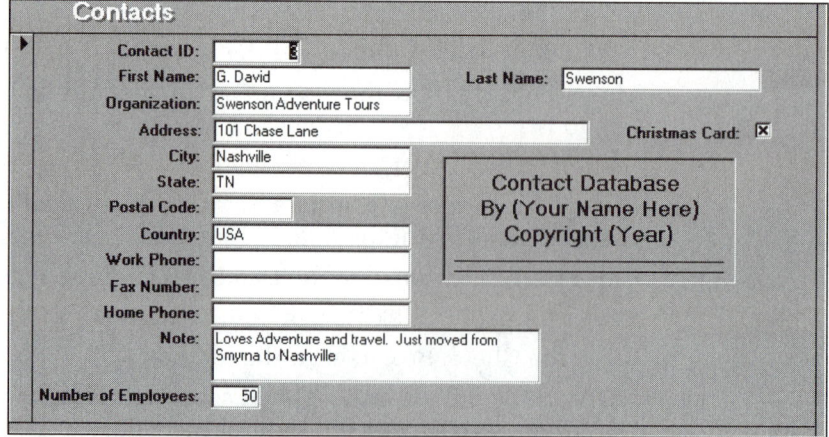

**Figure 10-8** **Form view with Check Box**

18. Add O'Leary to the Christmas Card list by clicking the check box when his record is on the screen.

19. Drop Kanzaki from the list by clicking the check box when his record is on the screen.

20. Close the form, saving the changes when prompted.

# Objective 3:  Creating a Command Button

There are some operations that you perform regularly on a form, such as go to another form or close a form. You can build a command button that will do these things for you automatically, instead of having to select a menu item or navigate your way around the Database window.

## Exercise 4: Creating a command button

In this exercise, you will put a command button on the Contacts form to close the form.

1. Open the Contacts form in Design mode.
2. Click the Command Button icon in the toolbox.
3. Draw a box for the button to the right of the Note field.

   The Command Button Wizard dialog box appears (Fig. 10-9).

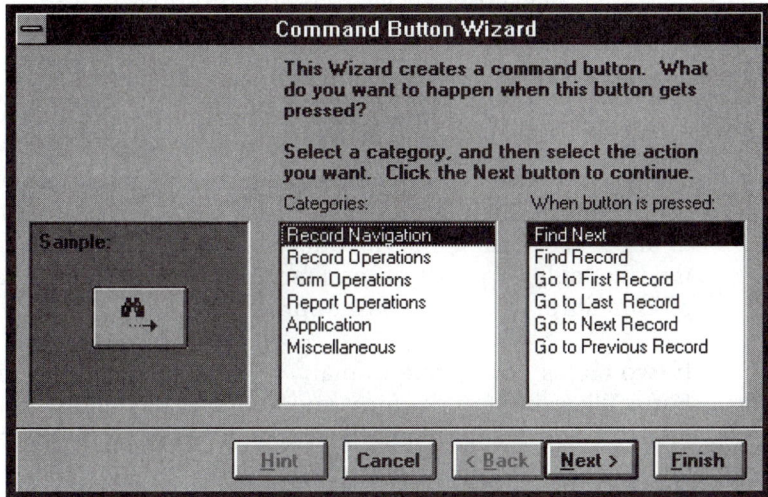

**Figure 10-9   *Command Button Wizard dialog box***

4. Select Form Operations from the Categories list, then Close Form from the list of actions. Click Next.

5. Choose any of the available options for the "look" of the button—a stop sign, an exit door, or just a text message. You can abbreviate the text to Close. Click Next.

6. Name your button cmdClose when prompted, then click Finish.

7. Position and size the button appropriately.

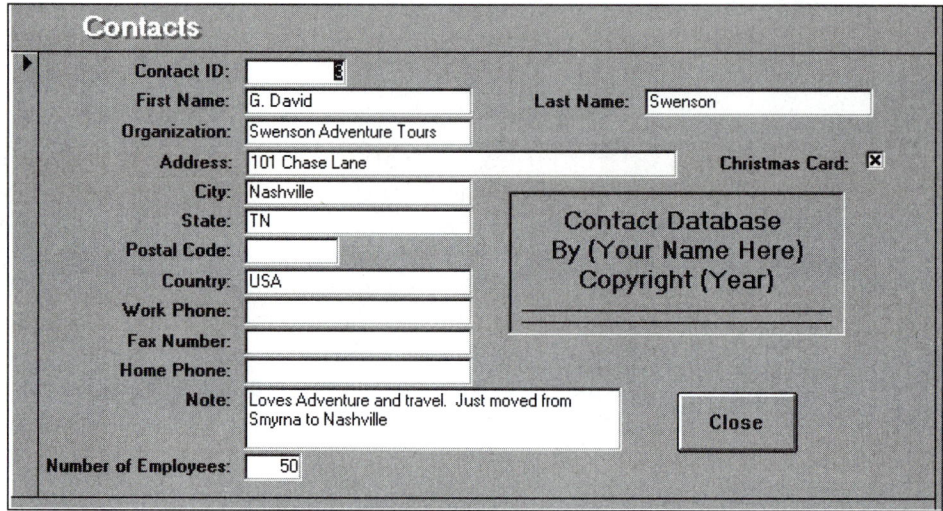

**Figure 10-10** **Form with command button**

8. Save the form with your changes. Switch to Form view (Fig. 10-10).

9. Click the Close button, and your form will close.

# Objective 4: Including Data from More Than One Table in a Form

The easiest way to display data from more than one table in a form is to base the form on a query. In the query, you select fields from related tables, then build a form using the query just as you would a table. The data from the two tables appears on one form. When two tables have a one-to-one relationship, this is the best approach.

**subform** If two tables have a one-to-many relationship a better method is to use a Form Wizard to build a form and *subform*. The main record (from the one) is displayed on the form and the associated data (from the many) is displayed on the subform. The subform is presented as a datasheet so that many records can be displayed at once.

## Exercise 5: A Multitable form

You will use the Form Wizard to build a form based on a query you created in Chapter 9. Then you will modify the PhoneType field to a combo box, as you did in Exercise 1.

1. Start at the Database window with the Form tab selected. Click New.

2. Select qryPhoneList and click the Form Wizard button.

   Make sure that you select the query, not the PhoneNumbers table.

3. Select the Single-Column Form Wizard and click OK.

4. Click the double arrow to select all the fields for the form, then click Next.

5. Select a style, then click Next.

6. For the form title, type Phone Directory. Accept the defaults and click Finish to see the form in Form view.

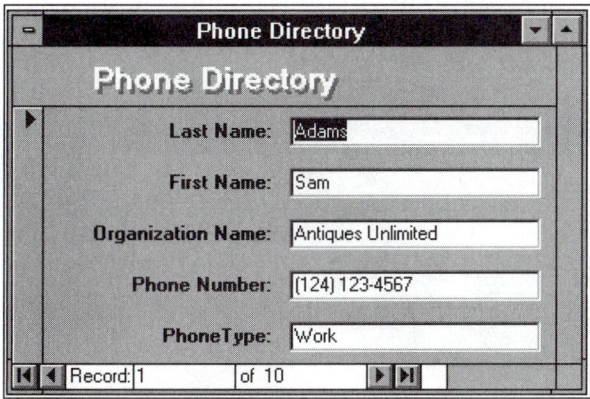

**Figure 10-11 Multitable form**

7. Switch back to Design mode.

8. Delete the PhoneType field and its label.

9. Create a combo box, as you did in Exercise 1, to replace the PhoneType field you just deleted. Use the same values for the list. The label will read Type of Phone Number. Adjust the size and placement of the combo box on the form. Switch to Form view (Fig. 10-12). Test the combo box.

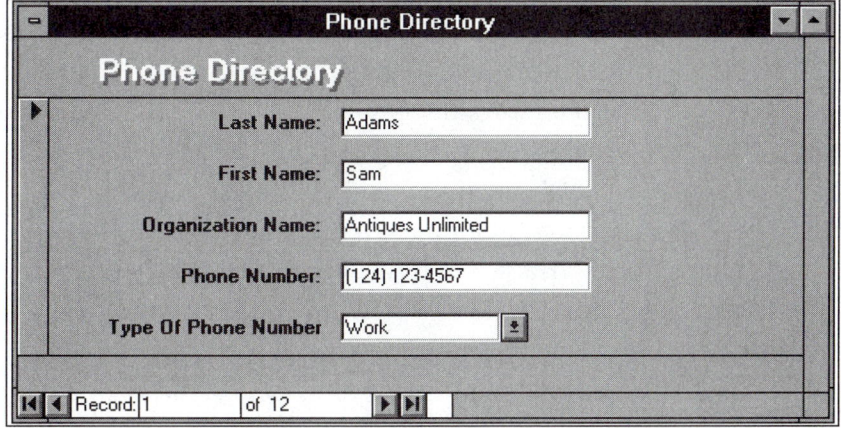

**Figure 10-12 Multitable form with combo box**

10. Save the form as frmPhoneList. Close the form.

## Exercise 6: Building a form and subform

In this exercise, you will use the Contacts and PhoneNumber tables to build a form and an associated subform.

1. Start at the Database window with the Form tab selected.
2. Click New, select the Contacts table, then click the Form Wizards button.
3. Select the Main/Subform Wizard and click OK to open the Wizard dialog box (Fig. 10-13).

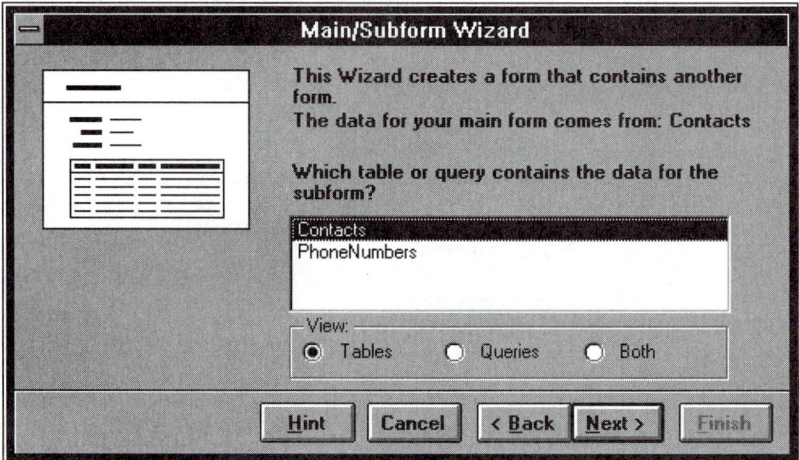

**Figure 10-13** *Main/Subform Wizard dialog box*

4. Select the PhoneNumbers table for the subform and click Next.
5. Select the following fields for the main form: LastName, FirstName, and OrganizationName. Click Next.
6. Select the following fields for the subform: PhoneNumber and PhoneType. Click Next.
7. Select a style for your form. Click Next.
8. For the form title, type Contacts + PhoneNumbers. Click Finish.

   A dialog box appears, telling you that you have to save the subform.
9. Click OK to close the dialog box.
10. Save the subform as frmSubPhones.

    The Wizard will finish building the form (Fig. 10-14).

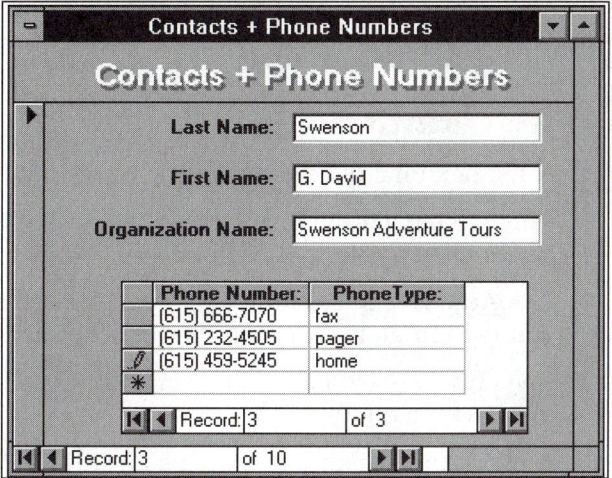

**Figure 10-14  Form with subform**

11. Browse through the records using the controls at the bottom of the main form.

    The numbers in the subform change as the Contact in the main form changes.

12. Find the record for David Swenson.

    Note the multiple entries in the subform.

13. Click File/Save Form As and save the form as frmContactsPhoneList.

14. Close the form, close the database, and exit from MS-Access.

## Chapter Summary

In this chapter, you learned how to create more complex forms that can assist you with your work. You learned how to limit the data input to a range of permitted values and how to pop up that list on the form when needed. You became familiar with using check boxes to display and change Yes/No values. Your form now includes command buttons to perform various functions. You learned another way to display data from more than one table—by using a form and subform.

## Review Questions

### True/False Questions

_____ 1. A list box on a form can show a list of values from a table.

_____ 2. When using a form with a subform, the field that joins the two tables must appear on the form.

_____ 3. The Auto Expand feature makes the box on a form bigger when you type in more text than the field can display.

_____ 4. The only way to show data from two related tables is to join them with a query.

_____ 5. A check box for a field contains an X if the field's value is Yes.

### Multiple-Choice Questions

_____ 6. You can create a command button on a form to
   A. close a form.
   B. add a new record.
   C. save a record.
   D. Any of the above.

_____ 7. For a multiple-choice question on a form with only one correct answer, you would use
   A. a check box.
   B. a toggle button.
   C. an option button.
   D. Either A or B.

_____ 8. To restrict a combo box to accept only permitted values, you would
   A. base the combo box on a table containing only the permitted values.
   B. type a list of permitted values in the Row Source in the Properties box.
   C. set the Auto Expand option to Yes in the Properties box.
   D. set the Limit to List option to Yes in the Properties box.

_____ 9. You can use a check box to display values from
   A. a memo field.
   B. a date field.
   C. a Yes/No field.
   D. an option field.

10. The values found in a combo box come from
    A. a list typed in the Row Source row of the Properties box.
    B. a table.
    C. a query.
    D. Any of the above.

## Fill-in-the-Blank Questions

11. A _____ box on a form can show a list of values or accept values that you type in the box.

12. You can turn the Auto Expand feature on or off by switching to _____ mode and changing the Auto Expand setting in the _____ box.

13. Pressing _____ zooms a box in which you are typing.

14. Associated records from tables in a one-to-many relationship can be shown on a form and _____.

15. A _____ button can be placed on a form and designed to perform an action on that form.

## Acumen-Building Activities

## Quick Projects

### 1. Building a combo box for MyBooks.

1. Open the Books database. Open the table MyBooks in Design mode.

2. Add two new fields—BookCover and ReadYet—to the end of the list of field names and assign each field the following data types, descriptions, and properties.

| FIELD NAME | DATA TYPE | DESCRIPTION | FIELD PROPERTIES |
|---|---|---|---|
| BookCover | text | Type of book | FieldSize: 20 |
| ReadYet | yes/no | Have you read the book yet? | Caption: Read Yet? Default Value: No |

3. Save the changes and close the Table Design window.

4. Open the form frmBooks in Design mode. Maximize the Design window. Make sure that the toolbox is visible and the Control Wizards button is depressed.

5. Widen the form to 5.5". Reduce the length of the BookCollectionID field. Lengthen the Title field. Place a combo box on the form alongside the Author field.

6. From the Combo Box Wizard, select the option to type in the values that you want for the list. Click Next. You want only one column in the box. Make the following entries, one per line, in column one: Hard Bound, Soft Bound, Paperback, and Magazine. Click Next.

7. Click the Store that value in this field option and store the value in the field BookCover. Click Next.

8. Type Book Cover: for the combo box label. Click Finish.

9. Adjust the size and placement of the combo box and label. Resize the window to normal and adjust the size of the window so you can see the combo box.

10.  Save the form. Switch to Form view. Fill in the categories as follows:

| | |
|---|---|
| Summer of the Danes | Soft Bound |
| Relativity | Hard Bound |
| Friday | Hard Bound |
| One Up On Wall Street | Soft Bound |
| Skinwalkers | Paperback |

## 2. Limiting input values with MyBooks.

This exercise is a continuation of Quick Project #1.

1. Return to Form Design mode and click the combo box to select it.

2. Open the Properties box and change the Limit to List option to Yes.

3. Close the Properties box and return to Form view.

4. Go to the third record (Friday), move to the combo box, and type Paper Back. Press ⏎ ENTER .

5. A dialog box appears because you entered an invalid entry. Click OK to remove the dialog box.

6. Select Paperback from the list in the combo box.

7. Save your work. Close the form.

## 3. Inserting a Yes/No field into MyBooks.

This exercise is a continuation of Quick Project #2.

1. Return to Form Design mode. In the Toolbox, click the CheckBox icon.

2. Position the cursor below the BookCover combo box and click once to place the check box.

3. Open the Properties box, click Control Source, and select ReadYet.

4. Click the label for the check box and type Read Yet? in the Caption row of the Properties box. Close the Properties box.

5. Size the label and position both the label and the check box appropriately.

6. Save your changes.

7. Switch to Form view and mark those books you have read.

8. Save your changes.

### 4. Building a Close Form command button for MyBooks.

This exercise is a continuation of Quick Project #3.

1. Return to Design mode and click the Command Button icon in the toolbox.

2. Place the button in the form header to the right of the title MyBooks.

3. From the Command Button Wizard, select FormOperations from the Categories list. Select CloseForm from the list of actions. Click Next.

4. Choose text and Close Form. Click Next.

5. Name this button cmdCloseForm. Click Finish.

6. Save your changes. Switch to Form view to test the button.

7. Click the Close button. Close the Books database.

## In-Depth Projects

### 1. Advanced forms for the CD database.

1. Open the CD database and go to the Query window.

2. Open the form frmCDCollection in Design mode and delete the Classification field and its label.

3. Create a new combo box to replace Classification. Position the cross-hairs at the upper left corner of the remaining shadow box and click.

4. In the Combo Box Wizard, select the option to type in the values that you want for the combo box list. There is only one column in the box, with the following entries: Cajun/Country, Classical, Country & Western, Easy Listening, Jazz, Movie Theme, Native American Flute, New Age Symphonic, Rock & Roll, and Symphonic Rock.

   Adjust the column width accordingly.

5. Store the combo box values in the Classification field.

6. For the label, type Classification. Click Finish. Adjust the size and placement of the combo box and label. Resize the shadow box.

7. Resize the window to normal and adjust the size so that you can see the Classification field. Save the form.

8. Switch to Form view. Test the new combo box. Close the CDCollection form.

9. Create a New form using the table CDCollection. Use the Form Wizards to build a main form and subform. Use the table Tracks for the subform.

10. For the main form, choose the following fields from the table CDCollection: Title, GroupName, and RecordingLabel.

11. For the subform, choose the following fields from the table Tracks: TrackNbr, TrackTitle, and TrackTime.

12. Choose your style. Name the form CDCollection and Tracks.

13. Save the subform and name it frmSubTracks.

14. Browse the main form. Find Cusco 2002 and add these track entries:

| 4 | Erosian | 5:39 |
|---|---|---|
| 5 | Ancient People | 4:25 |
| 6 | Unknown Paradise | 3:50 |
| 7 | Didjeridoo | 3:35 |
| 8 | From a Higher Point | 5:13 |
| 9 | Earth Waltz | 3:16 |

15. Save the data. Scroll through the new entries of the subform.

16. Save the form and name it frmCDPlusTracks.

17. Close the form. Close the CD database.

## 2. Advanced forms for the Dinner database.

1. Open the Dinner database. Open the query qryTripleJoin in Design mode.

2. Add DinnerID and GuestID to the query. Remove Sort in ascending order from the Date column. Choose Sort in ascending order on the FirstName column.

3. Run the query. Save the query. Close the query.

4. Create a New form using the table Dinners. Use the Form Wizards to build a Main/Subform. The query qryTripleJoin will be used for the subform.

5. For the main form, choose the following fields from the table Dinners: Place, Date, Time, Occasion, and Comments.

6. For the subform, choose the following fields from the query qryTripleJoin: GuestID, FirstName, and LastName.

7. Choose your style. Name the form Dinners and Guests. Open the form.

8. Save the subform and name it frmSubGuests. Browse the main form.

9. Switch to Form Design mode. Adjust the size of the main form and subform as necessary to show data for both. Switch back and forth between Form Design mode and Form View mode to look at the form as it will be used.

10. Save the main form and name it frmDinnerAndGuests.

11. Create a command button from the toolbox. Position it on the open space to the right of Date and Time.

12. From the Command Button Wizard select FormOperations, then select CloseForm.

13. Select the Exit picture and name the command button cmdExit. Click Finish. Position and size the button.

14. Save the form. Switch to Form view. Click the Close button. Close the Dinner database.

# CASE STUDIES

**Coffee-On-
The-Go:**

## Advanced Forms

In this chapter, you learned advanced techniques for creating forms. You will apply those skills to create a form for Coffee-On-The-Go.

1. Create a form which includes fields from both the Employee and the Benefits tables.
2. Create a combo box for the Location field that offers the user a list of choices.
3. Using the Form, add three new records.
4. Save your changes and close the database.

# CASE STUDIES

**Videos
West:**

## Advanced Forms

In this chapter, you learned advanced techniques for creating forms. You will apply those skills to create a form for Videos West.

1. Create a form which includes fields from both the Inventory and the Vendor tables.
2. Create a list box for the Vendor Name field that offers the user a list of choices.
3. Using the Form, add three new records.
4. Save your changes and close the database.

# Chapter 11

## Advanced Reports

*Objectives*
- Sorting Data
- Grouping Data
- Creating Calculated Fields
- Including Data from More Than One Table in a Report

*Key Terms*

| TERM | DEFINITION |
|------|------------|
| Grouping | logically organizing data in a report by dividing it into groups based on the value of a field in the report |

**grouping**

When you generate a report from a database, you want to organize the data, which can be sorted in various ways. Exactly how it is sorted depends on the data and the purpose for which it is being used. If you want a telephone directory listing, you sort by last name. A set of mailing labels is sorted by postal code. You can also group the data in your reports. *Grouping* means logically organizing data in a report by dividing it into groups based on the value of a field in the report. An example of grouping is a list of engine-part numbers, grouped by a prefix that indicates which factory makes each part.

A report often contains data which is calculated from other data. As you build more complex reports, you will find that you need to incorporate data from more than one table. You may need to change reports to sort and group the data in a different manner.

## Objective 1:  Sorting Data

In a database, data is stored in a certain order. However, as you have already learned, your report need not show the data in that same order. By changing settings in the report, you can control how the data is presented.

MS-Access makes this easy—there is a Sorting and Grouping icon on the top toolbar. When you open the Sorting and Grouping dialog box, notice the default values in the box. If you build a report from a query that has sorted or grouped data, the Report Wizard uses this information to define the sorting or grouping scheme in the report.

## Exercise 1: Sorting data

In this exerise, you will use the report that you built in Chapter 8 and modify it to sort the output in different ways.

1. Open the Contacts database and select the Report tab.
2. Open the report rptContactList in Design mode.
3. Click the Sorting and Grouping icon on the menu bar. The Sorting and Grouping dialog box opens (Fig. 11-1).

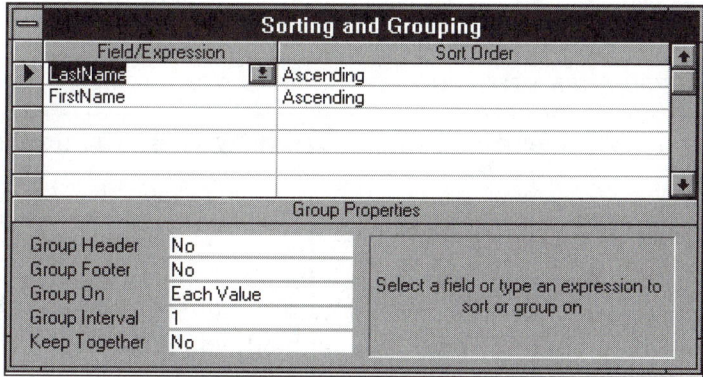

**Figure 11-1**  **Sorting and Grouping dialog box**

4. Use Print Preview to verify that the report is being sorted by LastName and then FirstName. Return to Design mode.
5. Click LastName in the Field/Expression list, then click the down arrow at the right of the box. Select PostalCode.
6. Click the margin of the box to the left of the F in FirstName.

   To delete an entry, you must select the entire line and then delete it.
7. Press (DELETE) to remove the FirstName sort. When prompted, confirm that you do want to delete this line.
8. Preview the report to verify that it is sorted by PostalCode. Return to Design mode.
9. Change the sort field to OrganizationName.
10. Preview the output (Fig. 11-2). Return to Design mode.

| | | | |
|---|---|---|---|
| **Name:** | Sam | | Adams |
| **Organization Name:** | Antiques Unlimited | | |
| **Address:** | 47 Main Street | | |
| **City:** | Boston | MA | 01738- |
| **Work Phone:** | (124) 123-4567 | **Fax Number:** | (124) 123-9874 |

| | | | |
|---|---|---|---|
| **Name:** | George | | Langford |
| **Organization Name:** | Langford Trucking | | |
| **Address:** | 1 Farm Road | | |
| **City:** | Mount Vernon | VA | 00111- |
| **Work Phone:** | (703) 234-1234 | **Fax Number:** | (703) 234-1111 |

| | | |
|---|---|---|
| **Name:** | Margaret | Moore |
| **Organization Name:** | Liberty Shield Insurance Inc. | |
| **Address:** | 145 Independence Ave., | |
| **City:** | Philadelphia | PA    01873- |

**Figure 11-2   The new report sorted by OrganizationName**

# Objective 2:  Grouping Data

You can sort records in a report without grouping them. You can define groupings only for sorted fields. Why? In order to separate the data into groups based on the value of some field, you must first sort the data on that field.

When you group data, you have the option of adding a header, a footer, or both to the group. For example, if you group by company name, you can add a header that shows the name of each company. You can keep a group of records all together on one page in a report. In other words, if all the records for a group do not fit on the current page, MS-Access begins a new page. This happens, except when there are too many records to fit on a single page. In that case, MS-Access simply ignores the request to keep all the records of the group together.

## Exercise 2: Grouping data

In this exercise, you will use the same report as in Exercise 1 to group the data. You will group on OrganizationName and add a group header to identify the group. You must specify what will be in the group header.

1. In the Sorting and Grouping dialog box, change the GroupHeader value to Yes.

   The symbol on the OrganizationName line changes from an arrowhead to the Sorting and Grouping symbol with an arrowhead. This indicates that the OrganizationName field is being used to group the data.

2. Move the dialog box out of the way and scroll until you see the OrganizationName header section.

3. Increase the height of this section to 0.6".

4. Click the Field List icon on the toolbar to open the list of fields.

5. Drag the OrganizationName field from this list and drop it in the OrganizationName header section. Click the Field List icon on the toolbar to close the list of fields.

6. Delete the label from the newly added field. Change the field font to Arial, 14 point. Enlarge the field, if necessary.

7. Preview the report. Find Precision Surveys, Inc. (Fig. 11-3).

   The header is shown once and then the four contacts are listed—but they are not in alphabetical order.

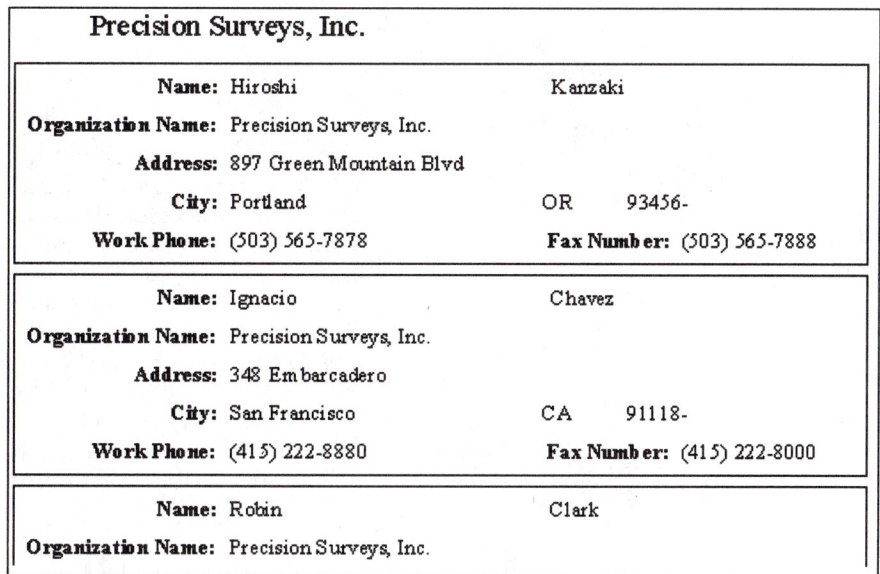

**Figure 11-3  The grouped report**

8. Return to Design mode. In the Sorting and Grouping dialog box, add a second sort line, using LastName in Ascending order.

9. Preview the report. Return to Design mode.

## Exercise 3: Keeping data together within groups

Sometimes on a report the records in a group are split between two pages. In this exercise, you instruct MS-Access to keep all the records in a group on a single page.

1. In the Sorting and Grouping dialog box, make sure that the OrganizationName line is selected.

2. Change the Keep Together value to Whole Group.

3. Preview the report. The contacts from Precision Surveys appear together. Return to Design mode.

# Objective 3: Creating Calculated Fields

In a previous chapter, you learned how to calculate totals and subtotals in queries. We said that any value that can be calculated from other data values should not be stored in the database. It is possible to calculate values in a report, so even if the table or query does not contain the value which you need, you can compute it on the report.

MS-Access has available a wide range of functions that may be used in the calculation of fields. These include SUM, AVG, and COUNT.

Calculated fields can be placed anywhere in the report. One common place for calculated fields is the group footer, where they summarize the records that appear in the Detail section.

## FEATURE

### Mail merge

You can use records from your database to print out "personalized" letters. This is called a mail merge. It is possible to send data from an MS-Access table or query directly into a word processor. However, you can do mail merge tasks completely within MS-Access. You can build a form letter in MS-Access and have it fill in the names and addresses of those people in your database to whom you want to send the letter. You build a query to extract just the names and addresses you need. Then you create the form letter, which is actually a report with a lot of text on it. On the report, you add the database fields that make up the inside address and salutation. You can add formatting for a professional appearance; you can even build your own letterhead. As a final touch, you can use the same query to generate a set of mailing labels to go with the letters.

## Exercise 4: Calculated fields in the group footer

In this exercise, you will add a group footer and specify what will appear in it. Start with a count of the number of records in each group.

1. In the Sorting and Grouping dialog box, change the Group Footer setting to Yes.
2. Scroll down the form to the OrganizationName footer.
3. Create a text box in the footer. You may need to open the Toolbox if it is not already visible.
4. Change the label for the text box to Number of Contacts in the Organization:. Enlarge the label if necessary.
5. Click the text box that is currently labeled Unbound.

   Unbound means that the box is not yet tied to a field or expression.

6. Replace Unbound, typing =Count (ContactID) in its place.

7. Click the text box again to select it. Click the Left-Align icon on the toolbar to align the value along the left edge of the box, close to the label (Fig. 11-4).

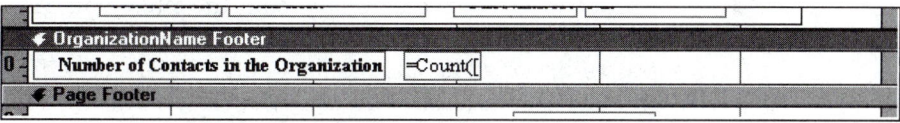

**Figure 11-4** **Calculated fields in the group footer**

8. Preview the report (Fig. 11-5). Return to Design mode. Close the Sorting and Grouping dialog box.

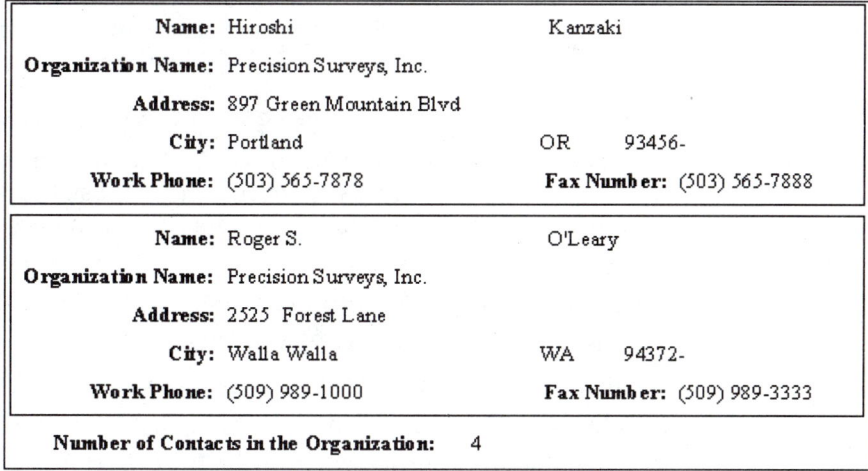

**Figure 11-5** **Calculated fields in the group footer of the report**

9. Save the report. Print the report. Close the report

# Objective 4: Including Data from More Than One Table in a Report

A report can be built from more than one table or query. The easiest way to build a report that includes data from multiple tables is to first build a query that selects the data from the tables. Then you can use the Report Wizard to build the report.

Often, for ease of data entry and efficiency in storage, you will use codes in your database. A typical example is the two-letter state code. Instead of storing California, you just store CA. Anyone who enters a large amount of data appreciates such abbreviations, but you may want to show the full word rather than the code on a printed report. Perhaps you are producing a report for clients who are unfamiliar with the shorthand codes used for product names or part numbers. How do you change a code into a full word? The best method is to use a reference or look-up table.

In Exercise 5, you will build a small reference table of states so that you can use it in a report. Once you have built the table, you can use it for other forms, reports, and queries. It can be tied to a list or combo box on a form, so you can pop up a list of states during data entry. MS-Access allows you to use tables from other databases, so you can refer to this reference table while working on other databases. This is known as attaching a table. Some database designers like to keep all their code reference tables—such as state codes, country telephone codes, postal codes—in one database. They attach to these tables from whatever other database they might be using. This has a real benefit: when you change a code or the meaning of a code, you change it in only one place. For every table in which that code is used, the value is automatically updated. Of course, if you plan to distribute your database applications to others, you have to remember to include the .mdb file with the code reference tables.

## Exercise 5: Building a report that uses more than one table

Previously you built a multitable query that combined the Contacts and Phone Number tables. In this exercise, you will use this query as the basis for the next report. The layout of the report reflects the relationship between the two tables.

1. Start a New report. Select qryPhoneList. Use the Report Wizards.
2. Select the Groups/Totals Report Wizard. Click OK.
3. Click the double arrow to move all the fields into the report. Click Next.
4. Select LastName as the field to group by. Click Next.
5. Leave the group order as Normal. Click Next.
6. Select PhoneType as the field to sort by. Click Next.
7. Pick a style for your report. Click Next.
8. Give the report the title Contacts and Phone Numbers.
9. Turn off the Calculate Percentages option. Click Finish (Fig. 11-6).

   The phone numbers for Swenson are listed as a subgroup under his name.

| Swenson Adventure Tours | | |
|---|---|---|
| | (615) 666-7070 | Fax |
| | (615) 459-5245 | Home |
| | (615) 232-4505 | Pager |

**Figure 11-6   Multitable report grouped by last name**

10. Print the report. Exit from Print Preview to return to Design mode.

# Exercise 6: Changing the grouping in the report

The last report was grouped by LastName. Now you will change the report to group by OrganizationName.

1. Click the Sorting and Grouping icon to open the dialog box.
2. Click LastName and change it to OrganizationName.
3. Change PhoneType to LastName and set the Group Header option to Yes.
4. Add a third row using the field PhoneType (Fig. 11-7).
5. Close the Sorting and Grouping dialog box.

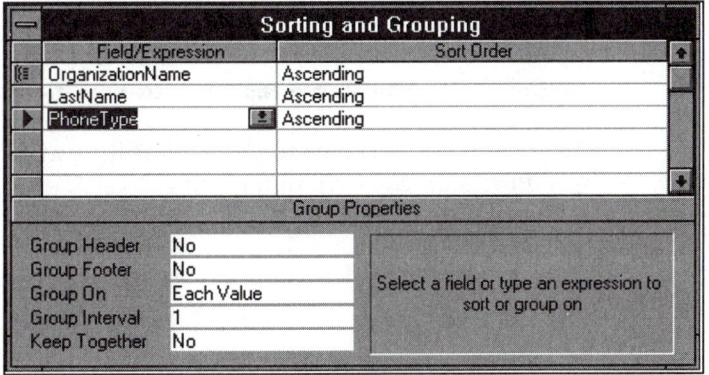

**Figure 11-7  Multitable report grouped by OrganizationName**

An extra header row appears. If you leave it blank, you will not see all the contacts in a company that has more than one contact. The report will print the LastName only when the OrganizationName changes, so you will see only the first contact at each company. There is a way to resolve this.

6. Use Print Preview to confirm the problem, checking the Precision Surveys listing. Return to Design mode.
7. Click LastName in the OrganizationName header. Hold down (SHIFT) and click the FirstName field to select it at the same time. Do not select the OrganizationName field.
8. Press (CTRL)+(X) to delete these fields and put them on the Windows clipboard.
9. Move to the LastName header section and press (CTRL)+(V) to paste these fields into that section (Fig. 11-8).

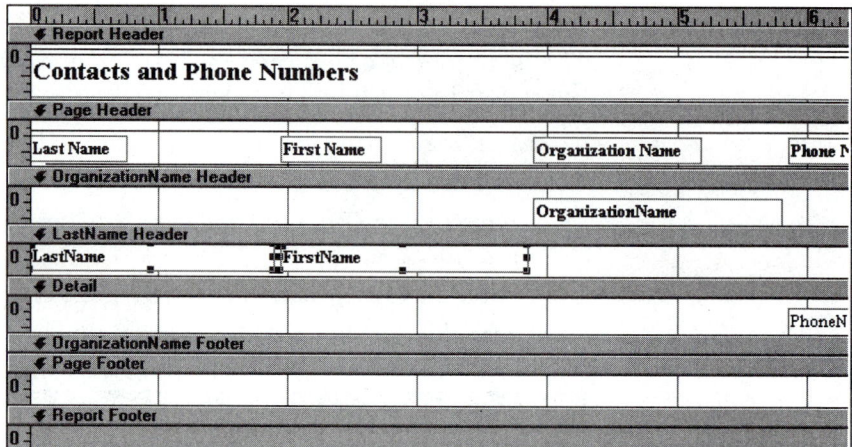

**Figure 11-8**   *Multitable report with modified group-by criteria*

10. Preview the report to verify that it now lists all the contacts at Precision Surveys in a group.

11. Save the report as rptBusinessPhone. Print the report. Close the report.

## Exercise 7: Building a reference table for a report

1. Start at the Database window with the Tables tab selected.

2. Click New. Click New Table to begin a new table layout.

3. Make the first field StateCode. Set it to a text field with field size 2.

4. Make the second field StateName. Set it to a text field with field size 24.

5. Switch to Datasheet view, saving the table as tblrefState when prompted. Do *not* create a primary key for this table. Enter the following pairs of values:

   | | |
   |---|---|
   | CA | California |
   | CT | Connecticut |
   | DC | District of Columbia |
   | ID | Idaho |
   | MA | Massachusetts |
   | OR | Oregon |
   | PA | Pennsylvania |
   | TN | Tennessee |
   | VA | Virginia |
   | WA | Washington |

6. Close the table and return to the Database window.

7. Click the Query tab. Click New. Click New Query.

8. Add the Contacts and tblrefState tables to the query.

9. Drag and drop the State field from the Contacts table onto the StateCode field in the tblrefState table to establish the relationship.

10. Include all fields from both tables in the query output by double-clicking the asterisk at the top of each table's field listing (Fig. 11-9).

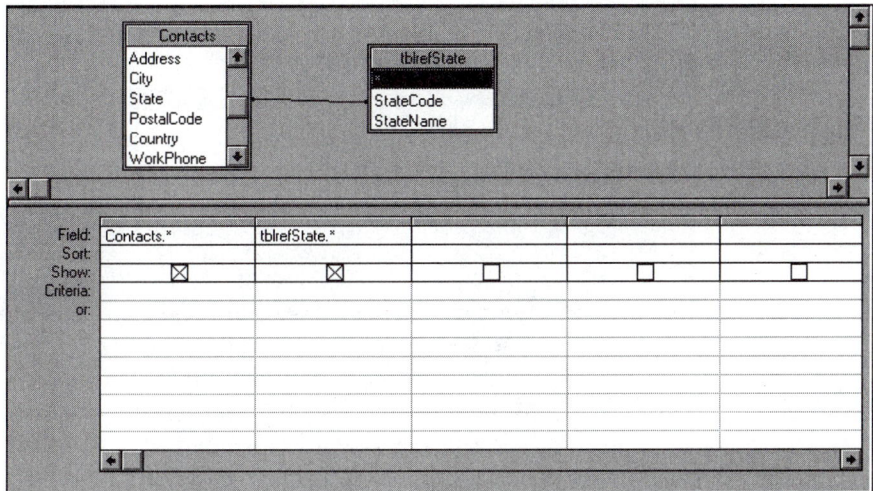

**Figure 11-9**    **Building the query with a reference table**

11. Close the query. When prompted for a name, save as qryContactsAndStates.

## Exercise 8: Including data from a reference table in a report

In this exercise, you will use the Mailing Labels Wizard. In addition to mailing labels, this wizard can produce a directory-type listing with multiple columns per page. In this exercise, you will build the report and then substitute the full state names for the corresponding state codes.

1. Start at the Database window with the Report tab selected.

2. Click New, select qryContactsAndStates, and use the Report Wizards.

3. Select the Mailing Label Wizard.

4. From the list of Available fields, select FirstName. Select Space.

5. From the list of Available fields, select LastName. Select Newline.

6. From the list of Available fields, select Address. Select Newline.

7. From the list of Available fields, select City. Select Space twice.

8. From the list of Available fields, select StateName. (Make sure that you select the StateName field, not the State field). Select Space twice.

9. From the list of Available fields, select PostalCode (Fig. 11-10).

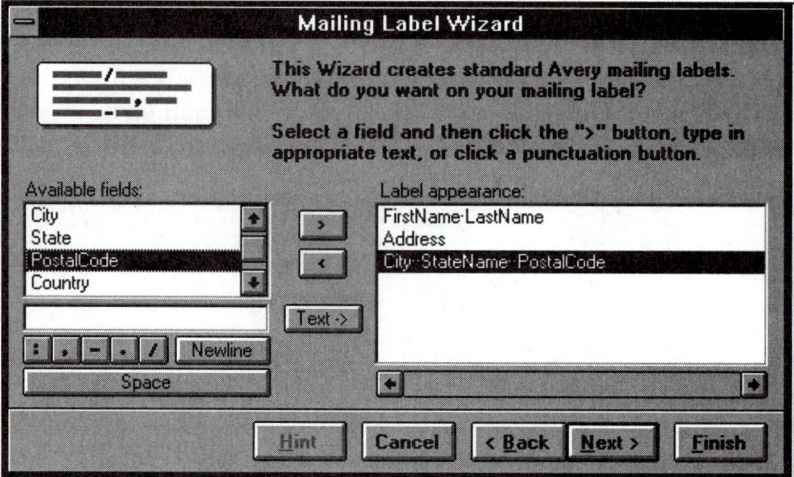

**Figure 11-10  Building the report with a reference table**

10. Click Next, choose sort by LastName, and click Next.
11. Choose the 5162 labels. Click Finish.

    Check the line that contains City, StateName, and PostalCode. The state names are shown in full (Fig. 11-11). Return to Design mode.

| | |
|---|---|
| Margaret Moore | Roger S. O'Leary |
| 145 Independence Ave., | 2525 Forest Lane |
| Philadelphia Pennsylvania 01873 | Walla Walla Washington 94372- |

**Figure 11-11  The report with full state names**

12. Use Format/Report Header-Footer to add a report header. Insert a label from the toolbar. Type your name in the label.
13. Print the report.
14. Save the report as rptContactsMailing. Close the report.
15. Close the database, then exit MS-Access.

## Chapter Summary

In this chapter, you modified your reports to group and sort data. You learned how to add calculated fields. Using a multitable query, you built a report that shows data from more than one table. You modified the report to change the sorting and grouping. The idea of reference tables was introduced. You built a reference table, used it in a multitable query to modify how the data was presented, and created a report with the modified data.

## Review Questions

### True/False Questions

_____ 1. You can sort data in a report without grouping it.

_____ 2. You can group data in a report without sorting it.

_____ 3. When a report is based on a query, the data on the report must be sorted in the same order as the data in the query.

_____ 4. To use a reference table from another database, you must copy it into your current database.

_____ 5. Calculated fields can be placed anywhere in a report.

### Multiple-Choice Questions

_____ 6. A report can be constructed from
- A. a query.
- B. a table.
- C. any number of queries and/or tables.
- D. Any of the above.

_____ 7. Arranging a list of data items in groups based on a common data value is called
- A. grouping.
- B. sorting.
- C. an array.
- D. ordering.

_____ 8. Arranging a list of data items in ascending or descending order is called
- A. grouping.
- B. sorting.
- C. an array.
- D. ordering.

_____ 9. By placing a calculated field in the footer section of a report, you summarize the records that appear in the report
- A. header section.
- B. footer section.
- C. grouping section.
- D. detail section.

_____ 10. If a field is unbound, it
- A. can be moved anywhere on the report.
- B. is not tied to a field or expression.
- C. has no limits on the values which it can accept.
- D. has no validation rules.

## Fill-in-the-Blank Questions

11. A field on a report does not have to be stored in the database, it can be _____ from other fields.

12. If you want to group records in a report based on the value of a field, you indicate this in the _____ in the Report Design screen.

13. If you want to add up the number of records displayed in a group, you use the _____ function in the report footer.

14. A table that is used to decode values from other tables is called a _____ table.

15. If you want to use a table from another database, you can _____ it to the database you are currently using.

## Acumen-Building Activities

### Quick Projects

### 1. Sorting data in a report for MyBooks.

1. Open the Books database. Go to the Reports window.
2. Confirm that rptBookList is sorted by Title.
3. In Report Design mode, click the Sorting and Grouping icon.
4. Change the sort field from Title to Author and leave it in ascending order.
5. Run the report and check the sort order. Return to Design mode.

### 2. Building a group header for MyBooks.

This exercise is a continuation of Quick Project #1.

1. In the Sorting and Grouping dialog box, change the Group Header value to Yes to open an AuthorHeader section in the report.
2. Delete the label from the Author field. Drag the Author field from the Detail section into the AuthorHeader section and position it on the left side of the Header section. Make it bold and italic.
3. Preview the report. Return to Design mode.

### 3. Inserting page breaks into the report for MyBooks.

This exercise is a continuation of Quick Project #2.

1. Close the Sorting and Grouping dialog box. Open the Properties dialog box.
2. Click in the AuthorHeader section. Make sure the Properties box reads Section:GroupHeader0.
3. Set the ForceNewPage property to BeforeSection.
4. Preview the report. Return to Design mode.

### 4. Calculating totals in the report for MyBooks.

This exercise is a continuation of Quick Project #3.

1. Close the Properties dialog box. Open the Sorting and Grouping dialog box.
2. Change the Group Footer setting to Yes.
3. Place a text box on the right edge of the footer. Resize the label and modify it to read Number of Books by this Author:.
4. Modify the text in the Unbound box, changing it to read =Count (BookCollectionID).
5. Left align Count(BookCollectionID). Preview the report.
6. Return to Design mode. Close the Sorting and Grouping dialog box.
7. Save the report. Close the report. Close the Books database.

## In-Depth Projects

### 1. Advanced reports for the CD database.

1. Open the CD database. Go to the Query window.
2. Modify query qryCompound. Remove the selection criteria from any of the columns. Add GroupName after Title; add Length to the end of the query.
3. Run the query to check it. Save the changes. Close the query.
4. Create a New report using qryCompound and the Report Wizards.
5. Make it a Tabular report and use all fields available. Sort by Title. Pick your style. Type CD Collection Detail Report as the name of the report.
6. Exit Print Preview. In Design mode, in the report footer, change the =Sum(YearReleased) to =Avg(YearReleased). Preview the report.
7. Print the report. Exit Print Preview. Close the report. Save it, naming it rptDetail.
8. Create a second New report using qryJoin and the Report Wizards.
9. Make it a Groups/Totals report and use all fields available. Group by Title, then GroupName. Use Normal grouping for each. Sort by TrackTitle. Pick your style. Type CD Report as the name of the report.
10. Print the report. Exit Print Preview. Close the report. Save it, naming it rptGroup.
11. Close the CD database.

### 2. Advanced reports for the Dinner database.

1. Open the Dinner database.
2. Create a New report using qryGuestByCity and the Report Wizards.
3. Make it a Tabular report and use all fields available. Sort by FirstName. Pick your style. Type Listing of Guests By City as the name of the report.
4. Print the report. Exit Print Preview. Close the report. Save it, naming it rptGuestsByCity.

5. Create a second New report using qryTripleJoin and the Report Wizards.

6. Make it a Groups/Totals report and use only the Date, Place, FirstName, and LastName fields. Group by Date. Use Normal grouping. Sort by FirstName. Pick your style. Type Dinner Report as the name of the report.

7. Exit Print Preview. In Detail view, left align the Date field in the Date Header section. Preview the results.

8. Print the report. Exit Print Preview. Close the report. Save it, naming it rptGroup.

9. Close the Dinner database.

# CASE STUDIES

**Coffee-On-The-Go:**

### Advanced Reports

In this chapter, you learned advanced techniques for creating reports. You will apply those skills to create reports for Coffee-On-The-Go.

1. Create a report which includes data from both the Employee and Benefits tables.

2. Group the data in the report by the Location field.

3. Sort the records by Last Name within each location.

4. Calculate the average of all the salaries.

5. Print the report.

6. Save the report and close the database.

# CASE STUDIES

**Videos West:**

### Advanced Reports

In this chapter, you learned advanced techniques for creating reports. You will apply those skills to create reports for Videos West.

1. Create a report which includes data from both the Inventory and Vendor tables.

2. Group the data in the report by the Type field.

3. Sort the records by Title within each type.

4. Calculate the total number of videos in the quantity field.

5. Print the report.

6. Save the report and close the database.

# Chapter 12

## Macro Basics

*Key Terms*

| TERM | DEFINITION |
|---|---|
| **Macro** | a set of instructions that performs a sequence of tasks |
| **Macro Group** | a group of associated macros that run independently but are usually related or similar in function |
| **Autoexec Macro** | a macro that runs every time the database opens |

**macro**  A *macro* is a set of instructions that performs a sequence of tasks. If you have experience with a word processor, you may have used macros. But macros in MS-Access differ from macros in a word-processing program. When you create a macro in a word-processing program, you record it by performing a task once while the program keeps track of the steps. Then you can replay the recorded macro. There is no macro recording option in MS-Access. The macros must be built by the database designer. Fortunately, MS-Access provides a lot of help during this process. In word-processing programs, macros are run by pressing a key combination—for example, Alt+P to print the current page. MS-Access uses command buttons and other controls to run macros.

# Objective 1: What Is a Macro?

In MS-Access, a macro consists of a set of instructions stored in the database that can be used whenever required. In the Database window, one of the tabs is marked Macro. This is where the macros are stored. You can run macros directly from this tab list, but, more commonly, macros are associated with controls on forms. In this chapter, you will build a macro, put a command button on a form, and associate the command button with the macro so that when you click the button, the macro will run.

Another way to run a macro is to connect it to a field on a form. When you enter data in the field, the macro automatically performs some action, such as checking to see if an item is in stock.

**autoexec macro** The *autoexec macro* is a unique macro. When you open a database, MS-Access looks for the autoexec macro and runs it. You can use this special macro to open a form when you start an MS-Access database.

**macro group** MS-Access allows you to put associated macros in a *macro group*. The macros within a group run independently but are related. For example, you may choose to put all the macros for one form in a group. This grouping makes it easier to maintain the database.

# Objective 2: Creating a Macro

When you build a macro you must decide what you want the macro to do and how it will be activated. The first step is to create the macro in the Macro Design window of the database. Then you build controls or command buttons and connect the macro to these controls or command buttons.

In Exercise 1, you will build a macro that will be activated by a command button on the Contacts form. When you push the button on the Contacts form, the macro opens the frmPhoneNumbers form and shows you the phone numbers for the person who is currently displayed on the Contacts form. Then you will build a second control button on the frmPhoneNumbers form, which will be attached to another macro. This second macro will close the frmPhoneNumbers form and return you to the Contacts form.

## Exercise 1: The Macro Design window

In this exercise, you will familiarize yourself with the Macro Design window.

1. Start at the Database window with the Macro button selected. Click New.

   The Macro Design window opens (Fig. 12-1). The toolbar for this window is very different from others you have seen.

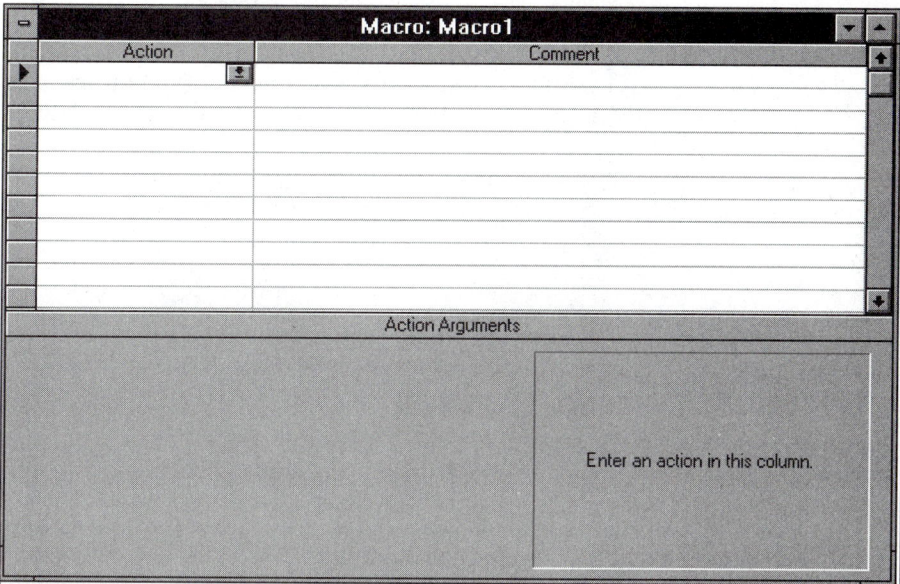

**Figure 12-1    The Macro Design window**

2. Use the balloon help to check the five buttons on the left of the toolbar (Fig. 12-2).

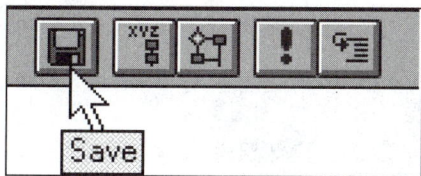

**Figure 12-2    The Macro Design Window toolbar**

The first button is the Save button, which is used to save the macro to the hard disk. The second and third buttons add the names and conditions columns to the Macro Design window. The fourth button runs the macro. The fifth button runs the macro one step at a time; this is used for debugging.

## Exercise 2: Creating a macro

In this exercise you will build your first macro.

1. Make sure that the Macro Name column is in the Design window; if not, click the Macro Names button on the toolbar to add it.

2. In the first row of the Macro Name column, type OpenfrmPhoneNumbers.

3. Move to the Action column, click the down arrow, and select the action Open Form.

The Action Arguments box opens at the bottom of the window (Fig. 12-3). The arguments in this box describe the action you have chosen.

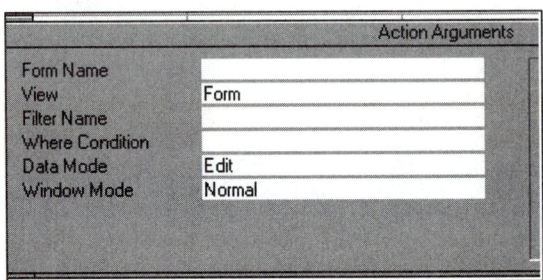

**Figure 12-3   The Action Arguments box**

4. In the Action Arguments box, click the Form Name row and then select frmPhoneNumbers.

5. Click the Where Condition row, then click the little button with the three dots, which appears at the right side of the row.

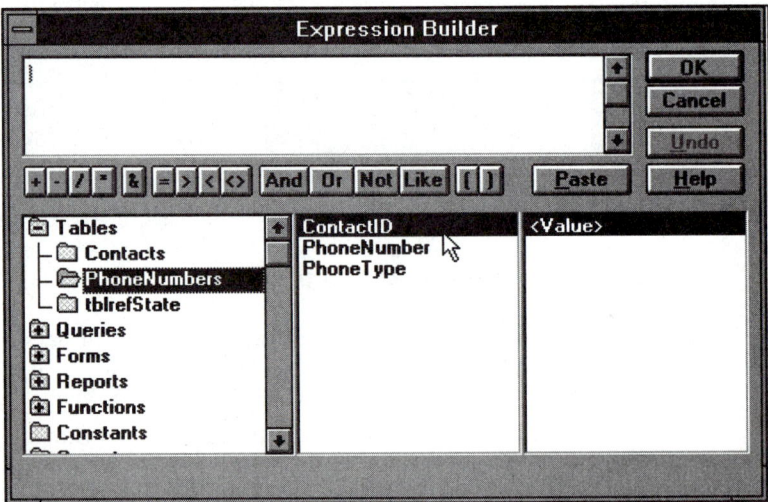

**Figure 12-4   The Expression Builder**

The Expression Builder opens (Fig. 12-4), where you set up the link that opens the frmPhoneNumbers form with only the records related to the record on the Contacts main form.

6. Double-click Tables in the lower left window. When the sublist opens, double-click PhoneNumbers.

7. Double-click ContactID in the middle window.

The first part of the expression appears in the upper window.

8. Click the button with the equals sign.
9. In the lower left window, double-click Forms.
10. In the sublist, double-click AllForms. Double-click Contacts.
11. Double-click ContactID in the center window.

   The expression is complete (Fig. 12-5). It states that the ContactID value should be the same on both the Contact form and the frmPhoneNumbers form.

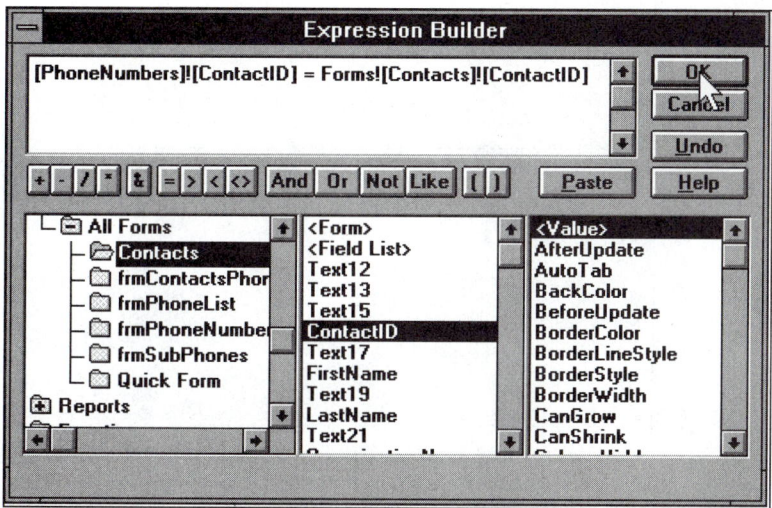

**Figure 12-5** **The Expression Builder with the completed expression**

12. Click OK to close the Expression Builder and return to the Macro Design window. Type Open the frmPhoneNumbers form. in the Comments column.
13. Click on the second row of the Action column below the OpenForm command. Select the action Maximize.

   This will maximize the frmPhoneNumbers form when it is opened by the macro.

14. Type Maximize the frmPhoneNumbers form in the Comments column.

# Objective 3: Saving a Macro

You must save a macro before you can use it. The name you give the macro when you save it is not the same as the macro name that you supplied while building the macro. What you are saving and naming is actually the macro group. A macro group can contain more than one macro. Think of the name you supplied earlier as the name of a macro and the group name you will supply in Exercise 3 as a macro family name.

## Exercise 3: Saving the macro

1. Click the Save icon to save the macro. Name it mcrConPhone (Fig. 12-6).

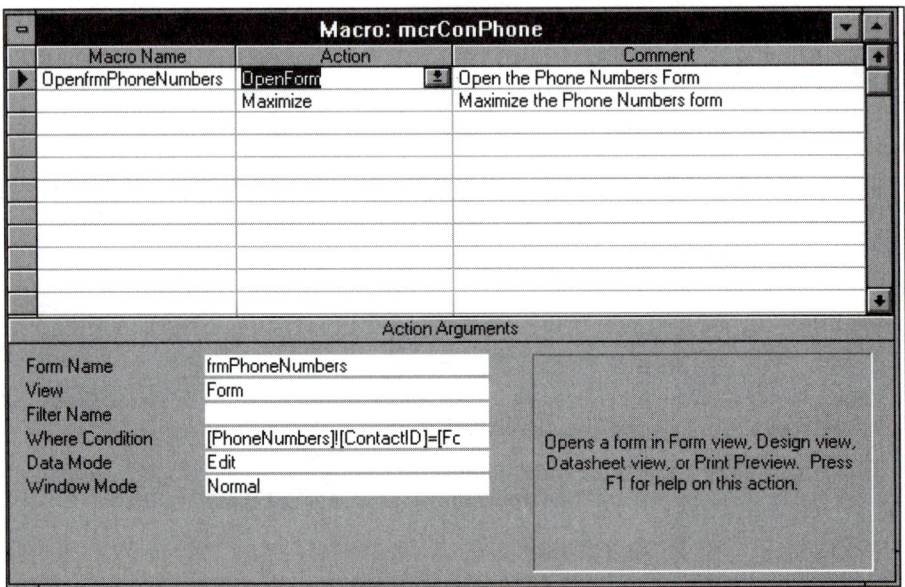

| Macro Name | Action | Comment |
|---|---|---|
| OpenfrmPhoneNumbers | OpenForm | Open the Phone Numbers Form |
| | Maximize | Maximize the Phone Numbers form |

**Action Arguments**

| | |
|---|---|
| Form Name | frmPhoneNumbers |
| View | Form |
| Filter Name | |
| Where Condition | [PhoneNumbers]![ContactID]=[Fc |
| Data Mode | Edit |
| Window Mode | Normal |

Opens a form in Form view, Design view, Datasheet view, or Print Preview. Press F1 for help on this action.

**Figure 12-6** **The Macro Design window with the completed macro**

2. Close the Macro Design window.

# Objective 4: Running a Macro

Usually, macros are not run from the Macro window. Most often they are run by pressing an associated command button. This makes sense since most macros are designed to perform a specific task within a form.

### Exercise 4: Running the macro

In this exercise, you will run the macro from the Macro window. The macro prompts you for a value for ContactID because, running alone, it cannot get the value of ContactID from the Contacts form. In order for this macro to work, the Contacts form must be open, which it currently is not.

1. At the Database window with the Macro tab selected and mcrConPhone highlighted, click Run.

2. When the dialog box appears requesting a value for ContactID, click Cancel.

## Exercise 5: Connecting the macro to a form

In this exercise, you will add a command button to the Contacts form that will run the macro and open the PhoneNumbers form with the data from the contact name shown on the Contacts form.

1. Open the Contacts form in Design mode. Make sure that the Toolbox is visible.
2. Place a command button on the form, just above the Close button.
3. When the Command Button Wizard dialog box opens, select Miscellaneous. Select Run Macro (Fig. 12-7). Click Next.

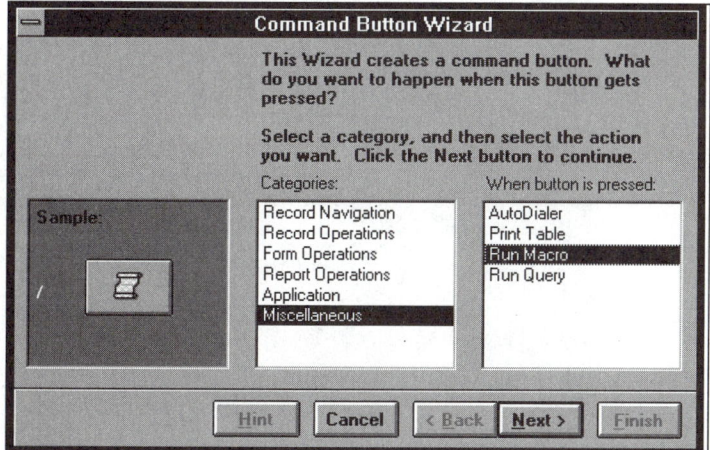

**Figure 12-7    The Command Button Wizard dialog box**

4. From the list of macros, select mcrConPhone.OpenfrmPhoneNumbers (Fig. 12-8). Click Next.

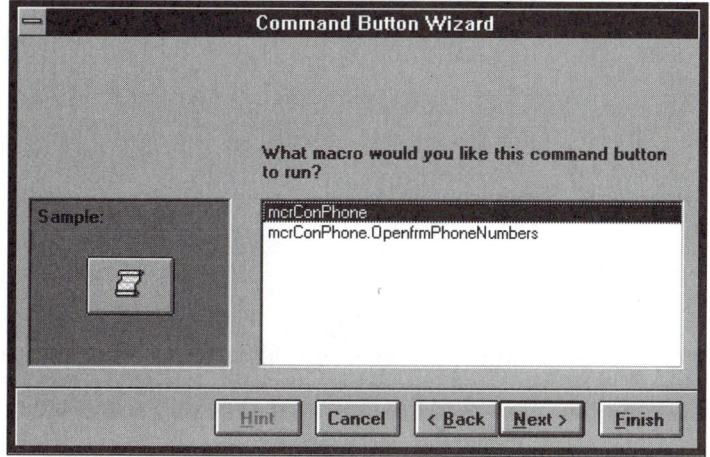

**Figure 12-8    The Command Button Wizard dialog box with a list of macros**

Note the naming convention. The macro you selected is named *macro family name.macro name*.

5. Click the Show All Pictures option and select Phone 1 from the list. Click Next.

6. Name the button ConPhone. Click Finish.

7. Switch to Form view (Fig. 12-9).

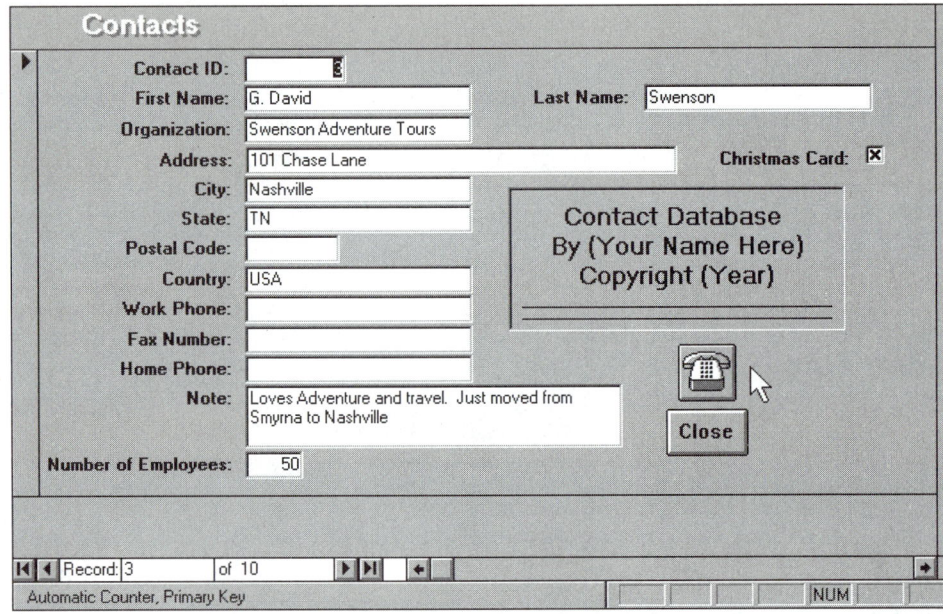

**Figure 12-9    The Contacts form with the macro button**

8. Find Swenson's contact record and click the button with the telephone on it.

The frmPhoneNumbers form opens.

9. Browse through the records. Notice that they all belong to Swenson. You cannot see the phone numbers for any of your other contacts.

10. Close the frmPhoneNumbers form.

You have to use File/Close or click the box in the upper left corner of the form.

12. Close the Contacts form, saving your changes.

# Objective 5:  Modifying a Macro

It is not very convenient to use File/Close or click the box in the upper left corner of the form each time you want to close the secondary form. To remedy this, you will put a close button on frmPhoneNumbers. You will add this macro as a second macro in the macro group you created earlier.

While you are making changes to mcrConPhone, there is another subtle change you should make. Remember what happeneed when you tried to run this macro on its own? The results were not what you expected. You can ensure that the macro will not accidently execute by inserting a blank line above the first line of instruction in the macro group.

## Exercise 6: Making multiple macro modifications

In this exercise, you will put a button on frmPhoneNumbers that will call a macro and close the form.

1. Open the macro group mcrConPhone in Design mode.
2. Click anywhere in the top row of the macro. Then click Edit/Insert Row.
   A blank row is inserted at the beginning of the macro group.
3. Position the cursor in the Macro Name column two lines below the end of the OpenfrmPhoneNumbers macro and type ClosefrmPhoneNumbers.
4. Click the Action column and select Close.

**FEATURE**

### Macros and event procedures

You may be wondering about the difference between the Close Form button you built in Chapter 10 and the one in this chapter, which runs a macro. The first one, which you built with the Command Button Wizard, actually has some program code behind it. If you examine the properties of this button, you will find something called an Event Procedure in the On Click property. This means that it runs a code snippet—a DoCmd Close—each time the button is clicked. The code, which is shorthand for "do the Close command from the menu bar," works as if you had selected File/Close. This is part of the programming language called Access Basic, which underlies everything that happens in MS-Access.

The last tab in the Database window is Modules. What is a module? Like a macro group, it can be a collection of small programs or code snippets. Each can be called from within a form or a report. While the macro is built by specifying a series of steps, the module is written in Access Basic.

5. In the Object Type row in the Action Arguments window, select Form. Then in the Object Name row, select frmPhoneNumbers.

6. Type Close frmPhoneNumbers in the Comments column (Fig. 12-10).

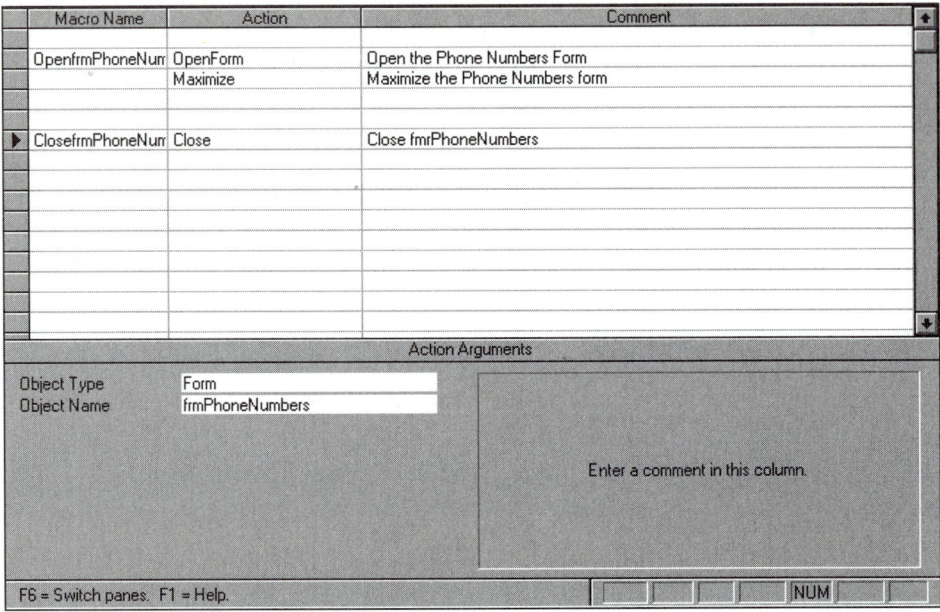

| Macro Name | Action | Comment |
|---|---|---|
| OpenfrmPhoneNum | OpenForm | Open the Phone Numbers Form |
| | Maximize | Maximize the Phone Numbers form |
| ClosefrmPhoneNum | Close | Close frmPhoneNumbers |

Action Arguments

Object Type    Form
Object Name    frmPhoneNumbers

Enter a comment in this column.

F6 = Switch panes.  F1 = Help.                    NUM

**Figure 12-10  The macro with changes**

7. Close the macro, saving your changes.

8. Open the form frmPhoneNumbers in Design mode. Place a command button on this form below the PhoneType field.

9. When prompted, select Miscellaneous, then select Run Macro.

10. When asked for the name of the macro, select mcrConPhone.ClosefrmPhoneNumbers. Click Next.

11. When prompted for the button face, check the Show All Pictures box and select the Exit Door button. Click Next.

12. Call the button cmdClosePhoneNumbers and click Finish.

13. Close the form, saving your changes.

14. Open the Contacts form in Form view.

15. Scroll to Swenson's record, then click the Phone button to open the Phone Numbers form.

16. Click the Exit Door button to close this form and return to the Contacts form.

17. Close the Contacts form by clicking the Close button on the form.

# Objective 6:  The Autoexec Macro

The autoexec macro performs a special function. When you first open your database, MS-Access looks for this macro. Whatever instructions are in this macro are run automatically. The most common use of the autoexec macro is to open a form so that the user can begin to browse or enter data. But you could use autoexec to generate a report every morning as you open the database with the previous day's sales figures and automatically e-mail it to your head office. In Exercise 7, you will build a simple autoexec macro to open the Contacts form.

## Exercise 7: Building the autoexec macro

1. Start at the Database window with the Macro tab selected. Click New.

   In this example, the autoexec macro has only one entry in its macro group.

2. On the first line of the Action column, select or type OpenForm.

3. In the Name row of the Action Arguments form, select the Contacts form.

   This is the form that will open automatically when you open the Contacts database.

4. On the second line of the Action column, select Maximize.

   This will enlarge your Contacts form to fill the screen.

5. Click File/Save As to save the macro as autoexec.

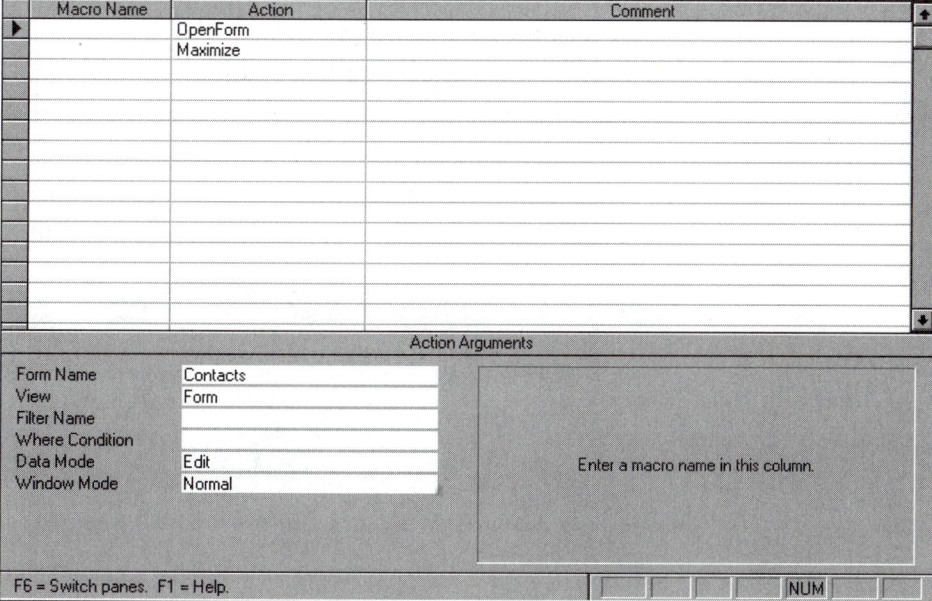

**Figure 12-11** **The autoexec macro**

6. Close the macro and return to the Database window.
7. Highlight the autoexec macro. Click Run.

   The Contacts form opens and fills the screen.

8. Click the Close button to close the form.
9. Click File/Close Database to close the database. Click File/contacts.mdb to open it again. Do not exit from MS-Access.

   The database opens to a maximized Contacts form.

10. Close the form.

***TIP*** Once the autoexec macro is in the Macro list, the database will open automatically at the form designated in the macro. To bypass autoexec, hold (SHIFT) as you click the database name to open it. You can disable autoexec by renaming or deleting it.

# Objective 7:  Debugging a Macro

There may be times when your macro does not work as you expected. How do you find the cause of the problem? The best method is to use the built-in macro debugger to step through the macro—that is, to execute each instruction and then pause to see what happens.

### Exercise 8: Stepping through a functioning macro

In this exercise, you will step through a macro that works correctly. This will give you an idea of what to expect in the debugging process.

1. Start at the Database window with the Macro tab selected. Open mcrConPhone in Design mode.
2. Depress the Single Step button on the toolbar.
3. Close the Macro Design window, saving the changes when prompted.
4. Open the Contacts form in Form view.
5. Click the button to open the Phone Numbers form.
6. Click Step repeatedly to execute the macro one step at a time (Fig. 12-12).

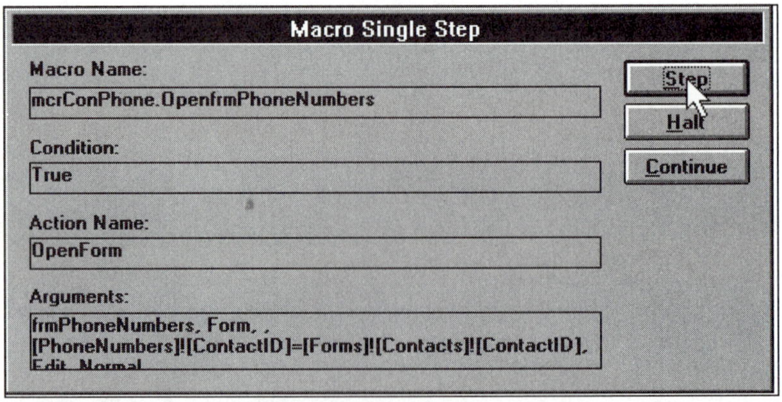

**Figure 12-12  The Macro Single Step window**

7. Click the button to close the Phone Numbers form.

8. Click Step to run the second macro.

9. Close the Contacts form.

## Exercise 9: Stepping through a macro with an error

Now, you will introduce an error into the macro and step through it. In this case, you know where the problem is, so watch what happens.

1. Open the macro mcrConPhone in Design mode.

2. Change the Action Arguments of the Open Form action so that the form name reads xxfrmPhoneNumbers. (There is no such form.) The Single Step button should still be depressed.

3. Close the macro, saving the changes when prompted.

4. Open the Contacts form in Form view.

5. Click the button to open the Phone Numbers form. Step through the macro.

   After the first step, a dialog box appears that reads, "There is no form named 'xxfrmPhoneNumbers'" (Fig. 12-13).

**Figure 12-13**  **An error dialog box**

6. Close the dialog box.

   The macro halts, showing you the instruction it was executing when it encountered the first error (Fig. 12-14). If you were truly debugging a macro you would fix this problem, then step through the macro again until it ran correctly.

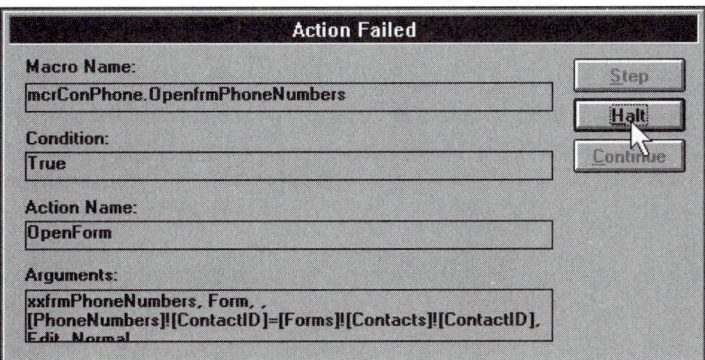

**Figure 12-14**  **The Macro Action Failed dialog box**

7. Click the Halt button to stop the macro.

8. Close the Contacts form.

9. Open the macro mcrConPhone in Design mode, remove the xx from the form name, and click the SingleStep button so that it is no longer depressed.

   Now the macro will run correctly.

10. Close the Macro Design window, saving your changes.

11. Close the database, and exit from MS-Access.

## Chapter Summary

In this chapter, you learned how to automate your application with macros. Macros can make moving between forms easier and can execute sets of instructions for you whenever you require. You learned that macros have to be built and then tied to a command button or a field on a form. The special autoexec macro runs automatically when the database is opened. To debug a macro, you can step through it one instruction at a time until you find the cause of the problem.

## Review Questions

### True/False Questions

_____ 1. You can record an MS-Access macro and play it back later as needed.

_____ 2. When you step through a macro, you will see every error as it happens.

_____ 3. Each macro within a group performs only one action.

_____ 4. You can bypass the autoexec macro by holding down Shift as you open the database.

_____ 5. MS-Access macros can be run with an Alt+key combination.

### Multiple-Choice Questions

_____ 6. An MS-Access macro is

   A. a sequence of strokes on the keyboard.

   B. a set of instructions that performs a sequence of tasks.

   C. program code.

   D. a form or report with embedded graphics.

_____ 7. The macro that MS-Access runs when the database opens is called

    A. autoexec.bat.

    B. autoexec.

    C. autoexec.mdb.

    D. mcrAutoexec.

_____ 8. Macros can be used to

    A. open a form.

    B. print a report.

    C. dial a telephone number.

    D. Any of the above.

_____ 9. When building a command button with the Command Button Wizard, you can place on the button

    A. a picture.

    B. text.

    C. text and a picture.

    D. text or a picture.

_____ 10. The instructions used to further define a macro action are called

    A. Macro Actions.

    B. Macro Arguments.

    C. Action Arguments.

    D. Argument Actions.

## Fill-in-the-Blank Questions

11. A set of related macros is called a _____.

12. The _____ is used when building a macro and constructing the code needed to link two forms.

13. The _____ command in an Open Form macro makes the form fill the screen when it opens.

14. The parameters that you specify to describe an action in a macro are called _____.

15. To debug a macro, you _____ through it instruction by instruction.

## Acumen-Building Activities

### Quick Projects

### 1. Create a Sort-by-Title macro and command button for MyBooks.

1. Open the Books database. Go to the Query window.
2. Create a New query without using the Query Wizard. Use the table MyBooks.
3. Drag each field from the table onto the Query window. Sort by Title in ascending order. Test the query.
4. Save the query, naming it qrySortByTitle. Close the Query Design window.
5. Go to the Macro window. Create a New macro.
6. Skip the first row in the Macro Design window. In the second row of the Macro Name column, type SortByTitle. In the Action column choose ApplyFilter. In the Comments column, type Sort the Books by Title. In the Filter Name row of the Action Arguments box, type qrySortByTitle.
7. Save the macro, calling it mcrSort. Close the macro.
8. Go to the Forms window. Open frmBooks in Design mode and maximize the form.
9. Place a command button on the form near the top at the 5" line.
10. From the Command Button Wizard, select Miscellaneous, then select Run Macro. Select mcrSort.SortByTitle. Put text on the command button and type Sort By Title. Name the command button cmdSortByTitle. Click Finish.
11. Resize the button if necessary. Save the changes.
12. Switch to Form view. Test the button. Close the form.

### 2. Create a Sort-by-Subject macro and command button for MyBooks.

This exercise is a continuation of Quick Project #1.

1. Go to the Query window. Create a New query without using the Query Wizard. Use the table MyBooks.
2. Drag each field from the table onto the Query window. Sort by Author in ascending order. Test the query. Save the query, naming it qrySortByAuthor. Close the Query Design window.
3. Go to the Macro window. Open mcrSort in Design mode.
4. In the fourth row of the Macro Name column, type SortByAuthor. In the Action column, choose ApplyFilter. In the Comments column, type Sort the Books by Author. In the Filter Name row of the Action Arguments box, type qrySortByAuthor. Save the changes. Close the macro.

5. Go to the Forms window. Open frmBooks in Design mode and maximize the form.

6. Place a command button on the form near the SortByTitle button.

7. From the Command Button Wizard, select Miscellaneous, then select Run Macro. Select mcrSort.SortByAuthor. Put text on the command button and type Sort By Author. Name the command button cmdSortByAuthor. Click Finish.

8. Resize the button so it is the same size as the first button. Save the changes.

9. Switch to Form view. Test the button. Close the form.

### 3. Create a Print Preview macro and command button for MyBooks.

This exercise is a continuation of Quick Project #2.

1. Go to the Macro window. Create a New macro.

2. In the second row of the Macro Name column, type PrintPreview. In the Action column choose, DoMenuItem. In the Comments column, type Preview the form before printing. In the Menu Bar row of the Action Arguments box, select Form. In the Menu Name row, select File. In the Command row, select Print Preview. Save the changes, call the macro mcrPrint. Close the macro.

3. Go to the Forms window. Open frmBooks in Design mode and maximize the form.

4. Place a command button on the form.

5. From the Command Button Wizard, select Miscellaneous, then select Run Macro. Select mcrPrint.PrintPreview. Place the Preview Document picture on the command button. Name the command button cmdPrintPreview. Click Finish.

6. Resize and reposition the button if appropriate. Save the changes.

7. Switch to Form view. Test the new button. Exit from Print Preview. Close the form.

### 4. Create an autoexec macro for MyBooks.

This exercise is a continuation of Quick Project #3.

1. Go to the Macro window and create a New macro.

2. On the first line of the Action column, select Open Form. In the Comments column, type The autoexec macro. In the Form Name row of the Action Arguments box, select frmBooks.

3. On the second line of the Action column, select Maximize.

4. Save the macro, naming it autoexec. Close the macro.

5. In the Database window, highlight autoexec and click Run.

6. Close the form. Close the Books database.

## In-Depth Projects

### 1. Link CDs and Tracks for the CD database.

1. Open the CD database. Create a New macro.
2. Skip the first row in the Macro Design window. In the second row of the Macro Name column, type OpenTracks. In the Action column, choose Open Form. In the Comments column, type Open the Tracks form. In the Form Name row of the Action Arguments box, type frmTracks. Use the Expression Builder for the Where condition.
3. Double-click Tables and double-click Tracks. Double-click MusicCollectionID.
4. Click the equals sign.
5. Double-click Forms. Double-click AllForms. Double-click frmCDCollection. Double-click MusicCollectionID. Click OK.
6. Save the macro, naming it mcrOpenSub. Close the Macro Design window.
7. Open frmTracks in Design mode. Position the Form window in the lower right portion of the screen. Open the Properties box. Find the entry for PopUp and change it to Yes. Close frmTracks and save the changes.
8. Open frmCDCollection in Design mode and maximize the form. Place a new command button in the header area.
9. From the Command Button Wizard, select Miscellaneous, then select Run Macro. Choose the macro mcrOpenSub.OpenTracks. Select the picture Subform and name the command button cmdOpenTracks. Click Finish. Save your changes.
10. Switch to Form view. Test the Subform command button. Scroll through the tracks for the CD you have selected on the main form. Close the Track subform.
11. Go to the next CD on the main form. Click the Subform command button and scroll through the tracks for that CD. Close the Tracks subform. Close the CDCollection main form. Save any changes if prompted to do so. Close the CD database.

### 2. Creating an autoexec and a Print Report macro for the Dinner database.

1. Open the Dinner database and go to the Macro window.
2. Create a New autoexec macro. On the first line of the Action column, type OpenForm. In the Form Name row of the Action Arguments box, select frmDinnerGuest2. Add a comment to the Comments column.
3. On the second line of the Action column, select Maximize.
4. Save the macro as autoexec.
5. Create a second New macro.
6. Skip the first row. In the second row of the Macro Name column, type CurrentRec. In the Action column, choose Open Report. In the Comments column, type Print preview the current record before

printing. In the Report Name row of the Action Arguments box, type rptGuests; Leave the view as Print Preview. Use the Expression Builder for the Where condition and choose Tables/ DinnerGuests/ GuestID/ = /Forms/All Forms/frmDinnerGuest2/GuestID. Your expressions should look like `[DinnerGuests]![GuestID] = Forms![frmDinnerGuest2]![GuestID]`. Save the changes and call the macro mcrPrint. Close the macro.

7. Go to the Forms window. Open frmDinnerGuest2 in Design mode and maximize the form.

8. Lengthen the Detail section of the form. Place a command button at the bottom of the Detail section on the right side.

9. From the Command Button Wizard, select Miscellaneous, then select Run Macro. Select mcrPrint.CurrentRec. Place text on the command button and type Print Current Profile. Name the command button cmdCurrentRec. Click Finish.

10. Save the changes. Switch to Form view. Test the button. Exit from Print Preview. Close the form. Close the Dinner database.

## CASE STUDIES

### Coffee-On-The-Go: Using Macros

In this chapter, you learned to create macros. You will apply those skills to create a macro for Coffee-On-The-Go.

1. Create a macro of your own choosing which automates a task.
2. Test the macro.
3. Debug and edit the macro as necessary.
4. Save the macro and close the database.

## CASE STUDIES

### Videos West: Using Macros

In this chapter, you learned to create macros. You will apply those skills to create a macro for Videos West.

1. Create a macro of your own choosing which automates a task.
2. Test the macro.
3. Debug and edit the macro as necessary.
4. Save the macro and close the database.

# Acumen Advanced Features Milestone

## the Scouts Cookie Sale Database

Mrs. Wilson finds her Cookie Sales database to be very useful. She decides to build a multitable form so she can enter this week's cookie sales without having to switch back and forth between two different forms. She will add a command button so she can go directly to the Sales form and enter the type of cookie and number of boxes purchased. She is thinking about adding some combo boxes to assist with data entry, specifically on the scout's name and cookie type. Then she will build some new reports. One report will list all customers, what cookies they have ordered, and how much of each cookie type they have each ordered. A second report will list cookies by type and the total number of each cookie type sold. A third report will list the scouts and the cookies each has sold, grouped by type with a total number of sales for each scout.

Mrs. Wilson also wants to build an autoexec macro that will open this new multitable data entry form when she starts up the Cookie Sales database. She is thinking that she might like to have command buttons on the form that run macros to sort by different fields, too. Finally, Mrs. Wilson plans to make a backup of her database.

1. Build a multitable data-entry form. Make the Scout table the main form and the Customer table the subform. Put a command button on this form to go directly to the Sales form. Put the command button on the Sales form to return to the main form.

2. Build combo boxes on these forms to assist with data entry. Put a combo box on the Sales form to list the cookie types. Put a combo box on the Main form to facilitate choosing the scout's name. Add this week's cookie sales.

3. Create three new reports.

   - A list of all customers, what cookies they have ordered, and how much of each type.
   - A list of cookies by type and total number of each sold.
   - A report that groups cookie sales by scouts, then by what type of cookies each has sold. Add subtotals for the cookie groups and totals for each scout.

4. Create an autoexec macro to open the mutitable form when the Cookie Sales database is opened. Create a command button on the main form to sort by scout name, and a second command button on the Sales form to sort by cookie type. Make a backup of the Cookie Sales database.

## Group Project:

# the Community Rec Center Database

The Forms Designer decides to make some multitable forms to handle reservations and equipment issue. There will have to be command buttons placed on the forms to switch from one to the other. The Forms Designer must confer with the rest of the project team to design the forms so that they are easy to use and functional.

The Report Designer decides that the center needs to print equipment-issue receipts when a member checks out a piece of equipment. It would be best to do this directly from the Equipment Issue multitable form. Also, it would be very nice to be able to give each member a reservation slip when he or she makes a reservation to use a tennis court. The Report Designer wants to do this directly from the Reservations multitable form. In addition, the Report Designer would like to generate form letters with mailing labels to send to the members, notifying them of the annual Rec Center Holiday Party.

The Database Administrator decides to create an autoexec macro to bring up the Reservations multitable form when the Rec Center database is started. The entire project team will work together to enroll this week's new members into the Rec Center database and to record reservations and equipment issue. Then the Database Administrator will make a backup of the Rec Center database.

### The Full Project Team

Confer to design the best way for navigating through the new multitable forms for reservations and equipment issue. Compose the wording of the letter to the membership about the holiday party. Record this week's new members, reservations, and equipment issues.

### The Database Administrator

Create the autoexec macro so that the Reservations multitable form opens when the Rec Center database is brought up (if the rest of the project team agrees with this decision). Assist with the creation of any macros needed by the Forms Designer. Make a backup of the database.

### The Forms Designer

Create two new multitable forms, one for making reservations to use the courts, a second for recording equipment issue. Add command buttons to switch back and forth between the two forms as well as to navigate elsewhere in the database. Confer with the project team members as to the best design.

### The Report Designer

Create the equipment-issue receipts and confer with the Forms Designer about where and how to place a command button on the form to generate them. Create the reservations slips and confer with Forms Designer about where and how to place a command button on the forms to generate them. Create a general mailing to the membership, notifying them of the upcoming holiday party. Generate a set of mailing labels to accompany the letters.

# Appendix

# An Introduction to Windows

*Objectives*
- Start Windows
- Use the mouse
- Minimize, maximize, and restore Windows
- Use the menu bar
- Save and open files
- Exit Windows

## Concepts

If you are new to using Windows, this introduction was written for you! The purpose of this introduction is to give you an overview of basic Windows features before you start learning to use a Windows application.

### Starting Windows

Many computers are set up so that when you turn them on, Windows automatically starts. If a DOS prompt appears (such as C:\> or F:\>), type win and press (← ENTER) to start Windows. If you see something else, check with your instructor.

When you start Windows, the Program Manager window appears (see Figure I-1).

Program Manager is the starting point for all Windows applications. Instead of entering special commands to start programs, select applications from the Program Manager. Windows uses icons, or pictures, to represent applications.

### Using the Mouse

Use the mouse or the keyboard to perform Windows functions. To use the mouse, slide it across your desk. The mouse pointer moves in the same direction. After you have positioned the mouse pointer, there are three actions you can perform:

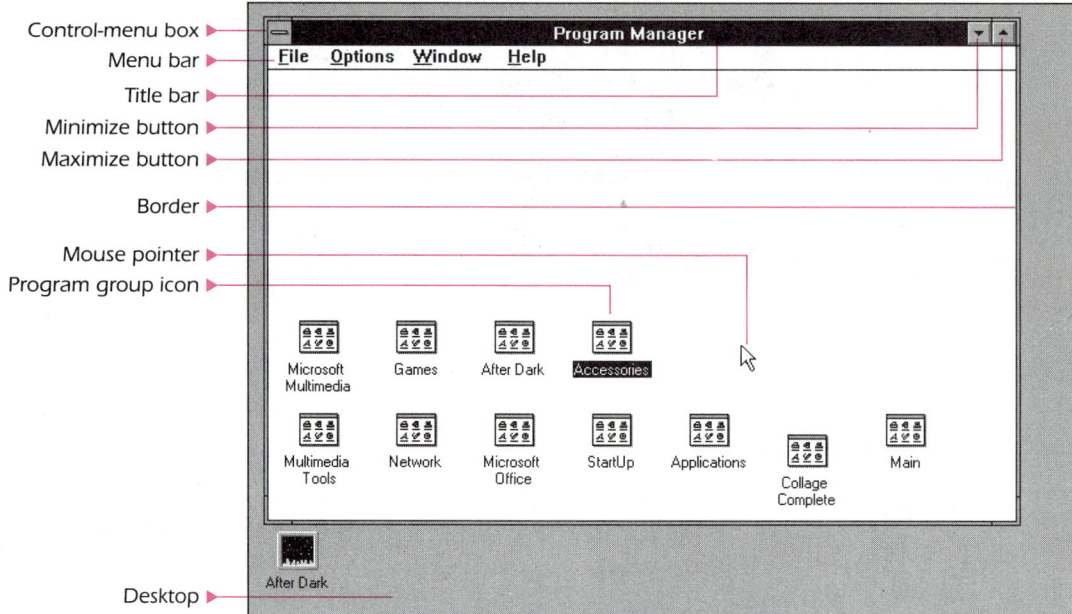

Control-menu box ▶
Menu bar ▶
Title bar ▶
Minimize button ▶
Maximize button ▶
Border ▶
Mouse pointer ▶
Program group icon ▶
Desktop ▶

**Figure I-1** **The Program Manager window**

| | |
|---|---|
| **Click** | Press the left mouse button and release it quickly. |
| **Double-click** | Press and release the left mouse button quickly twice. |
| **Drag** | Hold down the left mouse button and slide the mouse across your desk. This moves the selected icon or window. |

You will see the terms *click*, *double-click*, and *drag* used throughout this book. Unless the instructions specifically say to click the right mouse button, click the left button.

## Minimizing, Maximizing, and Restoring Windows

**A minimized window appears as an icon at the bottom of your desktop**

Opening multiple windows can clutter your desktop. To reduce the clutter without closing a window, *minimize* the window. Minimizing changes the window to an icon. The application is still loaded into your computer's memory. This can save several steps since you don't have to open the Program group icon, then the program item icon, and then the document.

To see more of a specific window, you can *maximize* it so that it fills the screen. Figure I-2 shows a maximized window.

The Maximize button then changes to a Restore button. Click this button to restore the window to its previous size.

## Using the Menu Bar

Use menu commands to perform functions such as opening and saving files, changing fonts, and printing. Open a menu by clicking the option, or by pressing (ALT) and typing the underlined letter (often referred to as the *mnemonic letter* or *hotkey*). See Figure I-3 for an example of the File menu.

Click a menu command to choose it, or type the underlined letter. Some menu options are followed by an ellipsis (. . .). Choosing one of these commands displays a dialog box, which means Windows needs more information. If a menu command is dimmed (light gray), it is not available at that time.

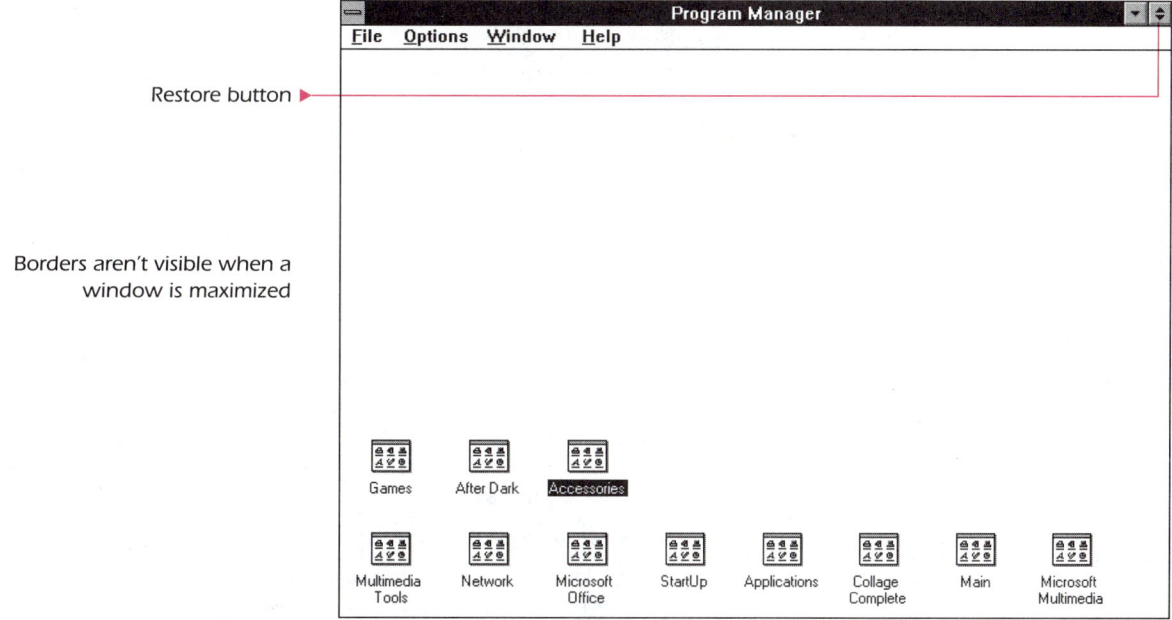

**Figure I-2   A maximized window**

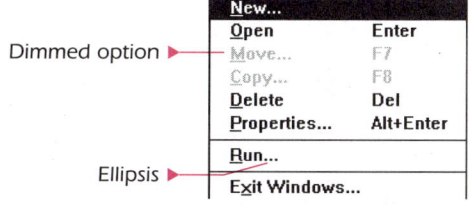

**Figure I-3   The File menu**

Key names, such as (SHIFT) + (F5), next to a menu command are *shortcut keys*. Press these keys to perform the command without opening the menu.

## Saving and Opening Files

When you are working on a document, it is stored in short-term memory, or RAM. You need to save your work to a floppy or hard disk. If you do not, it will be lost if you exit the application or turn off your computer.

When naming a document, follow DOS naming rules. A file name is one to eight characters long and cannot include a space. Applications automatically add a three-character extension onto the file name, separated from the file name by a period. You also cannot use these special characters . " / \ [ ] : * < > + = ; , ? The easiest way to make sure the file name is "legal" is to use only letters or numbers.

## Exiting Windows

After you have finished working with Windows, exit the program. Exit by double-clicking the Control-menu box or by choosing File, Exit Windows from the menu bar.

# Tutorial

In this tutorial, you will start Windows and practice using the mouse. You will learn how to minimize, maximize, and restore windows and use the menu bar. You will then save and open a file. When finished, you will exit Windows.

**LEARN BY DOING 1**

## Starting Windows

To start Windows, do the following:

1. Turn the computer on, if necessary.
2. If Windows is automatically started, go to Learn by Doing 2.
3. If the DOS prompt (C:\ >or F:\>) appears, type win and press ⏎ ENTER.
   ◆ The Program Manager window appears on your screen.
4. If a menu appears when you boot your computer or you cannot start Windows, see your instructor.

**LEARN BY DOING 2**

## Using the Mouse

Practice using the mouse by following these steps:

1. Hold onto the mouse, with your fingers positioned over the mouse buttons.
2. Slide the mouse across the desk, and notice how the mouse pointer moves in the same direction.
3. If you run out of room, pick up the mouse and reposition it, and then continue sliding the mouse.
4. Move the mouse pointer to each of the following window components (refer to Figure I-1 if you're not sure where these items are):

**Title bar**

**Control-menu box**

**Minimize button**

**Accessories group icon**

**Window border**

5. Double-click the Accessories group icon.
   ◆ The icon opens into a window (see Figure I-4).

6. Double-click the Write program item icon.
   ◆ The Write application window opens.

7. Place the mouse pointer on the Write application title bar.

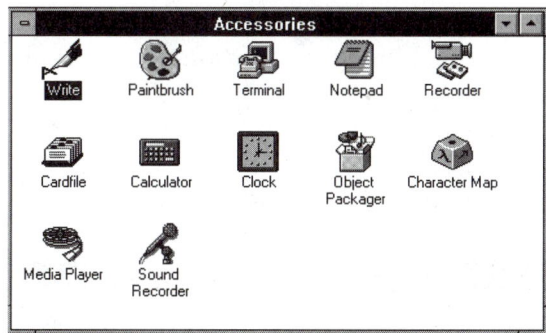

**Figure I-4   The Accessories group window**

8. Hold down the left mouse button, and drag the window to a new location.

9. Release the mouse button. The window is dropped at this spot. This technique of moving an object is referred to as *dragging and dropping*.

**LEARN BY DOING 3**   ## Minimizing, Maximizing, and Restoring Windows

Resize the Write window by following these steps:

1. Click the Minimize button in the Write window.
   ◆ The Write window is reduced to an icon.

2. Double-click the Write icon to open it.

3. Click the Maximize button.
   ◆ The window fills your entire screen.

4. Click the Restore button to return the window to its previous size.

**LEARN BY DOING 4**   ## Using the Menu Bar

To use menu commands, follow these steps:

1. In the Write window, click the File menu option.
   ◆ The File menu appears on your screen.

2. Click outside the menu to close it.

3. Press and release ⟨ALT⟩, then type e.
   ◆ The Edit menu appears on your screen.

4. Press ⟨ESC⟩ twice to close this menu.

5. Hold down ⟨CTRL⟩ and press b. This is a shortcut for bolding text.

6. Type your name in the document. The text is bolded.

## Saving and Opening Files

Practice saving and opening files by following these steps:

1. Insert a formatted floppy disk into your floppy drive.

2. From the menu bar, choose File, Save As.
   ◆ The Save As dialog box, shown in Figure I-5, appears on your screen.

3. A blinking vertical line, the *insertion point*, should be in the File Name text box. If not, click in the File Name box.

4. Type the file name **intro**.

5. Click the Drives box.
   ◆ A list of available disk drives appears.

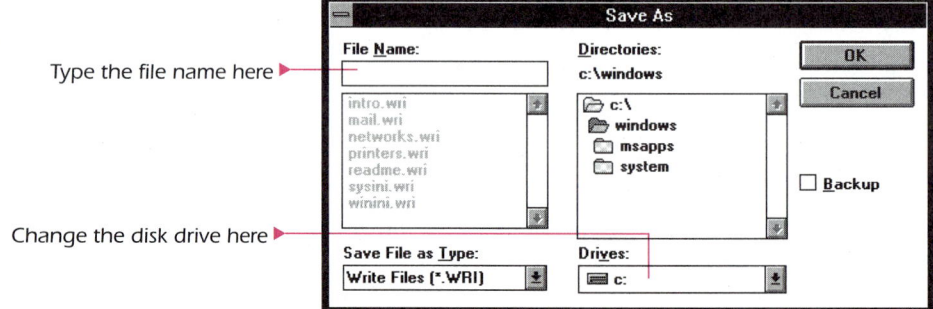

**Figure I-5    The Save As dialog box**

6. Click your floppy drive letter.

7. Click the OK button to save the file to your floppy disk.

8. Choose File, New from the menu bar.
   ◆ A blank document window appears. The intro file is cleared from memory.

9. Choose File, Open to open a file.
   ◆ The Open dialog box, shown in Figure I-6, appears on your screen.

10. Select your floppy drive from the Drives box, if necessary.

Highlighted command button ▶

File name ▶

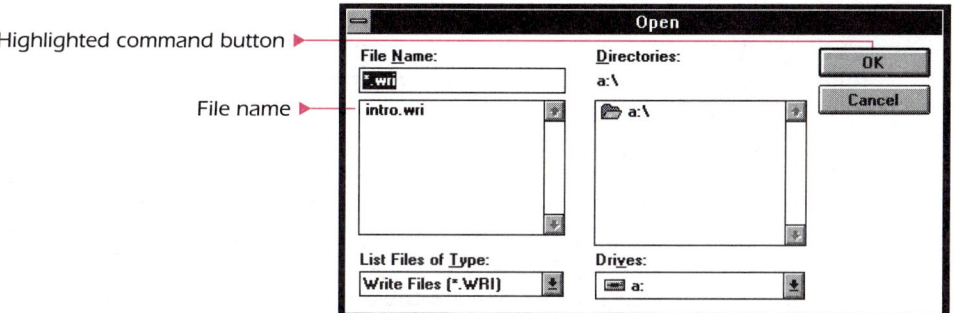

**Figure I-6  The Open dialog box**

11. Click the file name intro.wri under the File Name box. Notice that Write added the .wri extension to the file name.

12. Click the OK button. If OK is highlighted, you can also press ⟨↵ ENTER⟩.
    ◆ The intro.wri file appears on your screen.

**LEARN BY DOING 6**

## Exiting Windows

Follow these steps to exit Windows:

1. Close the Write window by choosing File, Exit.

2. Close the Applications window by double-clicking the Control-menu box (the minus-sign next to the Applications title bar).

3. Close Windows by double-clicking the Program Manager Control-menu box.
   ◆ A dialog box appears, telling you that this will end your Windows session.

4. Click OK or press ⟨↵ ENTER⟩.

## Command Summary

In this introduction, you learned some basic Windows functions. The steps to complete the tasks are:

### Starting Windows

1. Turn the computer on.

2. If a DOS prompt appears, type *win* and press ⟨↵ ENTER⟩.

### Using the Mouse

1. Slide the mouse across your desktop to position the mouse pointer.

2. To click the mouse button, press the button once and release.

3. To double-click, press and release the mouse button quickly twice.

4. To drag an object, press and hold down the mouse button. Slide the mouse to move the object, and then release the mouse button.

## Minimize, Maximize, and Restore Windows

1. Click the Minimize button to turn a window into an icon on your desktop.

2. Click the Maximize button to size a window to fill the entire screen.

3. Click the Restore button to return a Maximized window to its previous size.

## Use the Menu Bar

◆ Press and release (ALT), type the underlined letter in the menu name, and then type the underlined letter in the command.

◆ To access the command without opening the menu, press the shortcut key combination.

To use the mouse to access a menu command, do one of the following:

◆ If the menu is open, click on the menu command.

◆ If the menu is not open, click the menu, and then click the menu command.

## Save and Open Files

1. Choose File. Save As.

2. In the Save As dialog box, type the file name.

3. Click the Drives box to change the disk drive.

4. Choose OK.

5. To open a file, choose File, Open.

6. Enter the disk drive and file name in the Open dialog box.

7. Choose OK.

## Exit Windows

1. Close the Application and Group windows by double-clicking in the Control-menu box or by choosing File, Exit.

2. Close Windows by double-clicking in the Program Manager Control-menu box or by choosing File, Exit Windows.

3. Choose OK when asked to confirm you want to end the Windows session.

# *Index*